Samn Stockwell • Denslow Brown • Sabrina Bunks

Sarah Ives • Jo Brooks • Jill Harker • Diane Remy

Beth Reasoner • Randy Parker • Charlene LaVoie

Marcia Cameron • Alicia Woodson

Sandy Anderson • Barbara Beckelman • Libby Smith

Amy Allison • Anne Frye • Ellen Richard

Francesca (Ariel) Jenkins • Tina Yoxheimer • Ellen McCarthy

Laura Manby • Chloe Wheatley • Chanda O'Donnell

Julie Haddon • Esther Brienes • Sarah Giordano • Filis Rose

Anne Szost • Rachel Portnoy • Denise Hackney

Anne Arkin • Liz Seaborn • Cel Noll • Mev Miller

Fran Reed • Dora Odarenko • Ellen Mayer • Lynn Stenberg

Lys Guillion • Dawn Shewchuk • Robin Baena

Sarah Campbell • Judy Campbell • June Dunn • Kaia James

Karen Bernstein • Sharon Leslie • Dawn McDaniel

Jill Bornsec • Sandy Martin • Caroline Forbes

Judy Mortner • Susan Smith • Robin Baslow

Georgia Merola • Betsy Gooch • Marie Gall • Meg Profetto

Elaine Ward • Star Petrizzi • Nanette Raimond • Susan Grillo

Lindsay Nagy • Sarah Brown • Barbara Rodgers

Caroline Cowles • Carolyne Libby • Karen Cazary

Michelle Jarrett • Maryam Jubera • Beth McEntee

Lori Ensign • Siobhan Williams • Erin Kelly

Lauren Blanchard • Robin Whiting • Shirley Anderson

Sherilyn Pearce • Kristina Calvello • Teri Keiser

Heather Lyons • Kris Sabatelli • Jessica Glenn

Nancy Morgan • Amy Cheek • Nancy Judson

Carmen Russo • Erica Tetro • Maddie Sobel • Jodi Harlow

Robin Fukuyama • Donna Risolo • Sharon Berger

Nancy Berrero • Rosemary Redi • Zoe Cruz • Taylor Ross

Ildiko Makos Conley • Melissa Lardiere • Polly Molden

Emily Habansky • Maria dos Santos • Gail Cristiano

Jessica Pressley • Susan Hennessey • Debbie Gomes

Susan Myers • Yvette Nieves • Carolyn Schwartz • DJ Zupaniac

Alice Sun Tooley • Erin Strawn • Barbara McFerran

Madeline Martino • Vinda Daniels • Amy Weber

Jennifer Sisca • Angelita Pine • Caroline Griswald

Evelyn Turro • Purnima Ayarwal • Heather Stanko

Debbie Naples • Gail Ostrow • Daisy Quinones • Anita Senes

Courtney Carey • Jess Carey • Noelle Angers

Maggie Dunford • Karen Brown • Emma Middlebrook

Ana Velasquez • NykoleBlake • Elizabeth Bullis Weisse

Zoe Gardner • Sarah Koskoff • Lisa Strachan

Sheddi London • Amy O'Rourke • Shiobhan Dacres

Roxanne Delfino • Erma Elliot • Jovanna Garcia

Aminah Ashby • Cadence Carrol • Meredith Bell • Polly Walden

Rhiannan Alterio • Sarah Almodovar • Leanne Irwin

Alison Dunn • Connie Busch • Cindy Davis • Laura Diehl

Rose Lauture • Jennifer Leslie • Tori Mitchell • Heather Neil

Angelique Vanterpool • Melissa Wells • Lagusta Yearwood

Stephanie Zinowski • Victoria Forester • Lucilla Alton

Laura Cerato • Jennifer Laferlita • Jennifer Krawitz

Jessica Basista • Jennifer Doree • Nicole Deveau Jalbert

Dayna Mankowski • Kaitlen Austin • Christine Ferrer

Alison Fichera • Becky Gomes • Maya Kuznetsov

Jamie Records • Katie Ryckelynel • Nicole Strayer

Kate Traub • Nancy Clark • Gayle Colcone • Melanie Hardy

Autumn Leonard • Yuka Yazaki • Kate Habansky

The Best of
BLOODROOT

VOLUME TWO
Vegan Recipes

Selma Miriam & Noel Furie
with Lagusta Yearwood

Photography by Noel Furie

Anomaly Press
85 Ferris Street • Bridgeport, Connecticut 06605
203 576 9168 • www.bloodroot.com

We encourage the reproduction of up to five recipes and any of the introductory material, properly credited, for feminist and vegetarian purposes. Please write to us for more information and/ or recipe exchange.

Bloodroot drawing by Laura Louise Foster

©2007 Anomaly Press
a division of Mermaids and Crones Enterprises
85 Ferris Street
Bridgeport, Connecticut 06605

ISBN 0-9778549-1-4

Library of Congress Control Number: 200690834

Printed on 100% post-consumer recycled paper.
Printed in Canada

Anomaly: *deviation from the rule. Something out of keeping, especially with accepted notions of fitness or order. Exceptional, unusual, nonconforming, surprising, something that refuses to submit to classification or explanation.*

dedication

Feminism is the politics which informed the creation and maintenance of Bloodroot and our lives. Some time in the late 1990's, feminism as we knew it began to be disparaged. In particular, Catharine MacKinnon and Andrea Dworkin were maligned. Because we admired their work, we somewhat capriciously decided to name our two newly adopted rescued cats for them. We let Andrea know about our naming, and she was very pleased. She later relayed the information about their namesakes to Catharine.

Andrea spoke at Bloodroot several times, always to a packed audience. She was generous and brilliant, and what she wrote and cared about spoke to many women's experiences.

We dedicate these two books to her, in gratitude for her amazing courage.

acknowledgements

There are many people who deserve our recognition and appreciation for what they have given to make these two books possible and many also who through the years have contributed time and energy to Bloodroot herself.

Most important are our workers. Please note the two pages listing the names of women who have worked at Bloodroot in the past thirty years and who have enriched our lives in various ways.

Alison Dunn was our manager for over five years. She was a leavening agent, making manageable work schedules and cooking plans that were practical. She is an intuitive cook and passionate vegetarian and, though she moved to Illinois, we know our connection to her will be long lasting.

We love working with Rose Lauture. She has taken over the scheduling of staff and presides over the stove with skill and authority. She is a natural cook who, when she learns a new recipe says, "But this is so easy!"

Stephanie Zinowski, who runs a vegan café at Wesleyan University, works with us Saturdays and in summer. Her speed and efficiency cooking here, as well as her stocking and organizing are legendary. We're grateful for her warmth and generosity.

Suzanne Beck is a careful and focused cook. We're appreciative of her precision, her attention to detail and exceptional sense of responsibility. Carmen Russo has presided over the Tuesday-night stove for ten years. Angelita Pine worked here a decade ago and is back. It's a treat to have her particular warmth and intelligence. Angelique Vanterpool is also back and we are pleased she is. Kate Habansky brings graciousness and a sense of order to our kitchen. Lauren Mallon is warm, generous, and enthusiastic in her work. Dayna Mankowski, the crafty scientist, travels from Middletown on occasion to help out. We are fortunate for new workers: Jennifer Koenig, Julia Lundy, Sarah Verbil, and old friend Valerie Wilkie.

Charlene LaVoie has been with us a very long time. She worked here when we first opened in 1977. When she left to go to law school she promised to be back. We were skeptical, but indeed she came to work again. When she moved to Winsted,

Connecticut to work for the Nader Foundation we thought we wouldn't see much of her. However, we were again wrong. She comes here twice a month to rule over the counter in the kitchen. She is also our major source of legal help.

We've known Krystyna Colburn almost as long as Charlene. She lives in Massachusetts and comes here every month to do our payroll. What we treasure is her loyalty and her fierce feminist intelligence. She, Charlene, and Carolanne Curry are the advisors and stabilizers of our lives.

Carolanne has been here since 1988. She solves difficult and tricky problems for us with aplomb. We've entered the electronic age kicking and screaming; however Carolanne has organized a website for us as well as generally taken on myriad business problems as they have arisen.

Nancy Morgan, who used to work here but then moved to Pennsylvania, runs a little advertising service for us by sending out postcards to our mailing list every other month, listing menu selections and favorite new books. As can be imagined, it is a large and repetitive effort, greatly appreciated. This idea originated with Sabrina Bunks (Selma's daughter) who has consistently given us good business advice.

Bloodroot enjoys support from animal rights advocates. In particular, a Friday night group including Jack and Sheila Faxon (who come from Stockbridge, Massachusetts, each week), Pedro Hecht, Esther Meckler, Stephanie Underhill and many others. These people care intensely, as we do, about the creatures of this earth.

Our friend and customer Donna Andrade has liked our food and our feminism so much that she bought a house on our street so that she can visit often. We feel she understands our purpose particularly well.

We love discussing feminist and political issues with Ludger Viefhues and Kevin Bailey, who come weekly from New Haven.

For many years we had a women's night here—the G. Knapp Historical Society. It commemorated the only Fairfield County woman who was killed for being a "witch." Lucia Kimber was its membership chair and secretary, coming almost every week for Wednesday dinner.

Many others come weekly. Indeed they are our community. When our dining room ceiling was raised Anne Demchuk and Maelyn Bellemore brought ladders to paint it. A year later, they refreshed our outdoor trim, highlighting the mermaid over our door which was designed by Edie Platt and built by Kathy Thomas.

Over the years, we have been fortunate to become friends with several men in related businesses. John Moretti of Fountain of Youth Health Foods in Westport, Connecticut, helps us by adding items we need to his orders. We appreciate that he and his store remain determinedly vegetarian.

Some six years ago, we discoved Mike and Tony's organic farm, Urban Oaks in New Britain, Connecticut. Their beautiful, locally grown produce is delivered to us each week by Brian. It's a pleasure to have a business relationship with them.

And recently, The Fat Cat Pie Company has been selling our oatmeal sunflower bread at their restaurant and coffee shop. We appreciate the respect they have shown us as peers in this business and are delighted to be friends with them.

We are the recipients of many gifts that we treasure. Folks bring us pictures of mothers and sisters and grandmothers to decorate our wall. Michelle and Terry Cappellieri brought us Terry's grandmother's dining table (so that he could still dine at it) and a quality collection of soup pots. We are lucky to experience this generosity.

George Roberts (Pipe Dreams Plumbing) has been a friend for more than twenty years. Besides being a largish elf and lots of fun, he has kept our plumbing functional all this time.

We are fortunate and grateful that attorney Renn Gordon, a frequent customer at Bloodroot, has been willing to help with our business legal concerns.

Shane Taylor, our electrician, lights up our days in more ways than one. Our kitchen is especially bright because of him!

These books have had help as well in their assembling. Corrine Groark typed early drafts. Karen McInerney created the two cover designs. We're pleased for her enthusiasm for our food and for this project. The books are as beautiful as they are in part because of her efforts.

Thank you, thank you to all.

in appreciation

Neither of these two Best of Bloodroot books would exist if it were not for the efforts of Lagusta Yearwood. First and most important, she is a passionate "foodie," who is also a vegan and has been for 14 years. She operates a vegetarian meal delivery service between New Paltz and New York City as well as working with us one day every other week. Lagusta is regularly searching for and developing vegan dishes, as well as studying the history of food and cooking. And as a intelligent and unusually political person, she constantly mulls over how to lead a responsible life. Since we are trying to do something similar at Bloodroot, we do inspire each other! Secondly, Lagusta wanted these books to exist so much that she typed all the recipes in them, debating with us about ingredients and procedures since she was determined to make both as nearly perfect as possible. We are grateful—though our gratitude does not begin to express all we feel.

Table of Contents

Resistance is Fertile:
rethinking dairy from a vegan point of view

By Lagusta Yearwood

Note: This essay provides a perspective on the uses of coconut as an alternative to dairy. The ethics of meat and eggs are therefore outside the scope of this analysis, but this author wants to make clear that she sees no reason to eat either one. This and past Bloodroot cookbooks are resources for explaining precisely why feminists and all thinking people should not eat meat.

Part one: rethinking dairy

Westerners have been using milk of other animals for many years in our cuisine, but I see this as an accident of geography, not desirability—cows were here, so we used them. Now that other choices are available to us, I see no reason why we should continue to use the milk of other animals, especially when it has been widely documented that producing milk causes considerable strain on animals. Yes, high-quality dairy products—minimally pasteurized (sometimes even raw or fermented), humanely produced—are becoming more available, and this is a step in the right direction. But for those who believe that animals were put here for their own reasons,[1] dairy is not an option.

Throughout my fourteen years on the vegan path, my thinking about dairy has evolved. Like many vegans, I found dairy the hardest food to give up. I have come to believe, however, that this is mostly because we're used to it and excellent vegan alternatives to popular dairy dishes do not widely exist. If they

---

[1] As Alice Walker puts it in the preface to Marjorie Spiegel's *The Dreaded Comparison: Human and Animal Slavery* (1988): "The animals of the world exist for their own reasons. They were not made for humans any more than black people were made for whites or women for men."

i

did, undoubtedly many more people would be amenable to eating non-dairy meals. Out of habit, we use cow's milk, but this does not mean that it is the best choice. Ample evidence shows that it is, in fact, a terrible choice.[2]

What if, for example, coconut palm trees were as plentiful in North America as cows in factory farms are? It seems to me that in that case, cakes and cookies and all manner of foods would use coconut milk, and that would be thought of as the natural choice. Since my ethics preclude me from using cow's milk, the versatile coconut has worked its way into my cooking more and more, and I now believe it is the ideal candidate to replace cow's (and goat's and sheep's) milk altogether. This essay is the result of my studies on the topic, and before discussing the merits of the coconut, I will counter three possible negative assumptions about its use as a primary "dairy."

The coconut is not perfect. Obviously, eating what is indigenous to a particular area is preferable not only for environmental reasons, but because it is better for the body. For most of us in the United States, coconuts are not indigenous, and cows, while not native, are at least more local. Moreover, coconut milk comes in cans, and canned food, in addition to its wasteful packaging, cannot be said to have the same vitality as fresh food. However, given these issues, and despite the fact that it must be shipped a distance to get to us here, coconut milk is a better choice than cow's milk. Olives don't grow in Connecticut, but we at Bloodroot rely on olive oil on a daily basis. Cow's milk does not come from the soil and is not a truly seasonal product, thus using coconut milk in place of it does not have a more negative impact in either our planetary or personal health. Yes, coconut milk comes in cans, but organic coconut milk is widely available without any additives except a small amount of guar gum (a vegetarian emulsifier). It is heated to high temperatures as part of the canning process, but so is the vast quantity of milk on our

[2]See, for example, *The China Study*, by T. Colin Campbell, or *Diet for a New America*, by John Robbins. When one also notes that 70 percent of African-Americans, and 90 percent of Asian-Americans are lactose intolerant (source: John Robbins, foodrevolution.org), the USDA recommendation that all children drink milk every day seems not only unhealthy, but also racist.

shelves. Perhaps as the popularity of coconut milk for cooking purposes grows, it will be available fresh in health food stores.

It might seem that nominating the coconut for the title of Best Dairy Replacement is futile, as that crown has already been awarded: most vegans use soy milk in all ways that dairy milk is usually used. However, at Bloodroot we have found soymilk to have a bean-y and rather overly plastic flavor that we do not enjoy, and the comparatively long list of ingredients in many brands of soymilk does not compare favorably with coconut milk's three ingredients (two if you do not count water). Additionally, the increasingly corporatized natural food industry has oversold the health benefits of soy as a marketing tool. This oversimplification of "healthy" for the consumer has led to health-conscious people eating too much soy, especially processed, lifeless, soy products.[3]

Finally, one more potential flaw of the coconut should be discussed: it tastes like coconut. While most of the time this is a positive aspect, as the flavor of coconut is divine, when it is used in all the same ways cow's milk is used, there is a danger of "over-coconutization." Again, perspective is essential: most milk drinkers might not be able to pick out the flavor of milk in a dish, but this is because of its ubiquity and not because milk itself lacks flavor. To some, cow's milk vanilla ice cream tastes like vanilla; to most long-time vegans it would taste like cow's milk. That said, I do not make vegan vanilla ice cream using coconut milk, because I have to acknowledge that it would be coconut-vanilla ice cream.

However, the flavor of coconut is modified when paired with strong flavors. My chocolate truffles use coconut milk instead of cream, and the chocolate is so intense that the coconut is not noticeable. At Bloodroot, we make chocolate, coffee, and many other ice cream flavors using coconut milk as a base (see

---

[3]Fermented soy products that have been around for thousands of years, like tempeh and miso (and tofu, which is not fermented or a whole food, but is still relatively unrefined and traditional) are healthy and delicious, but highly refined, utterly unnatural soy derivatives such as soy protein isolate (found in all manner of "fake meats," protein powders, and other strange products) are common.

recipes), and coconut is not the primary flavor. To our palates, coconut has a cleaner flavor than soy or rice milk, and richer texture than nut milks.

The fat content of the coconut is a primary reason it is an ideal vegan product. I have found that most less-than-delicious vegan desserts are so because of a lack of fat. Fat contributes a texture that cannot be replicated. Vegans who eat a balanced vegan diet do not usually need to be concerned with fat, and the fats found in coconut are not unhealthy (this aspect is discussed below). Compared with soy, rice, or nut milks, coconut milk has more fat and is therefore much more tasty and makes desserts (as well as savories—see the recipe for Mushroom Stroganoff, for example) more satisfying. In ice creams as well as many other dishes, it also contributes a vastly improved texture. Fat (along with sugar and alcohol) prevents ice cream from freezing too hard, so coconut milk-based ice creams have a texture much more like that of similar dishes made with dairy cream.

It is at this point that a rather parenthetical discussion of "real" vs. "vegan" foods becomes relevant. Sometimes for example, well-meaning tasters of my vegan chocolate truffles proclaim them "just as good as 'real' truffles." I always want to ask them: Are they invisible? Cow's milk is popular, but it has not staked a claim on reality to such an extent that any other milk must be deemed an impostor. Soy milk, rice milk, coconut milk, and all manner of nut and seed milks have been used in many cultures for hundreds of years, and it reveals a Western bias to reduce them to the category of imitations. Let's stop comparing vegan dishes with "real" versions, and start comparing them to "cow's milk" versions (and then let's stop the comparisons altogether).

Another coconut product that is perhaps even more exciting for vegans is coconut oil (also called coconut butter). Many people have a negative impression of coconut oil because it is a saturated fat (it is solid at room temperature). However, it does not pose a problem for those who do not consume an excess of fat and/or cholesterol since more than half of it is composed of medium-chain fatty acids, which are used as energy and not stored as fat. Coconut oil does not contain toxic trans-fatty acids found in hydrogenated vegetable oils, which have been found to contribute to heart disease. Therefore, remarkably, this most luscious and luxuriously fatty food is not used as fat in the body but works as instantly available energy.

In addition, unlike most vegetable fats which are unsaturated and prone to destabilizing reactions with oxygen, coconut oil is highly stable and has a high smoke point. This is important because in order to get the nice caramelized brown color that makes vegetarian food so much more satisfying, oil must be heated very hot. When oil is heated, it can burn and become carcinogenic. Because coconut oil has a high smoke point, it is less likely to burn and thus much healthier than less saturated fats for searing, sautéing, and pan- and deep-frying. That this saturated fat is our best choice for frying seems to run counter to the general wisdom that unsaturated oils such as olive oil are always best for our health. It is important to keep in mind that the health benefits of unsaturated fats are only valid when those oils are stable, and for high heat frying, coconut oil provides a healthy alternative.

In addition to not being harmful, coconut oil has an important positive effect on the vegetarian body: it is one of the only vegetarian sources of lauric acid, which enhances brain function and the immune system and has anti-viral and anti-bacterial properties and is therefore beneficial for those with compromised immune systems.[4]

Now that you've bought your oil, a primer on the best way to use it is in order. For vegans looking for a butter substitute, coconut oil is perfect in almost all applications, and its fatty richness excels in baked goods. When replacing coconut oil for butter, shortening, or lard in recipes, the amount can be reduced by 25 percent (good news considering how expensive it is) because it is almost pure fat,[5] in comparison to butter and others, which contain significant percentages of moisture and/or milk solids.

---

[4] If you want the best coconut oil available, get organic Omega Nutrition brand, available via mail order. (800) 661-FLAX (3529).

[5] See recipe for coconut oil pie crust herein. The high fat content makes this crust superior in flakiness to butter crusts.

Because coconut oil is solid at room temperature in winter months, in cooler climates it can be melted prior to measuring, which makes it a little easier to work with. (In summer, it is liquid at room temperature.) Otherwise, it can be measured, packed down, in dry (flat-topped) measuring cups. If there are a lot of air pockets in the cup, the measurement could be off by a significant amount, so either pack it well or add grapeseed oil to fill up the cracks. Store coconut oil at room temperature.

Part two: resistance is fertile

The "coconut dairy" is an idea borne from the need for a new way of thinking about vegan food. Once we move beyond worrying about replicating animal products and using any means possible (chemical-laced margarines, etc.) to get there, we begin to explore the creative possibilities of vegan cuisine. This process—the creativity that results from immersion in an "alternative" culture like this—is typified by the phrase "resistance is fertile."

A novel we have enjoyed is Ruth Ozeki's *All Over Creation*[6] in which some of the characters in the book use "resistance is fertile" as a slogan. This sums up my own explorations in cooking from a political standpoint. I became vegan because I felt that if I could live without causing others to suffer, I had the moral duty to do so. For several years I was proud to be living my political beliefs on a daily basis in this way, but I was deeply unhappy with the food I was eating. I believed that making the choice to stop eating animals was enough—eating French fries at every meal and iceberg lettuce salads and "healthy candy bars" didn't matter, as long as they were vegan.

Slowly (thanks in large part to the women of Bloodroot) I came to have a more nuanced view of the politics of food. I saw that most food, even most food in health food stores, travels many hundreds of miles and is distributed by large agri-business corporations who often have political views I do not share (e.g. discrimination against lesbians and gay men, pro-globalization politics, exploitative marketing practices in

---

[6] Ozeki, Ruth, *All Over Creation*, NY, Penguin Books, 2003 (see also *My Year of Meats* by the same author, NY, Penguin Books, 1998).

"developing countries," etc.). I came to develop what Mary Daly calls a "biophilic" point of view, from "biophilia," meaning "love of life." Whereas I originally became vegan out of opposition to one practice (keeping and killing animals), I began to cultivate a philosophy of food with a wider progressive agenda. I saw that we could have a huge positive environmental impact by supporting local farmers, eating seasonally, and gardening. And of course, local, seasonal food tastes much better. Today, I feel that the **quality** of my food—the way it is grown, the way the workers who pick and process it are treated, the distance it travels, even down to the packaging it is shipped in—is just as important as whether or not it is vegan. When vegetarians and vegans limit politics to the realm of animal rights, we are doing ourselves a disservice. If Bloodroot has taught us anything in its almost three decades of existence, it is that feminism, progressive politics, animal rights, and environmentalism work best when they work together.

This is what "resistance is fertile" means to me: The Bloodroot atmosphere is fertile—women are teaching other women how to spin and knit, the air is laced with onions and garlic frying, books are being bought and discussed, the garden is teeming with gorgeous little green treasures. It is a site of resistance to the culture of violence and mediocrity that is the mainstream world. The more deeply I incorporate this culture of resistance into my life and work, the more fertile my life becomes—opportunities open up, creativity flourishes, hope is rekindled. In order to create the world we want to live in, we have to be able to imagine it.

Resistance is fertile.

SELMA, JANUARY 1977

Why vegan?

We wanted to demonstrate that being vegan is neither a sacrifice of taste nor of satisfaction. Although neither of us (Noel and Selma) are vegan, we are both animal rights vegetarians with a great respect for our vegan coworkers and customers. For many years now, in a desire to please them and also as a creative challenge, we have been producing more and more vegan dishes. Since we both eat our own restaurant food which is now 90% vegan, very little dairy or eggs ends up on our plates. And as we also notice the physical benefits of this lowered consumption of animal protein over time, we tend to want less of it.

The China Study[7] by Colin Campbell, published in 2005, makes the best health argument for a plant based diet. In the book Dr. Campbell documents the largest nutrition study in history which confirms that the diseases of affluence and of affluent societies—diabetes, cancer, obesity, heart disease—are a direct result of a diet based on animal proteins. Historically the people of Asia and Africa have no dairy tradition and meat consumption there has been very low compared to amounts consumed in the West and North. Therefore the incidences of the above named diseases have been low or nonexistent in these parts of the world. Of course the diets of peoples living near the sea have depended on fish and seafood, which are now so poisoned by pollution that they can no longer be considered a healthy food source.

But it's not easy to become a vegan. Many of us have had junk food eating experiences in our lives, and there is a lot of vegan junk food available to tempt us. Since we have become so familiar with American pseudo-foods, they attract us. Our friend and co-worker Connie Busch alerted us to the fact that many vegans consume junk food in excess. Artificial sweeteners, the over-reliance on soy (especially processed soy) and cups and cups of coffee in the vegan diet do not a healthy vegan (or vegetarian) make. Hopefully this book, combined with your own efforts, will be of help.

---

[7] T. Colin Campbell, *The China Study*, Dallas, TX, Benbella Books, 2005.

Limitation or Deprivation?

We encounter people who try to be vegetarian some of the time, usually for health reasons. For these folks, a vegan diet is too severe. So we ask the question: just what is deprivation?

We believe heartily in that great mother Necessity. The people of those cultures who have had very little diversity in their diets have learned to be artists with what they have. While we may celebrate how much there is available to us as cooks these days, it is mostly because we have the opportunity to learn about other people's home-style *comfort* foods. With access to such unusual items as shiso and daikon, ancho chilies and epazote, curry leaves and sticky rice, we also know that there is too much to choose from! So to limit one's menu to vegan foods seems constructive, and also a challenge. This is our work. A special challenge is to create desserts without eggs or cream. We know that as satisfying to the mouth as dairy is, it can cause real harm to our health. We have had many years to devote to developing delicious cakes, puddings, ice creams and mousses that are vegan. Without a focus on the idea of "limitation" we wouldn't have done it.

It is interesting to consider that *carnivores* are truly the ones suffering deprivation in their diet. Despite how trendy ostrich and buffalo meat may be, a dinner centered on meat(s) has very little variation. Think of how few meats there are, and how few ways they can be cooked: broiled, roasted, simmered or fried. Think of what passes for vegetables on the plate beside the meat. Then imagine just the grains possible in a vegan diet— the varieties of rice: white, basmati, Arborio, short-grain brown and wild rice. In addition, millet, quinoa, barley, corn, buckwheat groats, and of course, wheat. Think of the enormous cabbage family: broccoli, brussels sprouts, kale, Chinese cabbage, bok choy, mustard greens and collards. Think about the sweet roots: parsnips, carrots, turnips and beets. Think of the pulses: peas and lentils and beans in amazing numbers. Think of the chickpea flour dumplings of India and all the gravies called "dahls." Until we forgo the meats, we don't have time or stomach space to discover, to learn, to celebrate these riches of the earth. This is not deprivation, rather it is a door of "limitation" that opens to a new culinary landscape.

Changes

We opened Bloodroot in 1977. The seventies were a hopeful time. We had gotten out of Vietnam. There was a continuing civil rights movement whose goals were not yet accomplished, but that had impressive strength. There were the Stonewall riots (against persecution of gays) abortion was legalized, and second wave feminism was born.[8] We had a sense that we could have an effect on the future: in the words of the hymn, "We Shall Overcome."

In retrospect, it was also a quieter time. Children played outside despite the ubiquity of television (no video games, no 120 channels, no computers). At least amongst liberals, there was an assumption that public education was the most important domestic resource to be funded. "Home schooling" was nearly non-existent. The cost of college, while expensive, did not cause the indentured servitude as it does today. There was also the questionable assumption that psychotherapy of one sort or another could cure one's ills. Obesity was unusual, eating "disorders" unheard of, and there was no assumption of total accessibility by phone since there were no cell phones.

It was in the belief that something could be changed for women that consciousness raising groups began. The practice was developed by a South American cleric to prove to poor farmers that their problems were not isolated, but held in common because of a bad system.

Here's what some middle class white women talked about and debated, amongst much else: The idea that any success in life depended on marrying the "right" man, usually a rich one. We as women were in competition with each other. We might have best friends, whom we might betray. We despised our mothers; in fact, we despised ourselves. Mostly we knew that sex was the measure of us—that is, how sexually attractive we were. We all, the prettiest of us as well as the rest, were convinced that

---

[8] The first wave began in the 19th century, fighting for women's right to vote, which was finally won in 1920.

our bodies were ugly. If we were raped, it was our fault. Once you were married, rape was appropriate anyway. A woman's willingness or pleasure in sex was irrelevant. It was assumed that it was better for both parties if she was unwilling. Jobs were dead ends. Women weren't hired because they would probably get married and have babies. Lesbians (who were less likely to get married or have babies, at least then) weren't hired at all. If a woman went to a restaurant alone, it was assumed she was looking for a man to pay her in return for sex. If she were with other women, men would approach and ask the one deemed most pretty why she was alone! The few women doctors, lawyers and politicians (noted with surprise) were the exceptions to the men-only rule.

This awareness, discovered through our consciousness-raising groups, made us angry. We decided that we had to create a space for women (and any men who might be sympathetic) consonant with our beliefs. Therefore we decided to open a women's center where we might eat, read, buy books, talk with friends, organize. And so Bloodroot began.

At Bloodroot in the seventies, we carried a journal called *The Monthly Extract*,[9] which taught women how to look at their cervixes and do their own menstrual extractions, if need be. Hitchhiking was commonplace. We sold a bumper sticker which proclaimed, "Sisters Pick Up Sisters." Bloodroot had a women-only night on Wednesdays, and it was often our busiest meal, even in sleet storms. There are a lot of differences today. No hitchhikers. No call for a women-only night. A presumption that legal abortion will always be available. Then, women were in consciousness-raising groups. Now there's a proliferation of book groups (with no particular politics) and knitting groups called Stitch n' Bitch, perhaps with some feminist politics. Then there was very little discussion about organic farming. Now there is the rise of Community Supported Agriculture. On the one hand

---

[9] *The Monthly Extract, an irregular periodical* was an irreverent bulletin whose purpose was "to fire the Revolution by which women will rightfully reclaim our own bodies." It existed through the 70's, and was the work of New Moon Publications, the production by Lolly Hirsch with her daughters and Mary Lee Lemke.

the world is now more homogenized and outsourced. On the other hand, we have niche farming and biodynamic wines. We suspect that there were men in the seventies who enjoyed taking care of their babies and who were "soft," but they wouldn't admit to it. We think that, as a result of the woman's movement, men now feel free to show their potential for gentleness.

We love how diverse our country has become, and our city Bridgeport, Connecticut is full of relative newcomers. Before 1970 there were Italians, Puerto Ricans, Cubans, African-Americans, Hungarians, Poles, Germans, Jews and some Greeks and other Middle Easterners as well as the usual Anglo-Saxons. Today in Bridgeport there are also Brazilians, Indians and Pakistanis, and Mexicans, as well as people from many Asian and African nations. There's a Muslim mosque across the street from the old Romanian Church. This ethnic proliferation is a culinary horn of plenty to us. It is where our inspiration comes from.[10]

Over the years, we have seen many changes, but the one that concerns us the most is the rise of fundamentalist religiosity. In the nineteen eighties, Mary Daly called our culture a sado-society.[11] She believed that the church (any church, all churches) institutionalized patriarchy, and she wrote that Christianity in particular eroticizes sadism. So we are not surprised that there's a concomitant rise in pornography to match the rise in religiosity.

---

[10] For example, a customer born in Peru gave us seed of an herb called "Huacatay." It has an intense scent, somewhat like oregano. It grows up to ten feet tall each year and self sows in our garden. Our friend uses it on potato salads with fresh corn. If you want seeds, send us a stamped self-addressed envelope with your request to: Bloodroot, 85 Ferris Street, Bridgeport, CT 06605.

[11] In Mary's *Webster's First New Intergalactic Wickedary*, 1987, Beacon Press, she defined sadosociety as "n.: a society spawned by phallic lust; the sum of the places/times where the beliefs and practices of sadomasochism are The Rule; Torture Cross Society: Patriarchy, Snooldom." P. 94.

Pornography

In the past thirty years, women have made measurable progress in joining professions—"the ranks of the sons of educated men."[12] There are also more options for women living outside the structure of marriage. Meanwhile corporatization has increased worldwide and war, once thought to have been made unthinkable because of the destructive power of nuclear weapons, is currently considered the best political solution by our government. In fact, the horrors of war (and rape as its byproduct) have been increasing all over the world—a result, we believe, of the increasing fundamentalism of the three major patriarchal world religions: Christianity, Judaism, Islam.)[13]

Meanwhile, unnoticed by most good people, another aspect of violence, cruelty and hatred—pornography—has increased a thousand fold since 1990. The internet, as feminist lawyer Catharine MacKinnon points out, has made pornography vastly more accessible than any previous methods of communications could.[14] It is a "disease" which addicts boys at an increasingly younger age. Currently, there are more than 400 pornography websites directed toward children.

It's harder now to communicate with young women about the evil of pornography—we all swim in its sea and breathe its air. Magazines such as "Jane," "Self," "Fitness," et al., all sell the sexual desirability of soft porn—that is, the association of sexuality with violence, in their imagery. In its style pages, "The New York Times Magazine" is also offensive in this regard.

We see young women display the symbols (evidence) of pain (piercing) to make themselves what they believe is sexually

---

[12] See *Three Guineas* by Virginia Woolf (Harcourt Brace 1938). The book has long been considered an anti-war manifesto, as indeed it is. However it is also perhaps the most trenchant feminist analysis of women's lack of place in society: "Let us never cease from thinking—what is this "civilization" in which we find ourselves? What are these ceremonies and why should we take part in them? What are these professions and why should we make money out of them? p. 63.

[13] Fundamentalist Buddhism too!

[14] MacKinnon, Catherine, *Women's Lives, Men's Laws*, Cambridge, MA, Belknap Press of Harvard University Press, 2005.

alluring and/or to express their disconnection from their mothers' values. Rather than argue over free speech and whether or not there are negative effects from pornography, we want to make just one point: pornography is women hating propaganda. Just as the racist writings of the 1920's were propaganda that encouraged lynching (nice people, of course, didn't read it, they just looked the other way), and just as the anti-Semitic materials of the 1930's enabled the Holocaust (Germans were modern and intelligent Europeans—Jews couldn't imagine that they would believe Nazi propaganda)—so the pornographic depictions of women are intended to render our pain as ordinary: not important, not to be noticed by "nice" people. Pornography *is* women hating propaganda. Real women and children are used to make it, and it is "used" on other real women and children for men's pleasure. Pornography is called protected "speech"—but the women and children used in pornography are not protected people.

We do not want censorship, but we do want a society in which this kind of women hating is not possible—we want there to be no *market* for it, just as we want no market for racist or anti-Semitic materials. We must stand up and say that this is unacceptable and we expect that men who are truly our friends will do the same: making women-hating socially unacceptable on all levels.[15]

---

[15] As we wrote this, we discovered a recently published book: *Not For Sale*, edited by Christine Stark and Rebecca Whisnant, published by Spinifex Press, Australia, 2004. We are cheered to know that this book exists and that there are more than 30 contributors who are as angry as we are at the lack of acknowledgement of world-wide woman hating expressed by pornography and prostitution. Most important are the demonstrated interconnections between corporatized globalization, destruction of community, poverty, and the sale of women and children.

Resources

This new millennium has brought hard times for people with our political and ethical beliefs. Whether one reads newspapers, listens to radio or watches TV (or spends time on the internet), we are told only the worst about war, terrorism, etc. Fear is promoted. We have far less trust in our government than previously because it is more corrupted with lies than at any other time of our lives. The world has been corporatized. What we treasure—the earth, its atmosphere and its peoples and creatures—are in danger. We would be depressed all of the time (instead of just some of the time) if it weren't for levity. We came across the concept of levity in a book about biodynamic gardening.[16] Levity is the opposite of gravity. We have proof of gravity when we see things fall. We have proof of levity when we see things grow, like a bean sprout. It's an idea we like and it makes us laugh as well.

So we need other sources to help with the levity. What follows are some of our favorites. We hope you have others. We chose these not only because we admire them, but also because they seem to be unknown to most people whose values we share.

The magazine "Resurgence,"[17] from Great Britain is a favorite publication. It is the organ of the Schumacher Institute ("Small is Beautiful") that promotes a belief in keeping a human sense of scale and an earth-centered vision of governance, art and spirituality in opposition to the unsustainable religion of materialism. The editorials by Satish Kumar are always inspirational and we are pleased to find articles written by Vandana Shiva, the Indian physicist now environmental activist, in many issues.

The International Forum on Globalization[18] is dedicated to spreading information about native peoples, and how inter-

---

[16] *Biodynamic Gardening for Health and Taste* by Hilary Wright (London, Octopus Publishing Group, 2003); p. 16.

[17] *Resurgence*, Devon England, www.resurgence.org

[18] IFG *International Forum on Globalization*, 1009 General Kennedy Avenue, Suite 2, San Francisco, CA 94129.

national corporations (with help from the WTO and the World Bank) are stealing their resources. Indigenous peoples are fighting back in Central and South America, Africa and the Philippines. This news is essential.

Bioneers[19] holds a conference every Autumn featuring some of the best political speakers in the environmental movement. The Slow Food Organization,[20] which began in Italy, brings together both aesthetics and politics to counteract fast food. They call themselves an ecogastronomic organization supporting biodiverse sustainable food from local producers. In this country, Iowa Seed Savers[21] do more than offer a method for people who save heirloom seed to exchange their treasures. They are "saving the world's diverse but endangered garden heritage for future generations by building a network of people committed to collecting, conserving and sharing heirloom seeds and plants—while educating people about the value of genetic and cultural diversity."

Are there any mutual funds to invest in which hold political views we admire? As Paul Hawkin pointed out in Resurgence (Nov-Dec 2003): "All publicly held corporations live a lie. They believe we reside in a world where capital has the right to grow, and that that right is a higher right than the rights of people to their culture. There is something incalculably wrong with this view." Most funds that call themselves "green" or "alternative" invest in Wal-Mart and other scarcely admirable businesses. We have found only one fund operating with clear integrity and purpose as it invests only in alternative energy businesses with good politics, The New Alternatives Fund.[22]

On the radio, we try not to miss Diane Rehm's Friday morning NPR review of the week's news. Since she uses reporters/commentators with a range of political views, the program lends a perspective we don't find in any other medium.

---

[19] *Bioneers* Collective Heritage institute, www.bioneers.org.

[20] *Slow Food USA*, 20 Jay Street, #313, Brooklyn, NY 11201, (718) 260-8000.

[21] Iowa Seed Savers, Decorah, IA, (563) 382-5990.

[22] New Alternatives Fund–a mutual fund seeking growth and investment in various industries which are oriented toward a clean environment with a special interest in alternative energy. (800) 423-8383 or (631) 423-7373.

While her show presents opportunities for people with diverse opinions to express themselves, the comments of right wing reporters on her show clarify just how much at odds we are with their views.

Other magazines: *off our backs*[23] is surely the oldest and most continuously radical of feminist newspapers. We are so grateful it exists. We devour it each month. *Yes: A Magazine of Positive Futures*[24] recounts environmental efforts in the USA. *Conscience*[25] is a feminist Catholic publication which embodies real politics of conscience. *Tikkun,*[26] a Jewish magazine whose editors care about the fate of Palestinians, is well worth subscribing to for its positions on human rights issues.

Finally, here are four charities to which we want to call your attention: Unifem,[27] a global organization fighting for women's issues; United Farm Workers,[28] started by Cesar Chavez (a self proclaimed feminist) who struggled for dignity for farm workers—migrant or otherwise, the Farm Sanctuary,[29] a home for saved farm animals who won't be eaten or killed, and the Southern Poverty Law Center,[30] fighting racism and bigotry for 35 years.

We also have personal methods for creating levity. Paula Gunn Allen notes that the word "magic" derived from the word Mage—the two morphemes being Ma (universally mother) and Ge, or Earth, Gaia. What women do with what Gaia gives us—

[23] *OOB*, Washington, DC (202) 234-8072, www.offourbacks.org.

[24] *Yes*, Positive Futures Network, Bainbridge Island, WA (800) 937-4451.

[25] *Conscience*, Washington DC, (202) 986-6093.

[26] *Tikkun*, San Francisco, CA (415) 575-1200.

[27] *Unifem*, 1200 18th Street NW, Suite 1200, Washington DC 20036, (202) 721-1530.

[28] *United Farm Workers*, POB 62, Kaene, CA 93531-9989, (661) 823-6156.

[29] *Farm Sanctuary*, POB 150, Watkins Glen, NY 14891, (607) 583-2223.

[30] *Southern Poverty Law Center*, 400 Washington Avenue, Montgomery AL 36104, (334)956-8200.

this "transformation"—is magic.[31] Whether it is the cooking (the way the rice or lentils or broccoli is transformed into something delicious that gives us great pleasure in feeding ourselves and others), or the planting of the seed and the nurturing of the flowers and fruit which follows, or (especially for Selma) the spinning of wool or cotton or flax to a thread, then plying, dyeing, knitting and weaving, all this transformation is magic: a necessity, a healing, and a way to keep on going. While the product may be delicious or beautiful, it is the *process* which seems most beneficial, despite the apparent tediousness of weeding or chopping. Yes, there are a lot of stitches in knitting, but it's never tedious for Selma.[32] We both don't know what we'd do without our gardens — both at home and at Bloodroot. Noel captures the joy they give us with her photographs. They are so much work, but they are also the source of much magic and levity in our lives.

---

[31] *Grandmothers of the Light: A Medicine Woman's Sourcebook* by Paula Gunn Allen (Boston: Beacon Press, 1991) pp. 15-16. Also: "...the matter of the relation of ritual magic to women's lives and especially to the women's tradition: magic, as the word itself implies, is primarily a womanly enterprise. It's closest kin are the domestic arts." p 24.

[32] Knitting is very much the thing these days. Favorite classics are *The Knitting Workshop* and *Knitting Around* by Elizabeth Zimmerman, School House Press, Pittsville, WI. Also *A Treasury of Knitting Patterns* by Barbara G. Walker and the three *Treasuries* which followed it, long out of print but now reprinted and available from School House Press.

A Photographer's Perspective

Notice that our cat (named for Andrea Dworkin) is a bit out of focus in the photograph on the cover of this book. I (Noel) was taking a picture of the scene just beyond the door of Bloodroot— it was the mood of the moment there that I wanted to express. In the first photo of this series (the cover of Best of Bloodroot: Vegetarian), Andrea was lying on the stones looking out toward the water. This then, was the second shot, in which she had moved and was headed into the restaurant. The scene outside is still the main focus and is a stage for the cat. In this case the stage is the more important element. If the focus had been on the cat the photograph would have another meaning or intention.

The cropping or framing of this photograph is as important as the focus—the light outside the door draws the viewer there and is framed on two sides by the darker interior. The light draws the eye out while the movement of the cat suggests the viewer might want to explore the inside space as well.

Choice of focus, cropping, and shutter speed as well as a decision regarding depth of field[33] are variables used to create every photograph. Using this process of taking a picture as a metaphor, we can focus on what is biophilic, productive and beautiful in our lives. We can make conscious decisions regarding what we wish to include inside the frame and we can crop effectively so that whatever intrudes upon our creativity is left outside. Over time, we have found that by keeping the diversions of TV, junk food, inept presidents and computers outside the center of our lives (as much as possible) there is space for what Mary Daly calls telic focusing, which she defines as an "all pervasive principle within an organism entirely present in all parts of the organism. Source of deep purposefulness which makes possible growth, adaptation, creation."

We need to remember that we have a right to the joy such telic focusing brings us. Thinking in the photographic metaphor can be a way to help fight against those forces which would deprive us of that joy.

---

[33] How much of the image from the near plane to the distance is in sharp focus.

Autumn

Soups

Salads

Entrees

DESSERTS

portuguese kale and potato soup

Although this soup is traditionally served with Linguica, a Portuguese sausage, we find the sausage quite unnecessary. One of our Portuguese customers adds cooked red beans to this soup.

1. Peel and chop **1 large Spanish onion** and turn into soup kettle. Add ⅓ **cup olive oil, 2 large cloves crushed garlic**, and a **pinch red pepper flakes**. Sauté.

2. While onions are cooking, peel **3 to 4 medium size potatoes** and cut coarsely into 1½″ pieces.

3. Wash ½ to ¾ **pound kale**. Washing with hot water will get rid of any aphids you may find on unsprayed kale. Remove tough stems, roll leaves up tightly, and shred with a French chef's knife.

4. Add kale to soup pot with **1 quart water**. Bring to a boil, then lower heat and simmer until kale is cooked.

5. Add potatoes to soup with **3 to 4 tablespoons tamari**, ½ **tablespoon salt**, and **dash Tabasco**. Simmer until potatoes are done. Use a potato masher to crush potatoes somewhat. Add freshly grated **pepper** and correct seasonings.

6 servings

shiitake soup

This soup is the one to make for someone who doesn't feel up to par. It is more effective than the proverbial chicken soup since shiitake mushrooms are known to enhance the immune system. It also tastes wonderful.

1. Soak **12 dried shiitake mushrooms** in **2 quarts water** for ½ hour, or until they are soft. Remove them and squeeze the water back into the bowl. Soaking liquid should be reserved for the broth. Thinly slice the shiitakes. Set aside.

2. Chop **1 small onion**, thinly slice **1 carrot**, peel and slice **1 small yam**.

3. In soup pot, heat **1 to 2 tablespoons grapeseed oil**. Sauté the shiitakes until they turn golden, then add the onion and **1 tablespoon toasted sesame oil**. As the onions begin to brown, add the carrot and yam.

4. Next add **1 cup Chinese cabbage**, sliced thinly, **1 clove garlic**, chopped, and ½ **tablespoon fresh ginger**, grated. Turn all vegetables in the pot frequently. Add more **grapeseed oil** only if necessary.

5. When vegetables are well browned, add reserved shiitake soaking liquid and bring to a boil. Add a **few leaves fresh spinach**, ⅓ **cup tamari**, and fresh grated **pepper**. Taste and correct seasoning.

6. Serve hot, with sliced **scallions** on top.

   Optional: cooked **soba noodles** (Japanese pasta made of buckwheat) add a pleasant texture to this soup.

6 servings

quinoa soup
with cabbage and potatoes

This is an energy-producing soup. Quinoa is a high protein grain from the Andes.

1. Chop **1 large onion** and begin to brown in a soup pot in ⅓ **cup olive oil**. Peel and cut **5 to 6 carrots** in half, then into thin slices. Add to pot, stirring on occasion. Thinly slice **3 outside stalks of celery** and chop the **inside leaves**; add to pot, stirring.

2. Cut **half a small cabbage** into dice and add to pot. Thinly slice **2 cloves of garlic** and add. Stir vegetables seriously now, to be sure they brown well without burning. When this is done, add **3 quarts water**, 1½ **tablespoons salt**, and **1 cup quinoa** that has been rinsed in a strainer. Cover pot and bring to a boil.

3. If you like, peel and dice a **very small** (or half of a medium-sized) **rutabaga** and add to pot. When rutabaga is almost tender, peel and dice **2 small baking potatoes**. Add to soup pot. It is likely you will need to add more **water, 2 cups** should do.

4. When potatoes are cooked, serve the soup garnished with chopped fresh **cilantro**.

12 to 14 servings

spanish lentil and garlic soup

From Demetria Ocete via Sarah Giordano.

1. Soak **2½ cups green lentils** in **water** to **cover** for three hours, or until they have softened and are swollen. Drain and turn into a soup pot.

2. Shred **Swiss chard** and measure **4 cups**, packed. Dice **2 large red peppers**, peel and dice **2 potatoes** (2½ cups), **2 large carrots** (2 cups) and **1 large tomato**. Add all vegetables to the soup pot. Peel the cloves of a **whole head of garlic** and add to pot with **2 to 3 bay leaves** and **½ cup olive oil**.

3. Measure **12 cups water**, pour into the pot and bring soup to a boil. Turn flame down and simmer for 2 to 3 hours, or until lentils have virtually dissolved. Add **1 tablespoon salt** and simmer a few minutes longer. More salt or water may be needed.

10 to 12 servings

african curried butternut squash and banana soup

1. Peel and cut **1½ pounds butternut squash** into large dice. Place in a shallow pan with **1 ripe unpeeled banana**. Drizzle with **2 tablespoons grapeseed oil**, and roast at 350°F for 20 minutes or until squash is tender.

2. Meanwhile, peel and coarsely dice **1 carrot** and ½ **onion**. Slice **1 stalk celery** and **1 clove garlic**. Sauté the carrot, celery, and onion in **2 tablespoons olive oil** until softened. Add garlic, **1 teaspoon curry powder**, ½ **teaspoon ground coriander**, ¼ **teaspoon ground nutmeg**, and a **pinch cinnamon**. Cook all together for a few minutes. Turn off heat.

3. Remove squash and banana from oven. Peel banana and add to pot with squash pieces. Add **1 (14 oz.) can coconut milk** and an equal amount of **water**. Cook all together until well blended.

4. Turn soup into a blender in batches to purée. Return to pot. Season with **2 to 3 tablespoons tamari** and **3 tablespoons lime juice**, also **salt** and **pepper** to taste. Correct seasoning, and add water as needed to thin to proper consistency.

5. Serve hot with chopped **fresh cilantro leaves** and **pepitas** (pumpkin seeds).

6 servings

three sisters soup

Made of corn, beans, and squash, this rich and satisfying soup uses the native vegetables particular to North America. This recipe is adapted from Beth Brant of the Mohawk Nation. She serves the soup with fry bread and cabbage salad.

1. Soak ½ **pound red beans**, such as cranberry or pinto, overnight in water to cover. Or bring beans to a boil, turn off heat and let sit 1 hour, covered. Drain. Cover with water and cook until soft.

2. To make the stock, measure **2½ quarts water** (preferably from cooking potatoes) into a large soup kettle. Add **1 large onion, unpeeled, 1 scraped carrot, 2 to 3 outside stalks and leaves of celery, 1 scraped parsnip**, and a few **sprigs dill**. Bring to a boil. For added flavor you may add, if available, a few **bayberry leaves** or **1 dried ancho chile**, depending on whether you are from the Northeast or Southwest. Turn heat down to simmer and cook until vegetables are soft, about 1 hour.

3. Chop **1 onion** and **1 whole head celery**. Mince **2 to 3 cloves garlic**. Sauté vegetables in **2 tablespoons grapeseed oil** in another soup kettle, until they begin to brown, stirring often.

4. Turn contents of stock pot into a colander over the second pot or a large bowl. Press down on vegetables to extract flavor and then discard.

5. Add the soup stock to the sautéed vegetables. Stir in ½ **pound hominy** (lime-treated corn kernels, available in Latina markets. Do not use canned hominy). Simmer until quite done. You will probably need to add 1 quart **water**.

6. Add cooked beans. Peel ½ **large butternut squash**, and cut into wedge-shaped pieces. Add to soup with **1 tablespoon salt**, and simmer until squash is just done.

6 servings

STEPHANIE

sunchoke soup

To make when there are too many for salads. Sunchokes (Jerusalem artichokes) grow well in the garden, and can become a pest. Segregate these plants to a separate bed. This recipe is reminiscent of cream of chestnut soup.

1. Use a vegetable brush and water to clean soil from **sunchokes**. Cut up coarsely to yield **6½ cups**. Set aside. Peel and slice **1 large onion**.

2. Heat **2 tablespoons grapeseed oil** in a soup pot and sauté onions, stirring until wilted but not brown. Stir as needed. Add sunchokes and **2 cups water**. Cover and stew over low heat for 30 minutes or until sunchokes are quite tender.

3. Turn soup into a blender in several batches and purée. Return to pot. Season with **2 tablespoons tamari, 1 to 2 tablespoons lemon juice, fresh ground pepper**, and **fresh grated nutmeg**. Thin out with **1 to 2 cups** more **water** and correct seasoning. Reheat before serving.

4. Lightly toast **¼ cup pignoli nuts** at 300°F until light brown. These nuts brown easily, so be careful. Crush with a rolling pin or chop coarsely. Garnish soup with nuts.

6 servings

roumanian salad

From Fay Davidson.

1. Cover ½ **pound California Giant dried lima beans** with water and bring to a boil. Add **3 to 4 leeks**, well washed and finely chopped. Simmer several hours or until very soft. Mash with fork. Mixture should be loose since liquid will be absorbed.

2. Mince **1 small onion**. Chop **3 tablespoons straight leaf parsley** and add parsley and onion to the lima bean-leek purée. Add **2 teaspoons lemon juice, salt** and **pepper** to taste, and ¼ **to ½ cup olive oil**. Taste for lemon and salt. Chill.

3. Place a **whole eggplant** directly on a gas burner with the flame on high (or on a preheated electric burner). Turn the eggplant every few minutes so that it steams inside and turns black on the outside. It will be quite done in 5 to 10 minutes. Remove from stove (which will be a mess), slit open and scoop out eggplant flesh into a bowl. Chop ½ **small onion** very fine and add with **salt** to taste and ⅓ **cup grapeseed oil**. Stir together and chill.

4. Wash **2 pounds red and green bell peppers**. Use tongs to hold over gas flame or grill under broiler, turning often. When peppers are well blistered, remove to a paper bag. Close it and wait 5 minutes, then skin and remove seeds and drop into jars. Bring **1½ cups cider vinegar, 1½ cups water** and **1½ tablespoons sugar** to a boil. Pour over peppers and cool, refrigerate.

5. Serve lima bean-leek purée, Roumanian eggplant, and
   strips of roasted pickled peppers on a bed of
   shredded **lettuce** with **wedges of tomato** and **thin
   slices of cucumber**. Drizzle **vinaigrette** (see glossary)
   over the lettuce, tomato, and cucumber.

6 to 8 servings

LAGUSTA

three bean salad

From Denslow Tregarthen Brown.

1. Soak in water overnight in separate pots **1 cup dried chickpeas** and **1 cup dried kidney beans**. Cook the beans (separately) until soft. Allow an hour or more.

2. When the beans are done, steam or parboil **1 cup fresh green string beans** until barely soft. Do not overcook. Drain all the beans in a colander and mix them all together in a large enough bowl.

3. Make a vinaigrette while the beans are warm: mix **⅓ cup wine vinegar**, **1½ tablespoons olive oil**, **½ cup grapeseed oil**, **¾ teaspoon celery seed**, **2 cloves garlic**, crushed, **salt** and **pepper** to taste. If available, add **1½ tablespoons** chopped **fresh summer savory**.

4. Pour the vinaigrette over the beans while they are still warm. Add **3** chopped **scallions** and mix together. Refrigerate until ready to serve.

5. Serve cold on a bed of **Boston lettuce** with **red onion** slices, **alfalfa sprouts**, and **avocado slices**. Top with **gomahsio** (see glossary).

6 to 8 servings

tomatillo, pepita, and avocado salad

AUTUMN

We decided to grow tomatillos so that we could make Salsa Verde and because fresh tomatillos are infrequent in Northeastern markets. Raising them from seed is about as easy as raising tomatoes from seed, and in subsequent years we have found them as self-sown volunteers in our garden, so we have lots of tomatillos. Their botanic name is *Physalis Ixocarpa*. The epazote, which we cook with beans, is also a garden volunteer.

1. On a bed of **lettuce**, arrange peeled, washed, sliced **tomatillos**, **slices of avocado**, and **red onion** rings. Sprinkle **pepitas** (pumpkin or squash seeds) over the top and add a few chopped leaves of fresh **epazote**, if available, and a little minced **cilantro** (the white flowers are prettiest). Drizzle with **vinaigrette** (see glossary).

17

sweet and sour rice salad

1. Bring to a boil **1 cup long grain white rice,**
   ½ teaspoon salt, and **1⅔ cups water** in covered
   saucepan. As soon as water boils, turn down heat and
   cook slowly until water is absorbed and rice is fluffy.
   Let cool.

2. Make marinade: in a large bowl combine **⅔ cup**
   grapeseed oil, ½ cup red wine vinegar,
   2½ teaspoons agave nectar, ½ teaspoon dry
   crumbled **tarragon, 2 teaspoons salt, ½ teaspoon**
   pepper. Mix well.

3. Add the cooked rice to the marinade with **3 cups**
   mung bean sprouts, 1 cup slivered almonds,
   ¾ cup raisins and **½ cup red onion,** finely chopped.
   Mix well; refrigerate.

4. Arrange the salad on a bed of **lettuce.** Top with **red**
   onion rings and **fresh** snipped **tarragon,** if available.
   This salad will keep in the refrigerator several days.

10 servings

sunchoke salad

1. Either grow your own **Jerusalem artichokes** or buy them in a market. If you are harvesting your own after the first frost, scrub them thoroughly with a small brush under running water. Prepackaged ones need no cleaning and neither needs peeling.

2. For each diner, arrange a bed of **fresh spinach** on a dinner plate. Top with sliced **raw mushrooms** and thinly sliced **sunchokes**. Add a slice of **onion** separated into rings and finish with **vinaigrette** (see glossary).

crimson slaw with cranberries

1. Use a French chef's knife to shred ½ **head red cabbage**. Slice ½ **red onion** thinly and chop **3 scallions**. Combine vegetables with **6 oz. dried cranberries**.

2. Whisk together: ⅓ **cup olive oil, 2 tablespoons red wine vinegar, 2 tablespoons sugar, ½ teaspoon black pepper, 1 teaspoon salt, ½ teaspoon ground cumin, and ¼ teaspoon dried mustard**.

3. Pour dressing over cabbage and mix well. Refrigerate.

6 servings

avocado persimmon salad

Persimmons are available in November. Unless they are fully ripe (very soft to the touch), they will taste puckery instead of sweetly luscious as they should.

1. For each serving, make a bed of **lettuce** on a plate, using Boston, chicory and/or other favorite combinations.

2. Arrange on top of lettuce in a pinwheel pattern freshly peeled **grapefruit** sections, **avocado** slices, and **persimmon** slices. Top with **Bermuda onion** rings.

3. In a small jar, shake together ½ **cup grapeseed oil**, ¼ **cup lemon juice**, and **salt** and **pepper** to taste. Spoon dressing over salad.

Dressing makes enough for 6 salads

escarole salad
with pomegranate seeds

A surprisingly felicitous combination.

1. Choose a **small head of escarole**. Discard tough outer leaves, wash and break up inner ones into bite-sized pieces. Turn into a large salad bowl and set aside at room temperature.

2. Pull seeds from a **ripe pomegranate**. You will need ⅓ to ½ **cup seeds**. Set aside.

3. Make dressing: lightly crush **1 clove of garlic**. Use a small pot to heat the garlic gently in **3 tablespoons olive oil** for 5 minutes. Discard the garlic. Add **1 tablespoon sherry wine vinegar** (*or* **balsamic vinegar**) and **1 tablespoon dry sherry** to the oil with ½ **teaspoon salt** and a grating of **black pepper**.

4. Just before dinner, bring the dressing to a boil. Immediately pour it over the escarole and toss to mix. Top with pomegranate seeds.

4 to 5 servings

gingered broccoli stem salad

We save the stems from broccoli used in other recipes. They will keep at least a week in the refrigerator.

1. Whisk together in a large bowl: **¼ cup vinegar, ¼ cup Chinese sesame oil, 2 tablespoons agave nectar** *or* **maple syrup, 3 tablespoons tamari, ½ teaspoon fresh ginger**, grated, **1 clove garlic**, cut in half. Set aside.

2. Peel **2 bunches broccoli stems**. Discard the hard bottom of each stem. Slice the stems crosswise into thin rounds. (A food processor slicer works well for this.) Steam the sliced stems briefly so they remain crisp.

3. Put broccoli into bowl with dressing. Toss. Discard garlic pieces. Add **½ cup sliced mushrooms** and **½ cup slivered almonds**. Mix again and chill.

4. Serve on a bed of **lettuce** (we prefer Boston). A little shredded **carrot** on top adds color and sweetness.

6 servings

daikon-carrot salad

1. Cut **daikon** into quarters lengthwise and slice paper-thin. You will need **2 cups**, sliced. Peel and slice **1 carrot** paper-thin. You will need 1 cup. Place in a shallow container.

2. Combine ½ **cup rice wine vinegar**, ½ **cup water**, **1 teaspoon salt**, and **1 tablespoon agave nectar** *or* **maple syrup**. Whisk together well. Pour over carrots and daikon. Refrigerate.

3. Prepare a bed of **lettuce**. Arrange daikon and carrot slices on it. Slice **cucumbers** and add to salad. Top with **vinaigrette** (see glossary) and **sliced scallions**. Sprinkle with **gomahsio** (see glossary) if desired.

6 to 8 servings

autumn roasted vegetable platter

1. Plan on using two cookie sheets (trays) to roast vegetables, one for the ones that need long cooking, and another for the quicker cooking ones.

2. Peel and cut up **carrots** and **fennel bulbs**, cut a **white turnip** into wedges, and peel **small whole white onions. Fingerling potatoes** *or* **small Yukon Golds** don't need peeling, just scrubbing under water. Arrange these on one tray. Drizzle with **olive oil**, sprinkle with **Kosher salt** and **pepper**.

3. On the second tray, arrange halved **Brussels sprouts, cauliflower flowerets,** and fresh **shiitakes**, stems removed. Place the latter cap side down. Small **endives** go on this tray also. Season as for the first tray. Fresh **rosemary, thyme**, and **sage leaves** (use your choice of 2 out of the 3) will add savor.

4. Preheat the oven to 425°F. The first tray will need 30 to 40 minutes of cooking, the second 15 to 25 minutes. Turn vegetables over when they seem to be halfway done, and add **whole cloves** of peeled **garlic**. Be sure the **olive oil** is adequate!

5. Arrange vegetables in rows on a big platters, drizzle with **water-diluted balsamic vinegar**. Serve with **cranberry sauce** mixed with **horseradish**.

red kuri squash
and brown rice

Kuri squash is Japanese. It is a kabocha type of squash, dry textured
and sweet. It grows to be about the same size as pumpkin, which
can substitute for it.

1. Thinly slice **1 small onion** and mince **1 clove
    garlic**. Chop **½ teaspoon ginger root**. Sauté these
    vegetables over very low heat in **1½ tablespoons
    sesame oil**. Set aside.

2. Cut **½ small kuri** *or* **other squash** into thin crescent
    wedges, each ¼″ x 5″ to 6″. Don't peel, but do remove
    seeds. To cook, steam in batches in a large covered
    frying pan in a little **water** until squash is barely done
    and still crisp. Now trim off skin. Set aside squash and
    cooking liquid. You will need **2½ cups of liquid**.

3. In a pot combine: **3 tablespoons white miso**,
    ½ cup mirin, **½ cup sweet brown rice vinegar**,
    1 tablespoon umeboshi paste, and **⅔ cup tamari**,
    all available in health food stores. Bring gently to a
    simmer. Set aside.

4. Meanwhile, turn onion mix into a processor and
    purée into a paste. Add to saucepot containing miso
    mixture and add reserved squash-cooking liquid.
    Taste and correct seasoning.

5. Prepare **3 cups brown rice** by placing in a pot with
    5 cups water and **1 teaspoon salt**. Cover. Bring to
    a simmer and cook 40 minutes until done. Don't stir
    until rice is cooked.

6. Reheat squash in sauce together with ½ **pound tofu**, cut into thin triangles. Serve squash and tofu with the brown rice. We garnish this dish with **shiso leaves** (perilla). Shiso smells peppery and like basil. It is an annual which self-sows in our herb garden. The red variety is more decorative, the green tastier.

4 to 6 servings

WILLOW AND DARA

cabbage rolls
stuffed with sauerkraut, apples, and rye bread

Of Scandinavian inspiration.

1. In a 350°F oven toast **2 cups** cubed **rye bread** until crisped. Set aside.

2. Chop enough **onion** to measure 2½ **cups**. Set aside. Chop outside **celery stalks** and **leaves** to measure 1½ **cups**. Turn ⅓ **cup olive oil** into a frying pan and sauté onions and celery. When they begin to wilt, add **1 large clove garlic**, crushed, and continue to fry vegetables a few minutes more. Turn off heat.

3. Peel, core, and dice **2 cups** tart, crisp **apples**, such as Mutsu or Fortune. Set aside. Measure **2 cups sauerkraut**, packed. Rinse in a strainer and squeeze to remove excess water.

4. Add apples and sauerkraut to frying pan and turn heat to high. Add more **oil** if necessary. Add **2 teaspoons caraway seeds** and **2 tablespoons Sucanat** and fry until sauerkraut begins to brown a little. Turn off heat and immediately add ¼ **cup cider vinegar**. Season to taste with **salt** and **pepper**. Turn into a bowl and mix with reserved bread cubes. Let cool.

5. Choose a **cabbage** with leaves that seem loosely attached to the whole. Often Savoy cabbages are the best choice. Use a small knife to cut out the core. Bring a pot of water to a boil and place cabbage in, "stem" end down. Cook until leaves begin to soften. Remove cabbage to a colander in the sink and gently pull off as many leaves as are par-cooked. Return cabbage to pot as often as necessary until all leaves are par-boiled.

6. If center vein of leaf is thick, cut most of it out. Hold one leaf at a time in your hand or on a plate, top generously with filling, and roll up. Tuck sides in and place in a shallow baking dish. Repeat. The smallest inside leaves of the cabbage will hold just a little stuffing like a cup. Lightly brush tops of rolls with **oil** and refrigerate until serving time. Rolls will need ½ hour to 45 minutes in a 375°F oven to heat thoroughly and to glaze the tops, so allow time accordingly.

7. **Make creamy dill sauce:** in a pot heat **2 tablespoons grapeseed oil** with **2 tablespoons flour.** When bubbling, add **2 cups water, 2 teaspoons prepared mustard, 1 tablespoon tamari,** and **1 teaspoon nutritional yeast.** Bring to a boil, whisking until thickened. Season to taste with fresh ground **pepper** and **salt.** Add **1 tablespoon** chopped fresh **dill.** Cover and set aside off heat.

8. Prepare **rice** to serve with cabbage rolls. When done, serve cabbage rolls with creamy dill sauce and rice on the side.

6 servings

stuffed cabbage

Russian Jewish style.

1. **Make filling:** soak **1 package chunk soy protein** (approximately **3 cups**) in water to cover for 20 minutes.

2. Cut **1 large onion** into pieces and peel **3 cloves garlic**.

3. Put half the softened soy protein into a food processor. Sprinkle with **1 tablespoon nutritional yeast** and pulse to chop. Transfer to a bowl. Add the rest of the soy protein with ⅓ **cup tamari** and the onion and garlic and pulse to chop. Mix both batches together, adding a generous grating of fresh ground **black pepper.** Set aside.

4. **Prepare cabbage:** use a small knife to cut out the core of a **medium sized green cabbage.** Bring a pot of **water** to a boil and begin to cook cabbage. As leaves soften, use tongs to pull them off one at a time and put into a bowl. Reserve cooking liquid.

5. **Make gravy:** meanwhile, chop **1 large onion** and **3 to 4 cloves garlic.** Peel, core, and dice **1 apple.** Divide onion, garlic, and apple into two frying pans with a little **grapeseed oil** on each. Sauté over low heat while you make the cabbage rolls.

6. **Stuff cabbage:** fill cabbage leaves with stuffing. Roll up, tucking in ends. As each is finished, add to frying pan and turn rolls over so that they can brown while onion softens.

7. **Make sweet and sour sauce:** in a separate pot, combine **3 cups cabbage cooking liquid**, ¼ **cup tomato paste**, **3 to 4** cut up **peeled tomatoes** (fresh or canned), ¼ **cup tamari**, juice of **one lemon**, and **2 tablespoons brown sugar**. Whisk together and bring to a boil. Add **2 teaspoons** salt. Pour over cabbage rolls in frying pans, cover, and simmer one hour. Taste and correct for salt, sweet and sour seasoning.

8. Serve with **white rice** and chopped **dill**. Three cabbage rolls will serve one diner. Cabbage rolls will reheat nicely in a 375°F oven.

12 to 15 servings

31

sev pilaf

This dish from India uses "sev," a very thin, two-inch long broken wheat vermicelli (chickpea flour sevs are different). Italian or other vermicelli will not do, so a trip to the Indian grocery store is necessary. You can get fresh curry leaves and inexpensive cashews there also, as well as the necessary spices.

1. Thinly slice **1 medium onion**. Use a wok to sauté it over gentle heat in **2 tablespoons coconut oil**. Add ½ **teaspoon yellow mustard seed** and **12 fresh curry leaves**. Sauté for 10 to 15 minutes. At the end, add ½ **teaspoon hot chili powder** and **1 teaspoon ground coriander** and cook another minute or two. Turn out into a small bowl and set aside.

2. At dinnertime, peel and dice **1 large waxy potato**, such as Yukon Gold. Fry in the same wok over high heat in **2 tablespoons coconut oil**, turning potatoes often to brown all sides. Turn heat down. Add ½ **cup** coarsely chopped **cashews** and sauté another minute. Now add **6 to 7 oz. sev** (Indian vermicelli). Stir all together and when sev is light brown, return onion mix to wok. Add ¾ **cup water**. Cover and steam 5 minutes. Add 1½ **teaspoons salt**, or to taste.

4 side dish servings, or 2 small supper servings.

chicken of the woods

Finding the Chicken of the Woods mushroom, *Polyporus sulfureus*, is always a serendipitous experience. It is a large ruffled orange mushroom which tastes like chicken or lobster when young and tender. We hope our readers are conscious of the danger of ingesting an improperly identified mushroom. Be sure you or a competent mycologist is certain of what you are harvesting!

1. Cut **8 cups** tender edges of **wild polypore mushroom** and sauté in ¼ **cup olive oil** over high heat until browned. Add ¼ **cup unbleached white flour** and stir a minute or two longer.

2. Add **2 teaspoons white** (or "mellow") **miso**, **2 tablespoons lemon juice, 4 cups water**, and ¼ **cup tamari**. Stir all together and bring to a simmer. Chop ⅓ **cup parsley** and fold in. Add freshly ground **black pepper** to taste, correct seasoning.

3. Cook **4 cups** white rice in 5½ **cups water** and **2 teaspoons salt**. When tender, serve mushroom mixture over **rice**. Garnish with more chopped **parsley**.

8 servings

arborio rice pilaf
with swiss chard, kale, and butternut squash

1. Peel and dice enough **butternut squash** to yield **2 cups**. Steam in **1 cup water**. Drain, reserving cooking liquid.

2. Coarsely chop **1 large onion**. Set aside.

3. Strip leaves from stems of **kale** and shred the leaves. You will need **3½ cups**. Bring a pot of **water** to a boil and blanch the kale. Drain into a colander. Shred **3½ cups Swiss chard**. Heat **3 tablespoons olive oil** in a frying pan and sauté onion until it wilts and turns golden. Now add the kale and Swiss chard together with **2 cloves garlic**, peeled and sliced. Stir all over high heat until wilted.

4. Add **1¾ cups Arborio rice** and continue stirring and frying until rice becomes translucent. Now add reserved squash cooking water, cover, and turn heat to low. It is likely you will need more liquid. When cooking Arborio rice, it is best to add it gradually. Use plain water or potato cooking water, if available. Lift the cover often to see what is needed. Season with **2 tablespoons tamari** and **½ teaspoon salt**. Add reserved squash to the pan and fold in. Correct seasoning.

5. This pilaf becomes a special dish by serving special **mushrooms** on top of it. If you can find fresh Portobello mushrooms, chanterelles, boletus edulis, *or* shiitakes, buy **1 pound**. They will be expensive, but will make this meal exceptional. Slice and fry in **2 to 3 tablespoons olive oil** until crispy and brown. Season with **coarse salt**. Serve on top of the pilaf.

6 to 8 servings

three-grain pilaf

Serve with Spicy Corn Bread and Fried Kale (see following recipes).

1. Rinse ¾ **cup wild rice** and turn into a pot. Add **3 cups water** and bring to a boil. Turn heat down and simmer 20 minutes.

2. Add 1½ **cups orzo** (rice-shaped pasta) and 1½ **teaspoons salt**. Cover and simmer 20 minutes more.

3. Meanwhile, sliver **1 large onion** and chop **1 clove garlic**. Sauté in ½ **cup olive oil**. Add **1 tablespoon** fresh **thyme leaves** (*or* 1½ **teaspoons dried thyme**) and cook over moderate heat until golden. Turn off heat and set aside.

4. Add ¾ **cup bulgur** and **2 cups more water** to the rice and orzo once the 40 minutes have passed. Cover and simmer until all grains are done. Drain excess water if necessary.

5. Add vegetables to grains and finish seasoning the pilaf by adding **2 tablespoons tamari**.

6. **Serve with parsnip purée:** peel **2 pounds parsnips** and cover with **water**. Boil until tender. Place in processor (save cooking water) and purée with a pinch **cloves**, a pinch **ginger**, and a grating of **lemon rind**. Add cooking water as needed to make a soft purée, **salt**, and a generous grind of **black pepper**.

7. Fry **kale** (see following recipe) to serve with the meal. A wedge of cooked **winter squash** on each plate sweetens the dinner.

8 servings

fried kale

1. Bring **4 quarts water** to a boil in a large pot. Meanwhile, remove stems from **2 pounds kale**. Shred into thin strips and wash in cold water.

2. When pot comes to a boil, add greens. Stir them into the boiling water once or twice and turn out immediately into a colander.

3. In a large frying pan heat **2 tablespoons olive oil** over medium high heat. Add the kale and fry, stirring constantly until it begins to wilt. Add **1 large clove** minced **garlic**. Fry one or two minutes more to cook the garlic, and then add **2 teaspoons tamari**. Continue frying until liquid has evaporated. Taste for seasoning and add **salt** if necessary. Note that other greens—turnip, mustard, etc. may be treated the same way.

6 side dish servings

spicy cornbread

1. Preheat oven to 400°F. Steam **winter squash**. You will need **2¼ cups**. Set aside.

2. Dice **2 to 3 frying peppers** and **1 jalapeño pepper**. Sauté in **1 to 2 tablespoons grapeseed oil** until golden brown. Turn off heat and set aside. Set out an ungreased 12″ x 12″ x 2″ pan.

3. Combine dry ingredients, using a dry whisk: **2 cups cornmeal** (preferably freshly ground from a health food store), **1½ teaspoons sifted baking soda, 1½ teaspoons baking powder, 1 teaspoon salt**, and **2⅓ cups unbleached white flour**. Whisk well and set aside.

4. Combine wet ingredients: use a food processor to purée squash together with **½ cup maple syrup, ¼ cup grapeseed oil**, and **1⅓ cups soy milk**.

5. Turn wet ingredients into the dry, add peppers, and stir quickly together. Turn into prepared pan. Sprinkle **¼ cup pepitas** (squash seeds) over the top of the cornbread. Place in oven. When bread puffs, turn heat down to 350°F and bake until done.

9 servings

cauliflower fritters

Fritter recipe from Janet Habansky.

1. Cut out core of **1 cauliflower** and separate into flowerets. Parboil and let cool, reserving water. Measure water and add enough to make **2 cups**. When lukewarm, add **1 tablespoon yeast, 1 tablespoon salt, 1 teaspoon pepper**, and **1 clove garlic**, crushed. Leave 15 minutes. Add cauliflower pieces, cut up, and add enough **unbleached white flour** to make batter difficult to stir, **about 2 cups**. Let stand 15 minutes.

2. Steam **1 cup brown rice** to serve with fritters.

3. **Optional:** make **dijon mustard-french lentil gravy** (see following recipe) as a sauce or dip to go with the fritters.

4. Heat **2 cups grapeseed oil** in a wok and fry fritters by tablespoonsful in the oil. When done, they can be sprinkled with **gomahsio** (see glossary) or **salt**.

5. Serve with **rice**.

6 to 8 servings

dijon mustard-french lentil gravy

From Lagusta Yearwood, adapted from a recipe in *The Millennium Cookbook* by Eric Tucker and John Westerdahl.

1. Pick over ½ **cup French lentils** to be sure there are no small stones. Cover with **water** and cook, covered, over low heat, until very tender. This will take about one hour.

2. Meanwhile, coarsely chop **2 large onions**. Sauté onions in **2 to 3 tablespoons olive oil** over moderate to low heat. Stir occasionally. It will take 15 to 20 minutes for onions to begin to caramelize. Add ½ **tablespoon dry thyme leaves**, crumbled, and ½ **tablespoon dry tarragon leaves** while onions cook.

3. Add **12 oz.** of a **Belgian-style beer** and **2 tablespoons Dijon mustard**. Bring to a simmer and cook until liquid reduces to approximately ½ cup. Add **3 tablespoons dry sherry, fresh ground pepper** and **2 teaspoons salt**. Combine with drained cooked lentils. Adjust seasoning. Add **1 to 2 tablespoons tomato paste** and **2 tablespoons grapeseed oil**.

4. Turn mixture into a food processor to purée. Add **water** if gravy is too thick. Serve over mashed potatoes or rice, or with **cauliflower fritters** (see previous recipe).

makes about 3 cups

mashed potatoes and quinoa
with pepper and sun-dried tomato gravy

1. **Prepare mashed potatoes and quinoa:** peel **3 Idaho** *or* other baking **potatoes**. Cut each into quarters. Place in pot with **2 cups water** and bring to a boil. Cook 5 minutes. Thoroughly rinse **2 cups quinoa** (available in health food stores); add to pot, cover, and simmer until potatoes are tender and quinoa is fluffy.

2. Turn into a mixer to mash. Add up to **2½ cups more water**, as needed, to make a soft mixture. Add **scant tablespoon salt** and **¼ cup olive oil**. Turn into oiled pan and set aside.

3. **Prepare gravy:** dice **1 medium onion, 2 small green peppers, 1 red pepper**, and **1 fresh jalapeño pepper**, removing seeds first. Peel and chop **2 cloves garlic**.

4. Heat **2 tablespoons olive oil** in a large frying pan and sauté vegetables over high heat, adding **1 teaspoon dried oregano**, **½ teaspoon ground cumin**, and **1 teaspoon dried basil** to the pan. Fry until peppers are well browned. Turn off heat and set pan aside.

5. Place **⅔ cup sun-dried tomatoes** in a small pot. Add **¾ cup water**, cover pot and simmer 5 minutes. Remove tomatoes, reserving liquid. Chop and add to vegetables in the frying pan along with **2½ tablespoons tamari** and the reserved tomato soaking liquid. Dice **¾ cup seitan** (wheat gluten) and coarsely chop **1 tomato**, fresh or canned. Add these to the frying pan also, together with **1 cup water**. Cover and simmer 15 minutes. Correct seasoning.

6. **To serve:** reheat potato quinoa mixture in a 375°F oven. We steam **calabaza squash** (a winter squash available in Latina markets) and serve thin slices on the side of the plate. Heap the potato mix on each diner's plate, make a well to hold the gravy, and top with chopped **cilantro**.

6 to 8 servings

SELMA AND CHARLENE

banana leaf tamales
with mushrooms

We've found frozen banana leaves in Asian markets as well as Latina ones. Masa harina is available in Latina markets.

1. Defrost, wash, and wipe dry **1 pound frozen banana leaves**. Cut or tear into pieces approximately 14″ x 20″. For this recipe, you will need 20 pieces. Save discarded ends to line the steamer.

2. Prepare **ancho-guajillo sauce** (see index).

3. **Filling:** soak **2 cups dried shiitakes** in **warm water**. Cut **½ pound oyster mushrooms** into large pieces. When shiitakes are soft, stem, slice thinly, squeezing liquid out first (reserve liquid). Fry both mushrooms over high heat in a **few tablespoons grapeseed oil** until well browned. Set aside.

4. **Prepare masa mix:** in a standing mixer, stir together **4 cups masa harina, 1 tablespoon salt**, and **1 tablespoon baking powder**. Add **⅔ cup coconut oil**. Mix just to blend. Add **3 cups liquid**: mushroom soaking water, water, and/or tomato juice. Mixture should become a soft dough. Add more water if necessary.

5. Line up banana leaves. Spread each with **2 to 3 tablespoons masa** mix. Add **ancho-guajillo sauce** and reserved mushrooms and, if available, **squash flowers**. Fold in thirds; fold in sides. Line a large casserole or heavy pot with banana leaf discards and arrange tamales on top. When all are filled, add ½″ water to pot. Cover and steam over low heat for half an hour. Be sure water doesn't boil out!

6. Serve 2 tamales per diner. They can be refrigerated and steamed again if need be. Serve with **mexican red rice**, **tomatillo salsa**, and **refried beans** (see following recipes).

10 servings

tomatillo salsa

1. Rinse and remove husks from **8 tomatillos.*** Remove stem from a **large jalapeño chile**. Leave whole.

2. Preheat broiler. Place tomatillos and chile on shallow pan. Broil about 5 minutes, turning tomatillos and chile. When skin begins to blacken, remove and cool.

3. Turn all into blender. Add **2 tablespoons lime juice** and a handful of **mint leaves**. Blend to yield a coarse purée. Mince ¼ **cup onion** and add to salsa with **salt** to taste.

one cup

*Available in Latina markets.

ancho-guajillo chile sauce

1. Tear **9 dried ancho chilies*** into pieces, discarding the seeds. Similarly treat **6 guajillo chilies*** Toast, stirring, in a dry skillet. When they smell "roasted," turn into a bowl. Add **5 cups hot tap water** and let soak 10 minutes.

2. Peel **4 cloves garlic**. Turn garlic into a blender with chilies and the soaking water, **2 cups tomatoes** (canned), and the following herbs and spices: ½ **teaspoon oregano**,** **1 teaspoon** each **whole cumin, whole peppercorns**, and **whole coriander, 8 whole cloves, 3 bay leaves**, and **2 teaspoons salt**. Pulverize.

3. Heat **2 tablespoons grapeseed oil** in a large skillet and sauté ½ **teaspoon achiote seeds**.* When the oil turns orange-red, strain out the seeds and discard. Add sauce from blender to the oil together with a handful of fresh **epazote leaves**.* Cook until color changes. If gravy seems too thin, add some **masa harina*** and stir to thicken.

makes about 1 quart sauce

---

*Available in Latina markets.

**Preferably Mexican, rather than Mediterranean oregano.

refried beans

1. Soak **1½ cups dried kidney** or **pinto beans** overnight. When ready to cook, bring the beans to a boil in saucepot with water to barely cover. If beans cannot be soaked overnight, they can be brought to a boil in water, removed from heat and left covered for one hour. Beans will taste better and be more tender if soaked overnight. Either way, cook until tender with a few sprigs fresh **epazote**,* if available, about 45 minutes. Check beans periodically and add water if necessary, but keep the amount of liquid to a minimum.

2. Chop **1 large onion.** Fry in large pan in ¼ **cup olive oil.** When onions wilt, add **2 teaspoons** whole **anise seed** and **1 teaspoon** whole **cumin seed.**

3. When beans are done, use a slotted spoon to lift beans out of pot and into frying pan. Mash with potato masher and continue to cook. Some beans will remain whole. Season to taste with salt. When oil is absorbed, add ¼ **cup coconut oil.**

6 to 8 servings as part of tamale dinner

*Available in Latina markets.

mexican red rice

1. Heat ¼ cup **grapeseed oil** *or* **olive oil** in a frying pan. Add **1 cup rice** and ½ **onion**, chopped and **2 cloves garlic**, sliced. Sauté until rice becomes translucent. Add **2 teaspoons oregano*** while rice sautés.

2. Add **1 cup water** and the contents of a **28 oz. can of organic diced tomatoes**, such as Muir Glen. Add **6 sprigs of cilantro**, cover and reduce heat. Cook until rice is done. Stir in **1 teaspoon salt**.

5 to 6 servings as part of tamale dinner

---

*Preferably of Mexican origin rather than Middle Eastern oregano.

colcannon

This is a basic Irish dish which is well-seasoned and surprisingly satisfying. Potatoes are sometimes combined with cabbage, sometimes with kale. We like to use both. For a complete meal, serve Colcannon with a side dish of rutabagas and carrots, as well as Apple Chutney (see following recipe).

1. Peel and quarter **8 medium potatoes**. Boil in **water** to cover until tender, but not falling apart. Drain in colander. Return to pot and shake over low fire until mealy. Mash potatoes with a fork, potato masher, or in a mixer. Add **2 tablespoons olive oil**, **1 cup soy milk**, **salt** and **pepper** to taste. Set aside.

2. Finely shred **2 cups cabbage** and **2 cups kale**, well washed. Cover with **water** in a pot and bring to a boil, covered. Remove lid and boil uncovered 10 minutes. Drain well in a colander. Turn into frying pan with **2 tablespoons olive oil**. Fry for about 5 minutes until slightly browned. Add to mashed potatoes. Colcannon is now ready to be served as is, or can be reheated in a 350°F oven.

3. Dice **1 bunch carrots** (about **2 cups**) and an equal amount of **peeled rutabagas**. Add just enough water to steam vegetables. Add **2 tablespoons olive oil**, **salt**, and **pepper** to taste. Cover and cook until barely done. Uncover pot and raise heat, stirring, until vegetables are glazed and slightly brown.

4. Serve Colcannon with carrots and rutabagas topped with **shiitake-beer gravy** (see index) and diced scallions. Serve **apple chutney** on the side (see following recipe).

5 to 6 servings

apple chutney

Chutney will keep at least a month in a covered container in the refrigerator.

1. Peel, core, and dice **4 cups apples**. We prefer Staymen Winesap, but any crisp cooking apple will do. Coarsely chop **1 cup onions**.

2. Tie **1 teaspoon mixed pickling spice** in a piece of cheesecloth. Grind **1½ teaspoons mustard seeds** with a mortar and pestle or in a small coffee grinder.

3. In a stainless steel pot combine the apples, onions, pickling spices, and mustard seed with **¾ cup seedless raisins**, **⅔ cup dark brown sugar**, and **¾ cup cider vinegar**. Add a rounded **¼ teaspoon dry ginger** and **¼ teaspoon cayenne pepper**.

4. Bring mixture to a boil, stirring occasionally, then reduce heat and simmer for about 2 hours or until most of the liquid has cooked away. Be sure to stir frequently during this time to avoid burning.

5. Remove the cheesecloth with pickling spices. Cool, chill. Serve with **colcannon**.

makes about 2 cups

beer gravy

This variation on **Miso Gravy** (see index) contains more beer than the original and also makes use of nutritional yeast, a product available at most health food stores, which has a flavor remarkably like chicken bouillion. Do not confuse it with brewer's yeast which has a bitter taste. See which miso gravy you prefer.

1. Mince **1 small onion, 3 large mushrooms, and 1 large clove garlic**. In a saucepan heat ¼ **cup grapeseed oil**. Sauté vegetables until lightly browned.

2. Add ⅓ **cup whole wheat flour** and ⅓ **cup nutritional yeast**. Cook over low heat, stirring occasionally, about 10 minutes.

3. Add **12 oz. beer**, any inexpensive kind, or for especially full-bodied flavor, try **Guinness Stout**. Whisk gravy well, adding **1½ cup water**, ½ **teaspoon dried thyme**, crumbled, ½ **teaspoon dried basil**, **1 teaspoon agave nectar, 2 tablespoons cider vinegar, 2 bay leaves, 3 tablespoons tamari, 2 tablespoons red** *or* **brown miso**, and **2 teaspoons tomato paste**.

4. Cover and simmer approximately 20 minutes, stirring occasionally. If gravy becomes too thick, use **water** to reach desired consistency.

1 quart gravy

sweet potato cakes, maitake mushrooms, and soba noodles

Maitake mushroom (Hen of the Woods) is a wild mushroom, now available commercially in the Fall.

1. **First roast sweet potatoes:** wash **3 to 4,** place in a shallow pan. Coat lightly with **grapeseed oil** and sprinkle with **Kosher salt** and place in a 450°F oven. They will take 45 minutes to one hour to become soft.

2. Pull apart or cut up **1½ pounds maitake mushrooms.** Fry in several batches in a large frying pan in **grapeseed oil.** When each batch is crisp and a little brown, turn into a bowl. Repeat. Set frying pan aside and season maitakes with **salt** and **fresh ground pepper.** Combine in a 1 cup measure: **2 teaspoons toasted sesame oil, 1 tablespoon sherry wine vinegar, ½ tablespoon tamari,** and **1 tablespoon balsamic vinegar.** Sprinkle over mushrooms; toss and set aside.

3. **Make gravy:** mince **2 cloves of garlic.** Sauté gently in **1 tablespoon olive oil** in same pan used to fry the mushrooms. When garlic is soft, add ¼ **cup flour** and stir well to cook flour. If mix is dry, add a little more oil. Now add **1 cup water** and boil up, scraping up burnt mushroom bits. Season gravy with **2 tablespoons lime juice, 1 tablespoon tamari,** and ¼ **cup orange juice.** Mince **1 tablespoon cilantro leaves** and add to pot. Boil gravy and whisk well. Correct seasoning. Gravy should be rather thin.

4. Dice **1 small onion**, mince **2 cloves garlic**, and ½ of a seeded **jalapeño chile.** Sauté briefly in **1 tablespoon olive oil** in a small frying pan until wilted. Set aside.

5. Peel soft sweet potatoes and turn into a bowl.* Add onion and garlic mix to potatoes with ¾ **cup toasted breadcrumbs.** Mash sweet potatoes and add **salt** and **pepper** to taste. Divide mix into 6 to 8 balls. Dip each in **coarse cornmeal** and flatten to make cakes. Refrigerate until serving time.

6. Just before dinner, cook ¾ **pound soba noodles** till just done. Sprinkle soba with **1 tablespoon tamari, 1 tablespoon toasted sesame oil**, and **1 tablespoon sesame seeds.** Set aside.

7. At dinnertime, reheat the maitakes briefly, uncovered, at 350°F. Reheat gravy. Sauté one sweet potato cake per person in **hot grapeseed oil**, preferably in a cast iron skillet. Turn once to brown each side. Serve each diner one potato cake, a small nest of soba noodles and a small pile of maitake mushrooms. Spoon gravy over potato cake.

6 to 8 servings

---

*Don't discard the roasted skins. They make a delicious snack.

"meatloaf"

with shiitake mushroom gravy,
mashed potatoes, and peas

Soy paste is an important ingredient in this gravy. Find it in an Asian market.

1. **Meatloaf:** pick over **½ cup red lentils**. Turn into a small pot, cover with **water**, and cook covered over low heat until very soft. Drain in a strainer and set aside. Cover **½ cup dried porcini mushrooms** in hot tap **water**. Set aside. Turn **3 cups fine soy protein** into a bowl. Pour **1⅓ cups water** over the soy protein and set aside.

2. Chop finely: **1 large onion, 1 red *or* green pepper, 1 cup celery with leaves**. Turn into a medium-sized frying pan, add **3 tablespoons olive oil**, and fry over high heat, stirring constantly. Peel and slice **3 cloves garlic,** Add to frying pan. Add **1 teaspoon oregano, 1½ teaspoons dried basil**, and **1 teaspoon ground cumin**. Squeeze liquid from porcini and reserve. Chop the porcini. Add to the frying pan and continue sautéing until the vegetables begin to brown, stirring often. Set aside.

3. Add cooked lentils to soy protein bowl with **2 tablespoons nutritional yeast, ¼ cup tamari, 1 cup** fruit-sweetened **health food store catsup**, and the sautéed vegetables. Finally, add **3 tablespoons potato starch**. Mix all together well. Pack into a large Pyrex loaf pan (one that holds 5 to 5½ cups meatloaf mixture). Drizzle a little catsup over the top, and bake at 375°F for 45 minutes, or until browned on top. Let cool 15 to 20 minutes before turning out onto serving platter.

4. **Shiitake mushroom gravy:** soak together **8 to 10 dried shiitake mushrooms, 1 seeded ancho chile pepper,** and **2 large sundried tomatoes** in boiling water. Set aside. Slice **4 cups button mushrooms** and set aside. Chop **1 large onion** and **3 cloves garlic.** Pick out and squeeze shiitakes, reserving chile, tomatoes and liquid, and slice. Sauté onions, garlic, and both mushrooms in ¼ **cup grapeseed oil** over high heat until they begin to brown, stirring often. Add ⅓ **cup flour** and cook 2 minutes more. Now add **1 cup red wine** (optional), ⅓ **cup tamari,** and **3 cups water.** Purée ancho chile and sundried tomatoes in their soaking liquid in a blender and add to gravy pot with reserved porcini liquid. Add **2 tablespoons soy paste** (we use Kim Lan brand, available in Chinese markets) and **water** as needed. Bring to a boil, simmer 30 minutes, correct seasoning.

5. **Mashed potatoes:** peel and cut **5 potatoes** into thirds. Barely cover with water and cook until tender. Drain and turn into mixer. Mash briefly with a flat beater. Add **4 tablespoons olive oil,** ⅔ **cup soy** *or* **coconut milk, 1½ teaspoons salt,** and fresh ground **pepper.** Taste for seasoning. Turn into oiled Pyrex pan (mixture should be quite soft). Heat in a 375°F oven until potatoes form a brown crust.

6. **Peas:** meanwhile heat **1 package frozen peas** in **2 to 3 tablespoons water.** Don't overcook.

7. **To serve:** turn meatloaf out onto serving dish and slice. (Meatloaf may be reheated). Serve mashed potatoes with gravy and peas on the side.

8 to 10 servings

pasta and pepper tomato sauce
with broiled fresh shiitake mushrooms

Large Japanese shiitake mushrooms, *Lentinus edodes*, sometimes called Golden Oak Mushrooms, are incomparable. Their rich flavor justifies spending money for them when you can. We like to prepare them in this simple fashion as a garnish to a pasta dish.

1. **Make pepper tomato sauce:** clean and slice **8 frying peppers**, red ones if possible. Slice **1 very large onion.** Heat **3 tablespoons olive oil** and ½ **teaspoon red pepper flakes** in a pot, and fry peppers with onions over high heat until they wilt and begin to brown. Well browned vegetables give a natural sweetness to this sauce.

2. Add **29 oz. plain tomato sauce** to the pot with ¼ **cup tamari.** Rinse tomato sauce can with an equal amount of **water** and add to pot. Add ½ **can red wine, salt,** and **pepper** to taste. Simmer 20 minutes.

3. Finish sauce with **3 tablespoons pesto,** if available. Chop ½ **bunch straight leaf parsley** and add. Sauce should be thin and not very tomato tasting. Thin with equal parts **water** and **wine** as necessary.

4. **Cook pasta:** cook **2 to 3 pounds linguine** until just done. Drain well.

5. **Broil mushrooms:** just before serving, heat broiler very hot. Use **1 tablespoon olive oil** to lightly grease a shallow pan. Arrange **1 pound shiitake mushrooms** cap side down, in the pan. Sprinkle with **Kosher salt** and drizzle with very little **olive oil.** Broil without turning until mushrooms smell wonderful and edges begin to brown. Slice mushrooms into strips.

6. **To serve:** arrange pasta on a serving platter. Top generously with sauce, sprinkle more chopped **parsley** over the top, and place grilled mushrooms on top of platter.

6 to 8 servings

ANGELITA

harvest vegetable platter

We don't celebrate Thanksgiving because of its questionable association with the theft of Native American land. However, we do have a harvest feast on the fourth Thursday in November as an example of how well vegetarians can eat at feasting time.

1. **Make rutabaga-potato purée:** peel and cut into chunks **1 medium sized rutabaga** (yellow turnip). Cook in boiling salted water about 10 minutes. Add **2 medium potatoes**, peeled and cut into chunks. When both are cooked, drain and purée in food processor or mixer while still hot. In small pot, sauté **1 clove garlic**, crushed in **2 tablespoons grapeseed oil**. Add to purée together with ⅓ **cup olive oil**. Season to taste with **salt** and **pepper**. Can be reheated, uncovered, in a 350°F oven.

2. **Make roasted parsnips and carrots:** preheat oven to 450°F. Thinly slice **4 peeled parsnips, 1 medium onion, 5 scraped carrots**. Put into shallow roasting pan and moisten with a little **grapeseed oil**. Roast, stirring often, until browned. When almost done, add ¼ **to** ½ **cup sunflower seeds**. When well cooked, add ¼ **cup water** and **1 tablespoon tamari**. Cover with foil to keep warm or reheat covered.

3. **Prepare sweet dumpling squash:** slice **4 squash** in half lengthwise and scrape out seeds. (Discard seeds or roast in oven, sprinkled with a little oil and coarse salt for a snack). Now either slice squash crosswise in scalloped slices, or for a more elaborate dinner, stuff squash halves with chestnut stuffing (see below). If you are simply slicing them, put them in a roasting pan, add **1 cup water**, cover with foil and bake at 350°F until they are just soft. Don't overcook.

4. **Make chestnut stuffing:** dry enough homemade bread and chop by hand or in food processor to get **2 cups.** Cut an X in **20 chestnuts.** Sauté 5 to 6 at a time in **2 to 3 tablespoons oil,** stirring often, for 5 to 10 minutes. Let cool. Peel. Be sure to remove inner brown skin. Finely chop **½ cup onions** and **¼ cup shallots** and sauté in **2 tablespoons grapeseed oil** in large fry pan. Add breadcrumbs, **½ teaspoon dry thyme, 2 tablespoons chopped celery leaves, 3 tablespoons straight leaf parsley,** chopped, **1 teaspoon salt,** fresh ground **pepper, 1 teaspoon lemon juice,** and a **splash** of **brandy.** Slice the chestnuts into the mixture, which should be slightly moist. Add **soy milk** if needed. **Salt** and **pepper** the insides of the squash halves and moisten with **oil.** Heap stuffing into squash halves and place in pan. Add ½″ of water to pan, cover with foil and bake until squash are done, about 45 minutes, at 350°F. To reheat, uncover pan.

5. **Make apple cranberry sauce:** peel, core, and slice **6 tart apples.** Put in a pot with **½ pound cranberries.** Add **½ cup apple juice** *or* **cider,** **¼ teaspoon cinnamon** and cook covered until cranberries are popped and apples are soft. Now add enough **maple syrup** to sweeten.

6. **Make miso gravy** *or* **shiitake gravy:** see index.

7. When ready to serve, steam **1 head of broccoli flowerets** until barely done.

8. Serve rutabaga-potato purée and the squash with miso gravy. The roasted parsnips and carrots, broccoli and apple cranberry sauce all make a very pretty platter.

8 servings

shiitake soy paste gravy

Our favorite gravy. Kimlan Soy Paste should be available in Asian markets.

1. Place **6 dried shiitake mushrooms, 1 seeded dried ancho* chile pepper,** and **2 sundried tomatoes** in a bowl. Cover with boiling **water** and set aside.

2. Mince **1 small onion** and slice **1 to 2 cloves garlic.** When shiitakes have softened, squeeze liquid back into bowl and slice the mushrooms thinly. Sauté shiitakes, onion, and garlic in ⅓ **cup grapeseed oil.** When onions just begin to caramelize, add ⅓ **cup flour** and ¼ **cup nutritional yeast**** (optional).

3. Use a blender to purée ancho chile, sundried tomatoes, and reserved liquid. Add to pot together with **1½ cups water, 1 bottle** of a **honey brown ale,** ½ **teaspoon dried thyme,** ½ **teaspoon dried basil, 2 bay leaves, 2 tablespoons tamari,** ¼ **cup soy paste,** and **2 to 3 tablespoons tomato paste.** Bring to a simmer and correct seasoning. Add **water** as needed.

1 to 2 quarts gravy

---

*Available in Latina markets.
**Available in health food stores.

quinoa and butternut squash

From Janet Gordon.

1. Thinly slice peeled **butternut squash** and measure **3 cups**. Dice and steam. Set aside.

2. Rinse **1½ cups quinoa*** thoroughly and strain. Bring scant **2 cups water** to a boil with **1 teaspoon salt**, add quinoa and simmer covered until liquid is absorbed.

3. Meanwhile, toast ⅓ **cup pignoli nuts** in a 300°F toaster oven. Set aside when light brown.

4. Cut a small **red pepper**, seeded, into dice. Sauté in **2 tablespoons olive oil**.

5. When quinoa is done, add the peppers and the following: ¼ **cup currants, 3 tablespoons** more **olive oil**, grated **rind** of ½ lemon, **1 tablespoon lemon juice**, ⅓ **teaspoon ground cumin**, the pignoli nuts, and drained squash. Season generously with fresh ground **black pepper**. Toss all together. May be prepared ahead and reheated in an open casserole dish at 350°F.

6. We like to serve this with **2 pounds Brussels sprouts** which have been halved, steamed, and sprinkled with a mix of **tamari** and **rice wine vinegar** to taste, and **olive oil**.

8 servings

---

*See the glossary for information on quinoa.

tofu roast

We worked on many variations on this recipe with Stephanie Zinowski's help. She makes various tofu roasts at her vegan café at Wesleyan University. This is our favorite version. The result may be served hot as part of dinner, or cold as a snack or salad topping. Try the Lapsang Souchong smoked variation, it is delicious!

1. You will need **firm tofu** for this recipe. If your tofu is soft, cut 2 cakes (**2 pounds**) in half crosswise, arrange on a tray, cover with another tray and weight with, say, a big can of tomatoes for an hour. Drain liquid off. Slice tofu into thin triangles and place on a cookie sheet.

2. **Make marinade:** mince **2 tablespoons ginger,** crush **3 cloves garlic** and turn into a small pot. Add **3 tablespoons tamari, 3 tablespoons toasted sesame oil, 2 tablespoons brown rice vinegar, 1 tablespoon sugar,** and **1 teaspoon hot sauce.** Grate **black pepper** over. Bring to a boil and simmer 5 minutes. Chop **2 tablespoons fresh herbs** such as **basil** and **cilantro** (For a summer dish, use Thai basil and green shiso) and add to sauce. Spoon marinade over each tofu slice. Sprinkle with **sesame seeds.** Turn pieces, spoon marinade on other side and add more sesame seeds.

3. Chill at least 5 hours or overnight.

4. Preheat oven to 375°F. Tofu must roast as dry as possible, so if marinade remains, lift pieces out onto another cookie sheet. Brush lightly with **grapeseed oil** and roast at least 20 minutes per side (turn them over midway), or until chewy, almost crispy.

5. For a very interesting slightly smoked scent and flavor, transfer tofu to a rack which fits in an oven roasting pan. Open **3 to 4 Lapsang Souchong tea bags** and scatter the leaves in the pan below the rack. Cover the tofu with a loosely fitted tent of foil. Bake another 15 to 20 minutes.

3 to 4 servings as part of dinner

SWANS AT BLOODROOT

choucroute and "bacon"

We love Sandor Katz's book *Wild Fermentation*, and have been inspired to make our own sauerkraut as a result. Here's something wonderful to do with it.

1. You will need **2 pounds sauerkraut**. Place in a large glass baking dish. Moisten with ½ **cup apple cider** (if it has turned "hard," it's even better!). Set in a 350°F oven.

2. Pan-roast **2 teaspoons whole peppercorns** until crisp and nutty. Turn into a mortar. Add **6 juniper berries, 1 teaspoon chopped winter savory, 6 whole fennel seeds**, and **1 tablespoon chopped fresh rosemary**. Crush all together with the pestle. Sprinkle herbs and spices over the kraut, drizzle generously with **grapeseed oil**, and cover tightly with aluminum foil. Bake 1 hour.

3. Uncover. Top with **6 to 8 strips of faux "bacon"*** of your choice. Add more **cider** if mix seems dry. Continue roasting until "bacon" is crisp.

4. Meanwhile, scrub but do not peel **1½ pounds fingerling potatoes**. Cut in half lengthwise. Fry, cut side down, in a hot cast iron skillet in a little **grapeseed oil**. When brown, turn and fry the other side for 5 minutes. **Salt** and **pepper** potatoes.

5. Remove "bacon" from baking pan. Push kraut aside and add potatoes. Continue baking until potatoes are tender—another 5 to 10 minutes. Serve with bacon on top of casserole. Roasted **chestnuts** are a nice addition. **3 to 4 carrots**, sliced and cooked in **water** with a little **oil** and **agave nectar** until glazed, go well on the side.

6 to 7 servings

---

*Such as tempeh-based Fakin' Bacon or Morningstar Farms bacon strips.

new england boiled dinner

1. Prepare **sauce soubise**. See following recipe.

2. Prepare a cooking broth for the vegetables. Bring to a boil **1 quart water**, **⅓ cup tamari**, and **½ cup grapeseed oil**.

3. Cut up vegetables in large (2″) chunks. Start with **1 small rutabaga** and add to the broth. It should boil 15 minutes before adding **2 cups** peeled **baby white onions**. Turn heat to simmer and cook 5 minutes. Meanwhile, clean **1½ cups small white turnips**. Add to pot. Cook 10 minutes.

4. Clean **1 pound carrots**, cut in thirds and add to pot. When carrots are almost tender, add **6 to 8 red-skinned potatoes**, well-scrubbed but not peeled. Simmer 10 minutes. Cut a **small cabbage** in wedges and lay wedges at sides of pot. Simmer a few minutes and add **2 sweet potatoes**, washed and cut in thirds.

5. Meanwhile, if you like, cut X's in a **dozen fresh chestnuts**. Cover with water and bring to a boil. Peel while quite hot, removing brown underskin together with the shell. Add to stew pot.

6. To serve the boiled dinner, spoon out some of all the vegetables into deep dinner plates. Spoon **sauce soubise** over the top. Garnish with **chestnuts** and **fresh dill**. Serve more Soubise on the side, and offer **coarse mustard** for those who would like it.

6 to 8 servings

sauce soubise

1. Slice enough peeled **onions** to measure **6 cups**. Stew very slowly in a heavy sauce pot in ½ **cup grapeseed oil** for at least 30 minutes, stirring. Onions should not brown at all. Add scant ⅔ **cup flour** and cook over low heat 5 minutes more.

2. Add **2¼ cups water** and bring to a boil, cooking until thickened. Turn sauce into blender or food processor and purée. Return to pot, and if too thick, add up to ¼ **cup more water**. Return sauce to a simmer and add ¾ **tablespoon salt, pepper**, and **nutmeg** to taste, and **3 tablespoons Polish** *or* **coarse mustard**.

3. Rinse ¼ **cup capers**, salted or in brine, and chop coarsely. Stir capers into ½ **cup dry white wine** (*or* substitute ¼ **cup cider vinegar** and ¼ **cup water**), **2 tablespoons red miso**, and **1 tablespoon lemon juice**. Add to simmering sauce and correct seasoning.

4. Chop enough **fresh dill** to measure ¼ **cup** and add to sauce. Serve with **new england boiled dinner**.

makes about 3 cups

hazelnut pie crust

1. **Make flax seed "eggs":** soak ¼ cup flax seeds* in ¾ cup hot water in a blender for 15 minutes. Turn machine on until mix resembles grey caviar and most seeds are crushed. Store these "eggs" in the refrigerator.

2. **Make pie crust:** toast ¾ cup hazelnuts (filberts) at 300°F until light tan. Use a towel to rub skins off, if any. (Skinned hazelnuts are available in some markets.) Let cool.

3. Turn hazelnuts into a food processor. Measure 1½ cups all-purpose flour, 1 teaspoon baking powder, ½ teaspoon salt, 2 tablespoons sugar, and 1½ tablespoons potato starch. Turn processor on. Chop nuts fine and then add dry ingredients. Blend.

4. Add ⅓ cup coconut oil (either liquid in summer or solid in winter) and 1 rounded tablespoon of flax seed "eggs". Pulse briefly. Drizzle ¼ cup cold water into processor. Pulse. Don't overmix. A soft dough should form. If necessary, add a few more drops water.

5. Use flour to roll dough out. This can be done immediately, but it will be a little easier once chilled.

*makes enough for a two crust pie***

---

*Store flax seeds in the refrigerator.

**Leftover piecrust may be rolled out in a cinnamon sugar mix, cut into strips, and baked at 350°F to 375°F to make delicious cookies.

almond oat pie crust

1. Preheat oven to 375°F. Put **1 cup almonds** into food processor and chop coarsely. Turn off. Add: **¾ cup oat flakes**, **⅓ cup unbleached white flour**, **½ teaspoon baking soda**, **½ teaspoon baking powder**, and **¾ cup date sugar**. Process to mix. Turn off.

2. In a 1 cup pitcher, combine: **½ cup grapeseed oil**, **¼ cup soy milk** or water, and **1 teaspoon vanilla extract**. Turn processor on and add in a stream. Resulting mix will be a firm paste.

3. Use 2 spoons to pat out crust in a deep glass pie pan. Mixture that extends above edge can be pinched between thumb and forefinger to make a decorative fluted crust. Remaining dough can be shaped into flat cookies and placed on a small baking sheet.

4. Bake until light brown and crisp, about 20 minutes.

makes 1 crust and 4 to 5 cookies

coconut oil pie crust

This crust is the easiest of any to make, and the hardest to work with. It is more difficult in hot, humid weather. This recipe has been adapted from a lard version.

1. In a small bowl combine **1 cup all-purpose flour** and **½ teaspoon salt**. If you like, add **½ teaspoon ground cardamom**. Also add **2 tablespoons sugar**. Stir together with a dry whisk.

2. Measure a scant ⅓ **cup coconut oil** (it should be quite liquid. If it is not, heat it to liquefy.) Add **2 tablespoons water** to coconut oil and use a fork to stir oil and water together. Immediately dump liquids into flour mix and stir with fork. It will quickly form a very sticky ball.

3. Place pastry ball between 2 sheets of plastic wrap (or wax paper). Use a rolling pin to roll out a shape as close as possible to a circle. When it is thin enough, slide the plastic-wrapped sandwich onto a rimless cookie sheet. Carefully remove the top piece of plastic wrap and discard. Invert a 9″ Pyrex pie plate over the pastry, and carefully turn it all right side up. As you cautiously remove the second piece of plastic wrap, edge the crust into the pan. Use your **floured** fingers to shape the edge. Prick bottom with a fork. Sprinkle lightly with **flour.**

4. Refrigerate until cold, 5 to 10 minutes. Bake for 10 minutes weighted with foil and beans at 375°F. Remove foil and add fruit or other filling, or complete baking (about 15 to 20 minutes) and fill pie shell afterwards.

1 pie crust

coconut milk whipped cream

Sometimes a can of Thai Premium Organic coconut milk seems to be quite thick and ready to serve as is. This recipe is for the other times.

1. Turn contents (14 oz.) of a **can of coconut milk** into a small pot. Add ½ **cup water.**

2. Add **2 tablespoons sugar,** (*or* **1 tablespoon agave nectar**), **1 tablespoon coconut oil, dash salt, 1 tablespoon kudzu,** and **1½ teaspoon instant agar-agar** (see glossary). Stir. Bring to a simmer, stirring. When it thickens slightly, add ½ **teaspoon vanilla extract, 1 tablespoon brandy** and **1 tablespoon balsamic vinegar.** Cool, chill.

3. When mixture is solid, turn into a food processor to whip until fluffy. This will take a while. First it will separate and look curdled. It will take 3 to 4 minutes to become creamy. Store in refrigerator.

1½ cups

almond créme

A dessert topping.

1. Use a food processor to pulverize **1 cup almonds**, which needn't be blanched. When nuts are as fine as you can get them, slowly add **2 cups hot water** to the machine, to make an almond milk. Purée as thoroughly as you can.

2. Turn out into a cheesecloth-lined colander over a bowl. Twist the cheesecloth to extract as much almond liquid as possible. Discard almond pulp. Measure the liquid. You should have about 1½ cups of almond milk.

3. Turn into a small pot. Add **2 tablespoons plus 1 teaspoon light agave nectar** and **1½ tablespoons lemon juice**. Bring to a simmer. Meanwhile, mix together **1 rounded tablespoon kudzu starch** and **1½ tablespoons water** (you could use cornstarch if no kudzu is available at your local health food store). When créme is simmering, add starch and whisk until thickened. Remove from stove.

4. Season with **¾ teaspoon vanilla extract**, **⅓ teaspoon almond extract**, and **⅓ teaspoon salt**. Taste and correct seasoning if necessary. Refrigerate.

1½ cups topping

pumpkin tofu custard

1. Steam enough **pumpkin** *or* **Hubbard squash** to yield
   1½ cups. Preheat oven to 375°F. Turn squash into a
   food processor together with **1 pound tofu**, **⅔ cup
   maple syrup**, **⅞ cup water**, and **⅓ cup grapeseed
   oil**. Add **¾ teaspoon salt**, **⅔ teaspoon cinnamon**,
   ⅔ teaspoon ginger, **¼ teaspoon nutmeg**, **scant
   teaspoon vanilla** and a **dash cloves**. Blend until
   smooth.

2. Turn into custard cups and place in a pan. Pour water
   into the pan to a depth of 1″. Bake until custards
   darken and seem firm, about 20 minutes. Remove
   from the pan; refrigerate.

3. Serve with a little **coconut milk** over custards.

10 to 12 servings

dried apple, cranberry, and cider crisp

1. Measure out **4 cups dried apples** and cut into pieces. Check that there are no cores remaining. Put into a pot. Add **4⅔ cups fresh cider**, **½ teaspoon cinnamon**, dash **nutmeg**, and **2 tablespoons grapeseed oil**. Cover and bring to a simmer. Stew gently 5 minutes.

2. Add **2½ cups cranberries** and cook until they just pop.

3. Stir **2 tablespoons arrowroot** and **1 tablespoon potato starch** (*or* **cornstarch**) into **1 cup cold water**. Dissolve starches and add to simmering pot, stirring well until mixture thickens and clears. Turn into a 12″ square glass baking pan and turn oven on to 375°F.

4. **Make almond oat cake cookies:** coarsely chop **½ cup almonds** in a food processor. Turn off and add: **¼ cup walnuts**, **½ cup rolled oats**, pinch **baking powder**, pinch **baking soda**, **¼ cup flour**, and **½ cup date sugar**.

5. Pour into a 2 cup measure: **⅓ cup grapeseed oil**, **⅓ cup apple cider**, and **½ teaspoon vanilla**. Turn machine on, pour in liquids. Mixture should be a soft paste.

6. Use two spoons to drop topping mixture generously over apples in the pan. (Leftover batter can be patted into cookie shapes and baked separately. Add **raisins** if you like).

7. Bake until topping is lightly browned.

8 to 9 servings

cranberry walnut apple tart

1. Make **hazelnut pie crust** (see index). Roll out and place in pie plate; weight with beans and foil and pre-bake 10 minutes at 375°F.

2. Peel and dice **1 to 2 apples**. Chop ⅓ **cup walnuts**. In a bowl combine ¼ **cup flour**, ½ **cup sugar**, ½ **teaspoon cinnamon**, ¼ **teaspoon cardamom** and ¼ **teaspoon salt**. Grate **rind** of ½ **a lemon** over and stir together with a dry whisk. Add apples and walnuts and **3 cups of cranberries**. Set aside.

3. Remove foil and beans from partially-baked crust. Add filling. Roll out lattice strips to top pie. Return to oven and bake 20 to 25 minutes or until cranberries pop.

4. In a small pot bring ¼ **cup maple syrup** to a simmer. Add **1 tablespoon coconut oil** and **2 tablespoons rum** (optional). Reduce this mixture to 2 tablespoons. Pour into the openings in pie top. Dust with **confectioner's sugar**, using a sifter.

makes one 9″ tart

dried cherry apple strudel

Sweetening-free.

1. Coarsely chop a mixture of **dried unsweetened fruits** (apples, apricots, and sweet cherries) to measure **3 cups**. Dice **¾ cup dates** and turn fruits into a pot.

2. Make 2½ cups almond milk by blending or processing **2½ cups almonds** (organic, with skins) with **2½ cups hot tap water**. Pulverize and strain through cheesecloth. Add almond milk to pot. Grate **rind** of ½ **lemon** over fruits, cover and simmer over low heat 10 minutes.

3. Lightly toast **1 cup walnuts** in a 300°F toaster oven. Let cool and chop. Set aside.

4. Dissolve ¾ **tablespoon kudzu** in ¼ **cup cold water** and add to simmering fruit, stirring until thickened. Remove from heat and add a dash of **vanilla extract**.

5. Add **1 peeled and cored apple**, diced, and, if you like, ¾ **cup canned sour cherries**, drained. Mix well.

6. Lightly brush **6 to 8 sheets** of **phyllo pastry** (you will need ¾ pound total; see glossary for information on phyllo) with **grapeseed oil**, one at a time, stacking them up, and sprinkling each third sheet with breadcrumbs. Add fruit filling, sprinkle with **walnuts**, and roll up. Brush lightly with more oil and bake at 400°F until browned. Serve warm.

4 to 5 strudel rolls

apple strudel

A sweetening-free dessert.

1. Chop finely ½ **cup dried apricots** and ½ **cup dried apples**. Stew together in **apple juice** to cover until quite tender. Set aside.

2. Peel, core, slice, and dice enough **crisp, tart apples** to yield **6 cups** (Mutsu are best if you can find them). Turn apples into a bowl, add ¾ **cup currants**, **1 teaspoon cinnamon**, ½ **teaspoon nutmeg**, **2 cups** finely chopped **walnuts** *or* **pecans**, ¾ **cup** chopped **almonds**, grated **rind of 1 lemon**, **1½ teaspoons vanilla**, and enough of the apricot paste to sweeten the mixture.

3. You will need **1½ to 2 cups** of good quality **breadcrumbs**, preferably homemade. Open **1 pound** room temperature **phyllo** (see glossary) and stack about 8 sheets one on top of the other, brushing each with melted **coconut oil**. You will be using about ⅓ of the pound for each strudel roll you will be making. Now sprinkle generously with breadcrumbs. Add ⅓ of the apple filling to the long end facing you and roll up as tightly as possible. Carefully cut strudel roll into fourths and use a spatula to transfer to baking sheet. Repeat with remaining phyllo and filling. Brush tops of strudels with **coconut oil** and bake at 400°F until browned. This strudel is best served warm.

12 servings

jenovefa's gingerbread

From Jenovefa Knoop. We received a letter with this recipe in it sometime in the 1980's. We didn't get around to trying it until a few years ago, and then we couldn't locate the sender. Too bad; it's an excellent gingerbread.

1. Roast **1 sweet potato** until soft, or use a leftover one. Peel it.

2. Combine in a processor: ¾ **pound tofu**, grated **rind** of **1 orange, juice** of 1 lemon, and **juice** of **1 orange** (should measure slightly over ¾ **cup** combined juice) and purée together. Combine **agave nectar** and **molasses** to make 1½ **cups** sweetener and add to processor. Add sweet potato. Blend well. Scrape down and blend again. Preheat oven to 350°F.

3. Combine dry ingredients in a large bowl: 1½ **cups whole wheat flour**, ¾ **cup white flour, 2 teaspoons baking soda, 2 teaspoons baking powder,** ¼ **teaspoon salt, 1 teaspoon dried ginger, 1 teaspoon cinnamon,** ¼ **teaspoon nutmeg.** Stir all together with a dry whisk. Dice **1 cup dried apples** and chop ¾ **cup walnuts.** Add to mixture.

4. Lightly oil an 8″ x 8″ x 2″ Pyrex baking pan. Peel and quarter **3 apples.** Core and slice. Line the bottom of the pan with apple slices.

5. Quickly combine wet and dry ingredients. Don't overmix. Pour into pan. Bake 45 minutes to 1 hour, until dry in the center. Serve with **coconut milk whipped cream** (see index).

one 8″ square cake

mincemeat baked apples

1. Preheat oven to 325°F. Marinate **3 tablespoons raisins** in ¼ **cup apple jack brandy** (*or* **apple juice**). Cut **3 tablespoons dried apricots** into small dice and add. Chop ⅔ **cup walnuts** and add with ⅓ **cup sunflower seeds**, ⅛ **teaspoon cinnamon**, and a **dash nutmeg**. In a cup mash **1 tablespoon red miso** together with ½ **tablespoon water** and add to nut and fruit mix. Stir to blend well.

2. Peel 1″ off top of **7 Rome Beauty apples** or other large baking apples. Use an apple corer to cut out the core without cutting through the bottom of the apple. Core widely to make a nice hole for the filling. Push nut and fruit filling firmly into each hole and line up apples in a baking pan.

3. Pour **5 tablespoons apricot wine** *or* **dry sherry** over apples and into pan. Bake for 45 minutes.

4. Serve warm with **coconut milk whipped cream** (see index).

7 servings

sourdough applesauce spice cake

A sweetening-free cake.

1. In a small pot combine 1½ cups dried apple slices with 1½ cups apple juice. Cover and cook until apple slices are tender. Purée in a food processor. Let cool. You should have 2 cups of applesauce.

2. Combine in a bowl: ½ cup thick sourdough (see glossary), ¾ cup grapeseed oil, 2 teaspoons vanilla extract, 1 cup unbleached white flour, and 1½ cups fresh cider. Use a whisk to stir well and set aside.

3. Use a dry whisk to mix together dry ingredients: 2¼ cups unbleached white flour, 1½ teaspoons cinnamon, 2 teaspoons sifted baking soda, ½ teaspoon salt, 2 teaspoons baking powder, ¼ cup carob powder, 1½ tablespoons coffee substitute such as Pero or Cafix, ½ teaspoon allspice, ½ teaspoon nutmeg, and ¼ teaspoon cardamom.

4. Preheat oven to 375°F. Lightly oil a 9″ cake pan and line it with waxed paper. Peel and dice fresh apples to yield 2 cups and combine with 1 cup walnuts, chopped, the grated rind of 1 orange, and ¾ cup chopped dates.

5. Combine applesauce with sourdough mix, add dry ingredients and fresh apple mix. Stir just enough to blend. Turn into prepared cake tin. Bake 1 hour.

6. Let cake cool on rack for 10 minutes, then turn it out and peel off waxed paper and discard.

7. To make a **vanilla glaze**, bring **1 cup pineapple-coconut juice** to a boil with **1½ tablespoons cornstarch**. When thickened, flavor with a **dash salt** and ¾ **teaspoon vanilla extract**. Pour over cooled cake, or serve cake slices with glaze spooned on top.

makes one 9″ cake

LAUREN

pear pecan cake
with cranberry glaze

1. Lightly oil a 9″ round cake pan, and line with waxed paper. Preheat oven to 375°F.

2. **Combine dry ingredients:** place **1½ cups flour** in a bowl. Add **¼ teaspoon salt**, **1 teaspoon baking soda, sifted, 1 teaspoon baking powder, ¼ teaspoon cinnamon**, and **⅔ cup Sucanat** or sugar. Stir well with a dry whisk and set aside.

3. **Combine wet ingredients:** measure **½ cup sourdough** (see glossary) into a bowl. Add **½ cup oil, 1 teaspoon vanilla extract**, and **⅞ cup water**. Stir together and set aside.

4. Peel and core Bosc pears (eating varieties are too sweet for this cake). Cut into ½″ pieces. You will need **2 cups pears**. Set aside.

5. Coarsely chop **¾ cup pecans**. Quickly combine pears, pecans, wet ingredients and dry, stirring just enough to blend. Immediately turn tinto prepared pan and place in the oven. Bake 30 minutes.

6. **Meanwhile make cranberry glaze**: in a pot combine **1½ cups cranberries, ½ cup water, 3 tablespoons maple syrup**, and a dash salt. Extra diced pears may be mixed with the cranberries if desired. Add **1 tablespoon plus 1 teaspoon potato starch** and bring to a boil, stirring. When mixture thickens, remove from stove. If it seems too thick, use water or juice (such as cranberry) to thin the glaze.

7. Remove cake from the oven and cool 5 to 10 minutes on a rack. Run knife around sides and turn out onto a plate. Peel off waxed paper and discard. Spoon **cranberry glaze** over the cake.

one 9″ cake

pears poached in maple syrup and red wine

1. Prepare **almond oat cakes** (see index) if desired, to serve with pears.

2. In a saucepan combine **1 cup red wine, 1 tablespoon lemon juice, 2 tablespoons maple syrup** *or* **agave nectar, ¼ teaspoon cinnamon**, and bring to a boil. Turn off heat while preparing pears.

3. Peel, halve, stem, and core **3 large Bosc pears**.

4. Add pears to wine mixture, cover pot, reduce heat to a simmer and poach 8 to 10 minutes. Drain pears into a serving dish. Reduce poaching liquid until syrupy. Pour over pears and chill.

5. To serve, place a pear half on an **oat cake** and slice, keeping the shape of the pear. Spoon some cooking liquid over and top with **coconut milk whipped cream** (see index).

6 servings

cranberry tofu mousse

1. Pour **2 cups good fruit juice** into a pot and sprinkle with **2 tablespoons agar-agar flakes**. Let stand a few minutes to soften agar-agar flakes, then bring to a simmer, adding **½ pound tofu**. Let simmer 5 to 10 minutes.

2. Meanwhile use a coffee grinder to pulverize **¾ cup nuts** (Use walnuts, almonds, filberts [hazelnuts] or a combination. Sometimes we make up part of the measure with **coconut flakes**. The nuts provide richness and are the base of this dairy-free dessert.) Pulverize as finely as possible. Turn into a blender. Add tofu, berries, and juice with **¾ cup grapeseed oil**. Turn machine on. Mixture should become thick like mayonnaise. Scrape down. Add **⅓ cup maple syrup, 1 teaspoon lemon juice, 1 teaspoon salt,** and **1 teaspoon vanilla extract**. The smoothness of this mousse depends on how finely you are able to pulverize the nuts. Taste for lemon juice and for sweetness. Correct seasoning.

3. You will need 8 tea cups or custard molds. Pour mousse into molds. Cool, refrigerate.

4. Turn **2 cups cranberries** into a pot with **¼ cup maple syrup** and **¾ cup water**. Cook, covered, until the cranberries pop. Cool and chill. If sauce seems too thick, thin with juice or water. Top mousse with this cranberry sauce.

5. To serve, run a knife around sides of molds. Turn out onto plates and top with cranberry sauce.

8 servings

persimmon couscous cake

1. Rinse contents of a **1 pound box couscous** in a strainer. Line steamer with absorbent paper. Steam couscous 5 minutes.

2. Bring **2 cups apple juice** and **1¼ cups water** to a boil with a **pinch** of **salt**. Boil 1 to 2 minutes.

3. Turn couscous into a bowl and fluff up with a fork. Add boiled juice gradually—be sure it is absorbed. All juice may not be needed. Turn into a 12″ to 14″ glass pan. Cut **2 to 3 ripe persimmons** into wedges and cover top of cake.

4. In a pot combine **1 cup water**, **2 cups apple juice**, and a **pinch salt**. Sprinkle **4 tablespoons agar-agar flakes** on top. Bring to a simmer (don't stir). When agar dissolves, spoon over persimmons and cake. Let cool. Serve with slivered **toasted almonds**.

8 servings

spiced winter squash cake
with gingered pears

1. You will need **2 cups cooked Hubbard** *or* **Kuri squash**, well drained. Turn into food processor.

2. Add **1½ cups sugar**, pack **1 cup** measure almost full with **coconut oil**. Add **grapeseed oil** to the top. Add to processor with **1 teaspoon vanilla**, and **½ cup flax seed "eggs"** (see glossary). Turn processor on to blend thoroughly.

3. Preheat oven to 350°F. Combine dry ingredients: **3 cups all-purpose flour, 2 teaspoons baking powder, ½ teaspoon baking soda, 1 teaspoon salt, 1¼ teaspoons cinnamon, ½ teaspoon ginger (powdered), pinch** each **cloves** and **nutmeg, ½ teaspoon fresh ground pepper** and **¼ teaspoon dry mustard.** Stir well with a dry whisk.

4. You will need a 9″ square pan, ungreased. Gently but thoroughly stir contents of processor into bowl of dry ingredients. Batter will be very stiff. Immediately scrape into pan and put into oven. Bake until well done—1¼ to 1½ hours. Cool on rack.

5. Serve with **gingered pears** and **coconut milk whipped cream** (see index). For **gingered pears**: finely chop **2 tablespoons fresh ginger**. Grate **2 teaspoons lemon zest**. Peel and dice **3 cups Bosc pears**. Turn ginger, lemon zest, and pears into a medium-sized frying pan. Add **2″** of split vanilla bean* and **2 tablespoons grapeseed oil**. Sauté pear

---

*The vanilla bean is so superior to extract in this recipe that it is worth its high cost.

84

mixture over high heat until pears are softened. Remove from heat. Sprinkle with **2 tablespoons sugar** and **1 tablespoon lemon juice**. Fold into whipped cream or serve each separately.

9 servings

CODY AND CHARLENE

cranberry persimmon dessert sauce

To use over tofu mousse, lemon cake, sorbet, etc.

1. Place **2 cups cranberries** in a pot. Remove stems. Add ¼ **cup maple syrup** and ¾ **cup water**. Cover and cook over moderate low heat until cranberries pop.

2. Meanwhile, prepare **1 persimmon**. It must be very ripe, soft even at its stem end. Cut in thin slices and cut slices in half crosswise if persimmon is large.

3. Pour cranberry sauce over persimmon and fold together.

about 3 cups

persimmon dessert sauce

1. Cut up **3 large very ripe persimmons**, removing any pits and turn into a processor, skins and all. Add ¾ **cup orange juice**, ½ **teaspoon salt**, ¼ **teaspoon sugar** and **1 teaspoon powdered ginger**. Purée.

2. Add **1½ tablespoons lemon juice**, or to taste. Thin as needed with orange juice. Serve over **persimmon sorbet** or **lemon lotus ice cream** (see index).

autumn ice creams

Ice creams made from premium organic coconut milk are
surprisingly rich and delicious, and very satisfying.* A number
of recipes follow. The use of alcohol tends to keep the mixture
creamy rather than icy. The inexpensive home ice cream makers
(wherein the bowl is kept in the freezer) work well; our favorite
brand is the Girmi. It is most quiet. It's good to have a spare chilled
bowl since the ice cream grows in volume as the machine freezes
it, so you cannot fill the bowl to the top. On occasion, you may
need to do a partial second batch if you have too large a mixture.
That's when the spare bowl comes in handy. Otherwise, keep
the extra mix chilled and process it in the cold bowl the next day.
Agave nectar is an ideal unflavored sweetener; however maple
syrup and sugar work well also. Salt and pepper do a remarkable
job of pointing up flavor.

Sugar may be substituted for agave: ⅓ to ½ cup sugar for ¼ cup
agave, 1 scant cup sugar for ⅔ cup agave, 1 cup sugar for ¾ cup
agave. Or you can use maple syrup instead of agave, using the
same amount as agave.

We serve our ice creams with **gingersnaps** (see index).

all ice creams yield approximately 1½ quarts

---

*See the glossary for more information on coconut milk. Our coconut milk
comes in 14 oz. cans.

caramel rum ice cream

1. **Make caramel**: boil ½ cup sugar in ¼ cup water until caramelized (medium brown). Remove from heat. Add ½ **cup apple juice** or **cider**. Return to heat until caramel dissolves. Let cool.

2. Combine caramel with ¼ **cup Meyers rum**, ½ **cup sugar**, ½ **teaspoon salt**, ½ **teaspoon freshly ground pepper**, 2 **teaspoons vanilla extract** and the contents of 2 **cans coconut milk**. Chill until very cold, and freeze as per ice cream maker's instructions.

irish coffee ice cream

1. You will need **Jameson's whisky**, or another similar brand. Make a **coffee concentrate** by passing **1¼ cups** almost boiling **water** over **2¼ oz. ground coffee** in a filter to yield a total of **1 cup** concentrate.

2. Combine contents of 2 **cans coconut milk**, ⅔ **cup** of the **coffee concentrate**, ¼ **cup Jameson's whisky**, ½ **teaspoon salt**, ½ **teaspoon fresh ground pepper**, 2 **teaspoons vanilla extract**, and ½ **cup organic sugar**. Chill until very cold, and freeze as per ice cream maker's instructions.

3. **Make a syrup:** boil ½ **cup organic sugar** and ¼ **cup water** until caramelized (medium brown). Remove from heat. Add ⅓ **cup** remaining **coffee concentrate** and 2 **tablespoons Jameson's whisky**. Serve syrup over the ice cream.

persimmon ice cream

1. Be sure **persimmons** are very, very soft (ripe). Remove seeds if any; skin and all the flesh may be used. You will need **2½ cups** fruit. Turn into food processor. Add **½ teaspoon salt, ¼ teaspoon nutmeg, ¼ teaspoon powdered ginger, 1 tablespoon lemon juice, ¼ teaspoon fresh ground pepper, ¼ cup light agave nectar**, and, optional, **3 tablespoons Kirschwasser**. Purée all in processor.

2. Combine contents of processor with contents of **2 cans coconut milk**. Chill until very cold, and freeze as per ice cream maker's instructions.

pumpkin bourbon ice cream

1. Measure **1½ cups cooked squash** or **pumpkin**. We prefer Hubbard squash. Turn into food processor. Add **½ teaspoon ground cinnamon, ½ teaspoon ground dried ginger, ½ teaspoon salt**, scant **½ teaspoon fresh ground pepper, 2 tablespoons Wild Turkey bourbon, ⅔ cup dark agave nectar** and a grating of **nutmeg**. Purée all together.

2. Combine contents of processor with **2 cans coconut milk**. Chill until very cold, and freeze as per ice cream maker's instructions.

Winter

DESSERTS

black bean soup

From *Wings of Life* by Julie Jordan.

1. Soak **2 cups dried black turtle beans** overnight.* When ready to cook, bring the beans to boil in a soup pot with **5 cups water** and turn down to a simmer. Add **a bay leaf** *or* a few **sprigs of fresh epazote**,** if available. Cook the beans until done and set aside (allow 1 hour or more).

2. Chop **4 medium onions** and start to fry them over high heat in **4 tablespoons grapeseed oil**. Add **1 red sweet pepper**, finely chopped, **3 cloves garlic**, crushed, **1 teaspoon oregano**, ½ **teaspoon dry mustard**, and **1 teaspoon whole cumin seed**. Lower heat. Sauté vegetables, stirring often, for at least 10 minutes, or until onions just begin to caramelize.

3. Add the cooked beans to the soup pot, mashing some of the black beans with a potato masher. Add as much **water** as necessary to the soup so it is not too thick.

4. Turn the heat on high and add **1 cup canned tomatoes**, chopped and **2 teaspoons salt**. Let the soup come to a boil, turn down to a simmer, and let cook ½ hour or more to develop flavor. Taste for seasoning and add the **juice of 1 lemon** before serving. Serve with **slices of raw onion** and **avocado**.

8 servings

---

*If beans cannot be soaked overnight, they can be brought to a boil in water, removed from heat for 1 hour and then returned to stove and cooked until tender.

**Epazote can be found in Mexican markets.

winter miso soup

1. Soak **1 cup soybeans** overnight (this is essential).

2. Peel, quarter, and slice **2 very large onions**. Cut **2 carrots** in half lengthwise and then slice thinly. If you like, **2 parsnips** or a small **turnip** can be added also. Slice **6 mushrooms** and peel, quarter, and thinly slice **1 large sweet potato**. Place a **4 oz. piece of tofu** on absorbent paper. Top with more paper, a plate, and a weight.

3. Put **2 tablespoons grapeseed oil** in a soup kettle and fry all vegetables, but not the tofu, until slightly browned, stirring often. Turn off fire.

4. Now purée the soybeans in their water by putting small batches in a blender or food processor. Add ground soybeans and their water to the soup pot with **1 to 2 quarts water**. Simmer uncovered 10 to 15 minutes.

5. Soak approximately **1 oz. hiziki seaweed** in water 5 or 10 minutes, then drain and chop coarsely.

6. Cut the dried tofu into cubes or strips. Place **2 tablespoons Chinese toasted sesame oil** in a frying pan. Fry tofu pieces, turning them till light brown. Add hiziki and **1 clove garlic**, crushed. When hiziki ceases to give up its sea-like smell, add a few tablespoons **water**, and a dash **tamari**. Cover and simmer 5 minutes, then add to soup.

7. Put ⅔ **cup red** *or* **brown miso** in a bowl and stir with enough water to make a thin purée. Add miso to soup but don't boil again. Heat portion by portion so that miso does not boil.

8. Stir into each serving a little **tamari**, a splash **rice wine vinegar, sesame oil**, and top with sliced **scallions**.

6 to 8 servings

ALISON

wild mushroom barley soup

1. Soak **4 large dried shiitake mushrooms** in **water** to cover. Set aside. Separately, soak ¼ **cup dried porcini mushrooms** and **1 cup mixed dried wild mushrooms** in warm water to cover.

2. Scrape and then dice **1 to 2 carrots**; peel and chop **1 medium onion** and dice **2 stalks celery**. Slit **4 leeks** lengthwise; wash well and slice thinly.

3. Squeeze shiitakes and slice thinly. Reserve soaking liquid. In a soup pot, heat ½ **cup grapeseed oil** and fry shiitakes over high heat. Once they begin to brown, add all the other vegetables. Continue sautéing, stirring often, until vegetables brown slightly.

4. Meanwhile cook ½ **cup pearl barley** in **2 cups water** until barley is tender. Add to soup pot together with **6 cups water**, all the mushroom liquids, strained, and ⅓ **cup tamari**.

5. Wash and slice thinly ½ **head escarole**. Add to soup and simmer 15 minutes. Correct seasoning. Garnish with chopped **parsley** and **fresh ground pepper**.

6 servings

pot likker soup

This is a soup to make after you've cooked collard greens. Save the leftover juices, with a few cooked leaves as well.

1. Place **3 quarts collard greens' pot likker** in a large soup kettle. Add ⅔ **cup white rice** and bring to a simmer.

2. Slice **1 large onion** and peel and chop **3 cloves garlic.** Sauté onion and garlic in **2 to 3 tablespoons olive oil** with ¼ to ½ **teaspoon red pepper flakes.** Cook until very soft. Add to soup pot.

3. Peel **1 large sweet potato** and cut into half moon shapes. Simmer in a separate pot in **1½ cups water.** When rice is barely soft, drain.

4. When ready to serve, add sweet potato slices to each bowl and ladle soup in.

10 to 12 servings

cashew chili

Adapted from *Wings of Life*, Julie Jordan, Crossing Press, now unfortunately out of print.

1. Soak **1 cup dried red kidney beans** overnight. Rinse and cover again with **water**. Add a **sprig of fresh epazote** if available. Bring to a boil, turn heat down and simmer until done, about 45 minutes.

2. In a large soup pot, sauté **4 medium onions**, chopped, in ¼ **cup grapeseed oil**. Chop **2 green peppers** and **2 stalks celery**, including the **leaves**, and add to pot together with **3 cloves garlic**, crushed, **1 bay leaf**, **1 teaspoon dried basil**, **1 teaspoon dried oregano**, **1 teaspoon ground cumin**, and **2 tablespoons chili powder**. Stir the pot often with a wooden spoon.

3. When the vegetables have browned evenly and the beans have cooked, add beans to soup pot. Add **1 quart canned tomatoes**, chopped, ¼ **cup red wine vinegar**, ½ **cup cashews**, ¼ **cup raisins**, **1 teaspoon salt**, and some **fresh ground pepper**. Bring to a boil, adding as much liquid from bean pot or water as seems necessary to make an appropriate soup consistency. Simmer at least 1½ hours to develop flavor. This soup improves on reheating and long, slow cooking.

4. Before serving, adjust seasoning. Taste especially for salt and cumin, and add more chili powder if you like. Top each serving with extra **cashews** and serve with **cornbread** (see index).

6 to 8 servings

spicy peanut and mustard greens soup

Of North African inspiration.

1. Coarsely chop **2½ cups onions**. Dice **2 cups celery (including leaves)**, **1 red sweet pepper**, and **3 seeded jalapeños**. Turn all vegetables into soup pot. Add **¼ cup grapeseed oil** and sauté over high heat.

2. Mince **2 garlic cloves**. Once vegetables have wilted and are beginning to brown, add garlic together with **1 tablespoon Kosher salt**, **1¼ tablespoons chili powder**, and **⅓ teaspoon cayenne pepper**.

3. When vegetables are well browned, add **2 quarts water**, **3 cups canned tomatoes**, chopped, **½ cup millet**, and **8 oz. organic peanut butter**. Turn heat to low and simmer 20 minutes covered. Add water if soup is too thick.

4. Wash and chop **mustard greens**, discarding thick stems. You will need about **8 cups of chopped greens**. Use frying pan and **¼ cup olive oil** to fry the greens over high heat until wilted and slightly brown. Add to soup pot. Correct seasoning. Serve garnished with **whole peanuts**.

8 to 10 servings

WINTER

cannelini bean, kombu and potato soup

1. Pick over **2½ to 3 cups cannelini beans** to remove any stones. Soak in **water** to cover overnight.

2. Drain water, add **fresh water** to cover beans. Cook over lowest heat until beans are very soft. Add a **bay leaf** or two while cooking; and a strip of **kombu**.

3. Meanwhile, dice **2 large onions, 3 garlic cloves, 1 teaspoon ground cumin**, and **1 seeded jalapeño chile**. Sauté vegetables in ⅓ **cup olive oil** over lowest heat, stirring now and then until the vegetables begin to caramelize, at least 20 minutes.

4. When beans are very soft, remove the kombu and discard. It will have added a silky texture to the soup. Add onion, garlic, and pepper mix to soup with ¼ **cup tamari**.

5. Dice **4 cups Yukon Gold potatoes** and add to soup. When they are almost done and soup seems ready, lay in **2 to 3 more strips** of **kombu**. When they soften, remove them with tongs. Cut into 1″ dice and return to soup pot. Season soup with **fresh ground pepper**, and **salt** if necessary. Cook until kombu is just done; don't overcook it.

8 servings

russian potato and sauerkraut salad

1. **Make mustard vinaigrette:** combine ⅓ **cup good quality wine vinegar**, ½ **teaspoon salt**, and 2 **tablespoons prepared mustard** (we use Kosciusko). Whisk together thoroughly. Add 1½ **cups oil** (we use a blend of 25% olive oil, 75% grapeseed oil) and lots of freshly ground **pepper**. Whisk again until well blended.

2. Peel and dice 5 **potatoes**, 2 **carrots**, and 2 **beets**. Boil each separately until tender. Drain. Chill beets.

3. Combine carrots and potatoes in a bowl. Add enough **mustard vinaigrette** to coat generously. Add ½ **pound sauerkraut**, drained and lightly squeezed, 3 **diced scallions**, 1 **small** diced **cucumber**, and 3 **tablespoons** chopped **fresh dill**. Mix well and chill.

4. Arrange cold potato salad on a bed of **Boston lettuce**, garnish with chilled beets, onion slices, and **diced apples**. Add extra vinaigrette to each salad.

4 to 6 servings

endive, avocado, and watercress salad

A sensuous salad that can be eaten with the fingers.

1. For each diner, use **1 small whole Belgian endive**. Cut ¼″ off its base and separate the leaves, arranging them on a dinner plate in a fan shape. Slice the smallest inside leaves and heap at the base of the fan. Cut thin slices of **avocado** to fit into each leaf. Depending on the size of the avocado, you will need ¼ to ½ of the avocado for each plate. Slice ⅓ **bunch watercress leaves** (discarding stems) over endive hearts at base of fan. Cut a thin slice of **red onion** and separate into rings on top of the cress. Drizzle **vinaigrette** (see glossary) over the salad and serve immediately.

marinated tofu salad

1. Make marinade: combine **1 cup grapeseed oil,**
   ¼ cup Chinese toasted sesame oil, 2 tablespoons
   lemon juice, ¼ cup tamari, and **2 tablespoons rice**
   wine vinegar. Whisk well.

2. Cut **1½ pounds firm tofu** in half horizontally, then
   diagonally to form thin triangles about ¼″ to ½″ thick.
   Lay in a shallow container and spoon some of the
   marinade over. Cover, chill.

3. To serve, shred **1 head Chinese napa cabbage,** using
   a large knife. Arrange on plates. Top with tofu triangles.
   Center with shredded **carrots,** chopped **scallions,**
   and shredded **daikon** if available. Dress salads with
   marinade and top with **gomahsio** (see glossary).

4 to 6 servings

carrot salad with cumin

1. Toast **½ teaspoon whole cumin seed** in a hot dry pan,
   stirring until toasted. Let cool. Use a mortar and
   pestle to crush seeds. Combine with: **¼ cup orange**
   juice, ½ teaspoon Dijon mustard, 1 teaspoon Kosher
   salt, 3 tablespoons olive oil, and **1 tablespoon**
   raspberry vinegar. Stir well and set aside.

2. Slice **4 to 5 peeled carrots** into large ovals. Steam
   until barely soft, about 5 minutes. Combine hot carrots
   with vinaigrette. Let cool. Chop **1 tablespoon straight**
   leaf parsley and turn the parsley into the carrots.

3. Serve at room temperature or chilled.

4 side dish servings

spinach salad
with sherry dressing

1. Make salad dressing: in a jar combine ⅓ **cup dry sherry**, ¼ **cup grapeseed oil**, **3 tablespoons wine vinegar**, **1 teaspoon lemon juice**, ¾ **teaspoon tamari**, ¼ **teaspoon curry powder**, and a **pinch of crushed dry marjoram**.

2. Prepare croutons by drying cubes of leftover homemade bread at 300°F until hard. You will need ¾ **cup croutons**.

3. Clean, remove stems, and break up leaves from **1 to 2 pounds fresh spinach**. Place in salad bowl. Slice ½ **pound fresh button mushrooms** into bowl and add croutons.

4. When ready to serve, shake salad dressing, pour over and toss. Top the salad with **sprinkles of gomahsio** (see glossary).

6 to 8 servings

mushroom walnut pâté

Our intent was to develop a recipe for a dairy-free spread for bread. The resulting pâté is better flavored, we think, than the best liver pâtés. We serve it as a salad, though it could be made of softer consistency for a dip, can be frozen and defrosted with no change in consistency, and of course, is delightful spread on bread—especially rye, fresh out of the oven. The recipe which follows is tricky and somewhat time consuming. A good quality food processor is a necessity.

1. In a small coffee grinder, pulverize ⅓ **cup sunflower seeds** and **2 tablespoons sesame seeds**. These seeds are the recipe base and must be very finely ground. Use a processor if you don´t have a mill. Turn seeds into a bowl and set aside.

2. **Make mushroom-shallot duxelles:** coarsely cut ½ **pound mushrooms** (about 2½ cups) that are clean and dry in a food processor. Add about **3 tablespoons** peeled and coarsely chopped **shallots**, and chop finely by turning the machine on and off. Traditionally, duxelles are now turned into a clean dish towel over a small bowl, and the juice is extracted by twisting the towel slowly. Reserve this liquid. Heat **2 tablespoons grapeseed oil** in a frying pan and when hot, turn duxelles into pan and sauté over high heat, stirring, until mushroom-shallot mix is browned and separated. You can also just turn the mixture into the hot frying pan without extracting the juice, but expect to spend more time frying. Season duxelles with **salt** and freshly ground **pepper** and set aside.

3. Turn the ground seeds into the unwashed processor and add ½ **cup walnuts**, **1 small clove** peeled **garlic**, ½ **teaspoon dried oregano**, and ½ **teaspoon dried**

tarragon. In a measuring cup, combine ⅓ cup olive oil and ⅓ cup grapeseed oil. Squeeze **2 tablespoons lemon juice**. You will also need ¼ **pound tofu** (about ¼ of a cake), and most of all, patience!

4. Turn processor on and very slowly begin to add oil, until the mixture becomes a very stiff paste. This should be much slower than for making mayonnaise. Alternately add pieces of tofu, some lemon juice, and the oil as machine runs, stretching the oil addition to take about 10 minutes. If mixture becomes so stiff as to turn machine off, then pâté is proceeding properly. Add a little lemon juice to start it up again. Do not use all the lemon juice, taste to see how much is needed. Add ⅔ **teaspoon prepared mustard** and **1½ to 2 tablespoons tamari**. If pâté seems too stiff, add a little of the reserved mushroom juice or water. Remaining mushroom juice may be saved for soups. If oil was added too quickly, you may find signs of separation as machine works. Turn machine off, pour excess oil back into a measuring cup, and turn machine on. After a minute or two, begin dribbling oil in again until it is properly incorporated.

5. In a bowl, fold together the duxelles and contents of processor. Chill.

6. We serve the pâté in the center of a ½″ **thick green pepper ring** on a bed of Boston lettuce, surrounded by **cucumber slices** and **celery hearts**. The salad is lightly sprinkled with **paprika** and drizzled with **vinaigrette** (see glossary). Finally, the pâté is topped with a **fluted raw mushroom**.

makes 2 cups

beet and orange salad

1. Scrape **4 beets** to remove hairs and dirt. Rinse knife, but don't wash beets. Slice and place in a wide-bottomed pot. Add ½ **cup water**. Cover and cook over moderate heat until just tender. Cool, chill.

2. Make dressing: mix together **2 tablespoons lemon juice, 2 tablespoons orange juice,** and ¼ **cup olive oil.** Add ½ **teaspoon salt**, stir well, and set aside.

3. Grate the **rind** of ½ **orange** and add to dressing. Peel and slice **2 oranges**. Place in a dish and sprinkle lightly with a few **red pepper flakes**.

4. Pan roast ¼ **cup pepitas*** (squash seeds, available in health food stores) by shaking them in a small frying pan over high heat until light brown. When cool, crush in a processor or with a mortar and pestle.

5. To compose the salad, make a bed of greens using **lettuce, escarole hearts,** and **watercress**. Arrange beet and orange slices on top. **Green pepper** slices and **Portuguese olives** are optional additions. Pour dressing over and sprinkle generously with the ground pepitas.

6 servings

---

*Whole fennel or caraway seed can be used the same way.

curried shredded
parsnip salad

From Mary Prejean.

1. Cover **1 cup organic almonds** with water and bring to a boil. Cool in cold water and slip skins off. Turn into a blender.

2. Squeeze **2 tablespoons lemon juice**. Measure **1 cup grapeseed oil**. Add ⅔ **cup water** to blender and puree almonds at high speed. Add lemon juice and gradually add oil. Mixture will thicken into a mayonnaise.

3. Season "mayonnaise" with **1 tablespoon curry powder,** ½ **teaspoon salt, dash of Tabasco,** ½ **teaspoon prepared mustard**, and **2 to 3 tablespoons catsup**. Blend or stir all together.

4. Peel, then shred **4 to 5 parsnips**. Dice **3 stalks celery**. Drain liquid from a **can of pitted black olives** and chop them coarsely. Mince ⅓ **cup scallions**. Fold all vegetables and "mayonnaise" together. If mixture seems dry, stir in another tablespoon or two of water.

5. Serve parsnip salad on **wedges of avocado** on a bed of **lettuce**. A little **vinaigrette** (see glossary) will be necessary for the latter. **Alfalfa sprouts** may garnish the top.

6 servings

skordalia and gigande bean salad

From Ron Puhalski.

1. Skordalia is a Greek garlic sauce that can be served with various vegetables. It is particularly good with gigande beans, which should be available at Greek grocery stores. Pick over **3 cups gigande beans** to remove stones. Cover with water for 6 hours. Drain.

2. Place beans in a pot and cover with water. Add **2 to 3 whole bay leaves** (which Ron says helps prevent bean digestive problems) and bring to a boil. Reduce heat to simmer and cook until beans are tender, probably over an hour.

3. Meanwhile prepare Skordalia: cut **1 baking potato** in half, cover with water and cook until soft. Peel. **Soak several slices** *or* **½ a small loaf of Italian or French bread** in water until soft. Squeeze water out.

4. In a food processor, pulverize **1 cup almonds**. Add **6 cloves garlic**, peeled. Add cooked potato. Measure out **1 cup good quality olive oil** and begin to drizzle it in, alternating with pieces of the soaked, squeezed bread. Add **¼ cup wine vinegar** and the juice of **2 lemons, 1 teaspoon salt**, and lots of **fresh ground pepper**. Turn off processor and taste. Correct seasoning.

5. When beans are tender, drain and turn into a bowl. While still warm, add **½ cup olive oil, 1 teaspoon salt, a sprinkle of balsamic vinegar, fresh ground pepper**, and **2 tablespoons** minced **parsley**.

6. To serve, arrange lettuce on plates. Mound skordalia on the lettuce and place a spoonful of beans on the dish. A few **kalamata olives** and **slices of red onion** complete the salad. Drizzle with **vinaigrette** (see glossary).

10 to 12 servings

CAROLANNE

tofu and seitan en brochette

1. **Make marinade:** combine **9 tablespoons tamari, 6 tablespoons agave nectar, ½ cup minced scallions, 4½ tablespoons garlic**, chopped, **9 tablespoons sesame oil**, and **6 tablespoons dry sherry.**

2. Cover **1½ pounds firm tofu** with water and bring to a boil. Remove from water and let cool with a weight on the tofu—a tray will do. Then chill.

3. Cut enough **seitan** to yield **3 cups** into 1½″ pieces.

4. **Make dipping sauces** (see following recipes). We serve these brochettes with **peanut sauce** and **cucumber sauce**. Prepare about 24 1½″ squares of **green and red peppers** and clean about the same number of **button mushrooms.**

5. Use wooden skewers (available in Asian markets) to alternatively thread vegetables with tofu and seitan. We like to do one skewer with seitan, peppers and mushrooms, and one with tofu, peppers and mushrooms. Place on trays and set aside.

6. **Prepare brown rice:** in a pot put **3 cups short grain brown rice.** Add **5 cups water.** Cover and bring to a boil. Reduce heat to simmer and cook 30 to 40 minutes or until done.

7. During last 15 minutes, preheat broiler and pour marinade over skewers. Brochettes should not marinate longer than 15 minutes.

8. Broil brochettes, basting with marinade. Sprinkle the tofu ones with **sesame seeds** when they begin to brown.

9. For each diner, shape a cone of brown rice on a plate. Set skewers around the rice. Serve with little bowls of **cucumber sauce** and **peanut sauce**.

8 servings

cucumber sauce

1. Peel and cut out seeds of **6 small cucumbers**. Finely mince. Peel and mince **6 shallots** and **2 small red chile peppers** (seeded).

2. Combine **3 tablespoons agave nectar, 1 tablespoon salt, dash toasted sesame oil,** and **2 tablespoons cider vinegar** with the cucumbers, shallots and peppers. Add enough **water** to make sauce-like, up to **1½ cups.**

about 2 cups

peanut sauce for brochettes

A visit to an Asian market will provide ingredients which will make this dipping sauce exceptional. It is easiest to make the sauce · in a food processor though of course ingredients may be stirred together in a bowl.

1. You will need good quality peanut butter without added sweeteners or fat, which can be purchased in health food stores. Measure ¾ **cup peanut butter.**

2. Lemongrass is a desirable addition to this sauce. If available, mince **1 teaspoon lemongrass** (a processor cannot cut it up adequately).

3. Measure **1½ cups organic Thai coconut milk.**

4. Place in processor: **peanut butter, lemongrass, 1½ teaspoons agave nectar, 2 teaspoons tamarind juice** (*or* substitute lime juice), and **coconut milk.** Turn machine on. When well blended, add ½ **teaspoon chili-paste-with-garlic** (a spicy condiment available in small jars in Chinese markets), and **1 teaspoon salt.** Taste. More chili-paste may be added. Sauce will be quite thick, so dilute it to a consistency that you like. Also, chilling will stiffen the sauce, which must be refrigerated.

makes 2½ cups

seaweed and
bean thread noodle salad

Mixed dried seaweeds are available in health food stores that carry macrobiotic products.

1. Soak **2 cups mixed dried seaweeds** in **tepid water** to cover for 5 minutes. You can add **1 cup dried wakame** *or* **hiziki** *or* **arame** to the blend if you like. Separately, soak **2 oz. bean thread noodles** in **water** to cover.

2. Meanwhile, combine for dressing: **3 tablespoons rice wine vinegar, 3 tablespoons tamari, 1½ tablespoons toasted sesame oil,** and **½ tablespoon agave nectar.** If available add **½ teaspoon ground Szechuan pepper** (or other hot pepper). Whisk all together.

3. Don't let seaweeds soak too long. Drain and squeeze to remove excess moisture. Turn into a bowl. Use a knife to cut drained bean thread noodles. Add them to the bowl with the dressing. Shred **⅔ cup each carrots** and **jícama.** Use chopsticks to turn all ingredients together.

4. Serve salad on a bed of shredded **Napa cabbage.** Arrange **watercress sprigs** around the sides. Top with sliced or cubed **cucumbers** and **sesame seeds.** Drizzle dressing over salads.

6 to 8 servings

phyllo pastry mariposa (butterfly)
with gingered elderberry gravy

This is party food, a recipe we developed for New Year's Eve. There are a number of steps, but all (except folding the phyllo) are simple and can be done separately over several days. This is a rich, elegant meal.

1. **Make miso gravy:** finely chop **2 tablespoons onion** and sauté in saucepan in ½ **cup grapeseed oil** together with **2 cloves crushed garlic** and **6 minced mushrooms.** While sautéing, add ½ **teaspoon dried thyme** and ½ **teaspoon dried basil.** Cook over medium heat, stirring frequently, until well browned. Add ½ **cup unbleached white flour.** Cook several minutes, stirring. Add **6 oz. brown ale** such as Newcastle, and enough water to make gravy (vegetable cooking water is best if you have it). Add **3 tablespoons red** *or* **brown miso, 1 tablespoon tomato paste, 2 tablespoons dry sherry,** and **1 tablespoon tamari.** Simmer slowly ½ hour and correct seasoning.

2. Mince **2 teaspoons fresh ginger.** Sauté gently in **2 tablespoons grapeseed oil** over very low heat in a covered saucepot for 3 to 5 minutes, or until ginger is golden. Add **2 tablespoons flour** and stir over heat a few more minutes. Add: **1 cup water,** ¼ **cup tamari,** ⅓ **cup cider vinegar, 1½ tablespoons maple syrup, 3 tablespoons brandy** (optional), ½ **cup elderberry jelly*** and 1 cup of the miso gravy prepared in step

---

*We use our homemade elderberry jelly from our own bushes, made with very little sugar. A sour currant jelly or tart, unsweetened raspberry preserve could be substituted. Use less of sweet jellies.

one. Bring to a simmer and cook slowly 10 minutes. Correct seasoning and let cool. Refrigerate until needed.

3. **Make sauce soubise:** slice enough peeled **onions** to measure **3 cups.** Stew very slowly in a heavy sauce pot in ¼ **cup grapeseed oil** for at least 30 minutes, stirring often. Do not brown. Add scant ⅓ **cup flour** and cook over low heat 5 minutes more. Add **1 cup water** and bring to a boil, cooking until thickened. Turn sauce into blender or food processor and purée. Return to pot, and dilute with a few tablespoons more **water** if necessary. Return sauce to a simmer and add **1 teaspoon salt, pepper,** and **nutmeg** to taste, and ½ **tablespoon French** *or* **Polish mustard.** Rinse **1 tablespoon capers** and chop finely. Add to sauce with either ¼ **cup dry white wine** *or* **2 tablespoons vinegar** and **2 tablespoons water.** Also add **1 tablespoon red miso,** and **2 teaspoons lemon juice.** Let simmer and correct seasoning.

4. **Prepare mariposas:** bring **1 pound of phyllo pastry** to room temperature (you will use only half of it). Toast ½ **cup slivered almonds** until light brown in a 300°F toaster oven.

5. **Make mariposa filling:** cut ½ **medium cabbage** into 1″ dice. Set aside. Remove florets from ½ **head broccoli** and cut into small pieces. Set aside. Wash, then coarsely chop a **1 pound** package **fresh spinach.** Use a frying pan to sauté the cabbage in **1 tablespoon grapeseed oil** over high heat, stirring constantly until light brown. Turn out into a metal mixing bowl. Repeat with broccoli, adding **oil** only if necessary. Finally, stir-fry **spinach.** When all vegetables are in the

bowl, let cool. Stir in the soubise sauce and refrigerate mixture until ready to form mariposas.

6. Shape mariposas by making phyllo triangles. Keep phyllo under wax paper and a damp towel. Remove 1 whole sheet at a time. Brush lightly with **oil**. Fold one-third over to form a square and place 2 tablespoons filling on the doubled phyllo, in the lower center. Top with some almonds and fold phyllo over the filling from each side to form a long rectangular strip. Brush each again lightly with **oil**. Now fold the strip as you would a flag to form an isosceles triangle. Place on baking sheet and repeat. When all are formed, brush tops with **oil**. Refrigerate until ready to serve.

7. Cut **2 to 3 carrots** into fine julienne strips. Chill in refrigerator in ice water. You will need a bunch of **watercress** crisped in ice water to garnish each plate.

8. Preheat oven to 375°F. In a small pot reheat gingered elderberry sauce.

9. Place 2 phyllo triangles per diner on a baking sheet in the preheated oven for 10 to 15 minutes or until browned. Remove to plate placing triangles point-to-point to resemble a butterfly (mariposa) shape. Spoon elderberry sauce around plate. Place carrot strips where butterfly antennae would be and center watercress sprigs on "bodies."

10. Serve with a **salad rose** (see following recipe).

about 12 servings

salad rose

1. Arrange leaves of **Boston lettuce** and **radicchio** in layers to resemble a rose in full bloom. Place sprigs of **watercress** in the center with **radish slices** and **scallion slices**.

2. Make **vinaigrette** (see glossary) but substitute **balsamic vinegar** for the wine vinegar.

JO-JO, BECKY, ROSE AND YUKA

southern-style greens
with black-eyed peas and rice

In *The Taste of Country Cooking*, Edna Lewis writes: "The black-eyed pea is truly an African bean, first introduced into our area by Thomas Jefferson, via France."

1. **Make black-eyed peas first:** pick over **1½ cups dried black-eyed peas** to remove any stones. Put into a pot with **5 cups water** and **2 bay leaves** and bring to a boil. Simmer covered ½ hour. Coarsely chop **2 frying peppers, 1 seeded jalapeño pepper** and **1½ medium onions** and sauté in **3 tablespoons olive oil** together with **2 crushed cloves garlic** and ½ **teaspoon hot pepper flakes** until onions are quite brown, almost caramelized. When peas are cooked, turn onion mix into pot with peas. Add **1¾ cups white rice, 1 tablespoon tamari** and **1½ teaspoons salt**. Stir, cover, and simmer until rice is cooked. Add more water if necessary. Taste and correct seasoning.

2. **Prepare greens:** with a sharp knife strip leaves from stems from **4 bunches mustard greens *or* turnip greens**. Wash well. Coarsely chop **1½ medium onions** and fry in ⅓ **cup olive oil** in a 3 quart pot together with **4 cloves garlic**, crushed, and ½ **teaspoon red pepper flakes**. Sauté onions until golden brown and slightly caramelized. Break greens into small pieces and put into pot together with **1 tablespoon salt, 3 tablespoons tamari** and just enough **water** to cover. Bring to a boil, then turn down heat and simmer for at least an hour. If using turnip greens, scrape and cut turnips into fourths. Add to pot. When all is well cooked, season to taste with **salt** and freshly ground **pepper**.

3. At dinnertime, reheat rice and beans and greens in their pot liquor. Prepare **skillet cornbread** (see following recipe).

8 to 10 servings

JULIA AND CATHERINE

skillet cornbread

An 8″ or 10″ cast iron skillet will make a superior cornbread.

1. Preheat oven to 425°F.

2. Make **flax seed "eggs"**: place ¼ cup **flax seeds** in a blender. Cover with ¾ **cup hot tap water** and let sit, covered, 15 minutes.

3. Meanwhile, combine dry ingredients in a bowl: **1½ cups coarse organic yellow cornmeal**, ¾ **cup flour, 2 tablespoons sugar, 1 tablespoon baking powder, ½ teaspoon baking soda**, and **1½ teaspoons salt.** Stir all together with a dry whisk and set aside.

4. Drain liquid from a **15 oz. can** of **organic corn kernels.** Place corn in a food processor with **1 cup coconut milk,** ⅓ **cup coconut oil,** ⅓ **cup grapeseed oil** (you can use ⅔ cup grapeseed oil instead of half grapeseed and half coconut, and you can substitute soy milk for coconut milk. The cornbread will be a little less rich). Add ½ **cup sourdough starter** (see glossary).

5. Turn on the blender to create the flax seed "eggs." When seeds are crushed and mixture looks like grey caviar, turn off the blender. Measure ½ **cup** of the **"eggs"** and add to processor. Remaining "eggs" may be refrigerated, covered, for other uses. Turn processor on to blend wet ingredients. The corn kernels should not be puréed, so a pulsing action is called for.

6. Heat an 8″ to 10″ cast iron skillet on top of stove. Add **2 tablespoons grapeseed oil** and turn heat to moderate. Stir together wet and dry ingredients. Don't overmix. Turn into skillet and cook 1 to 1½ minutes on burner. Meanwhile, (optional) sprinkle top with **chili powder**. Place cornbread in oven. Turn heat down to 375°F and bake 35 minutes. Cornbread will be set in the middle and will have pulled away from the sides after 20 minutes but will be rather too moist. Another 10 to 15 minutes makes it just right.

6 to 8 servings

spicy haitian polenta
mais moulin avec pois

From Jacqueline Lauture.

1. Pick over and soak **1½ cups kidney beans** overnight or for several hours in water to cover. Drain and cook in fresh water until very tender.

2. Prepare herb-spice seasoning. The best chile for this is called "Jamaican hot pepper." It is similar to habaneros but is spicier and has a better scent. Place **3 whole Jamaican hot peppers*** (seeds and all, but no stems) into a food processor. Add **1** cut up **green pepper** (no seeds), **2 to 3 tablespoons fresh thyme leaves**, ½ cup packed **straight leaf parsley (leaves only), 2** cut up **scallions, 1** cut up **medium onion, 6 cloves of garlic,** peeled, ½ **teaspoon ground cloves.** Turn processor on and pulverize to a liquid. It will take 5 minutes.

3. Sauté about half of this herb-spice mix in a large pot in **2 tablespoons olive oil** and **3 tablespoons coconut oil.** The remaining mixture may be refrigerated for a week or frozen. Sauté over low heat, stirring often, for 10 to 15 minutes. When it just begins to turn golden brown, lift out 3 cups of cooked red beans and add to pot. Continue cooking, tossing the beans with the spice mix for another 5 to 8 minutes.

4. Meanwhile, measure **3 cups coarse cornmeal** (preferably Haitian*) into a bowl. Cover with **cold water** and swish cornmeal around in the bowl. Pour top cloudy water off, add water and repeat swishing and pouring off cloudy water.

*Available in Caribbean markets.

5. Add 3 cups of the bean cooking water to the herb and bean mixture. Stir well. Bring to a boil and add **1 tablespoon salt**. Pour off excess water from cornmeal bowl and add meal to pot, spoonful by spoonful, with **3 cups** more **water**. Stir constantly as it comes back up to a boil. Cover and let boil. Uncover and use a metal slotted spoon to stir vigorously, scraping pot bottom. Stir and cook, adjusting heat as necessary and adding water when polenta gets too thick. Cover between stirrings and cook for 15 minutes. Finally, cover and cook over low heat 10 minutes more. Taste. More **salt** may be needed to balance the hot peppers, and more water. Polenta should have a porridge-like consistency.

6. Serve this polenta with slices of **avocado**. You may also serve slices of **ripe plantain**, fried first, and we like **creamed collard greens** (see following recipe) on the side.

8 to 10 servings

creamed collard greens

1. Wash **2½ pounds collards**, cut leaves off of midribs and shred coarsely. (Discard midribs and stems.)

2. Dice **1½ cups onions** and slice **3 cloves garlic**. Use a 12″ frying pan to sauté onions, garlic, and ½ **teaspoon red pepper flakes** in **3 tablespoons olive oil,** until vegetables begin to brown. Now add handfuls of collards. Stir and turn over high heat, until they wilt, then add more. When all the collards are in, prepare stock: measure **3 cups water**, add **3 tablespoons tamari**, and pour over greens. Cover pan and turn heat to barely simmer for 1½ to 2 hours.*

3. Check collards to see whether they are tasty and tender. If broth remains, raise heat to reduce it to just a few tablespoons. Now add **1 cup** of canned organic **coconut milk**. Boil up. Season with **salt** and **pepper**, and serve.

6 side dish servings

---

*This is Southern cooking. The original pork-based recipe called for 3½ hours of simmering!

three-mushroom stroganoff

Mushrooms in variety reward vegetarians with great flavors. This recipe and the two which follow are examples of their uses. Both the sweet and the spicy Hungarian paprikas are essential for this dish.

1. Slice **2 pounds Portobello mushrooms, 1 pound fresh shiitakes**, and **1 pound button mushrooms**. Slice **4 large Spanish onions** and coarsely chop **4 garlic cloves**.

2. Fry onions in **grapeseed oil**. It's convenient to use 2 large frying pans at a time, each with at least **2 tablespoons oil** over high heat. As onions begin to melt and brown, you can begin to add mushrooms. Don't let pans become crowded; instead remove cooked vegetables to a saucepot and proceed with cooking the rest.

3. Meanwhile, add **4 tablespoons sweet Hungarian paprika** and **2 teaspoons hot Hungarian paprika** together with **2 teaspoons dried thyme**. Add garlic toward the end of cooking so that it does not burn.

4. When mushrooms are all well browned and have been turned into the saucepot, deglaze the frying pans by adding **1 cup dry sherry** and **2 cups water**. Stir well and scrape over high heat to dislodge browned bits to make a rich gravy. Turn liquid into saucepot. Add **3 bay leaves, ½ cup tamari, 1 (14 oz.) can Thai coconut milk, 4 oz. tomato paste, 2 tablespoons lemon juice, 2 tablespoons brandy**, and lots of freshly ground **pepper**. Heat mushroom stroganoff to blend all ingredients. Correct seasoning.

5. Serve with **farfalle noodles** and lots of chopped **parsley**.

6 to 8 servings

fancy mushroom ragoût
with soft polenta

1. Thinly slice and then dice **1 large onion**. Mince **2 cloves garlic**. Sliver **1 jalapeño pepper**. Sauté all in adequate **olive oil**, stirring until vegetables wilt and begin to caramelize. Turn into a sauce pan.

2. While onion mix cooks, prepare mushrooms: soak **¼ cup dried porcini** in **½ cup hot tap water**. Discard stems and slice **4 cups shiitake mushrooms**, slice **3 cups cremini mushrooms**, and slice **3 cups Portobello mushrooms**. Retain and use the stems of the latter two.

3. Fry sliced mushrooms in small batches in a large frying pan over very high heat adding **olive oil as needed**, turning often until well browned. As each batch is cooked, turn into sauce pan.

4. Drain porcini, squeeze out soaking water and slice thinly. Fry them as well. Deglaze fry pan with porcini soaking liquid. Also add **2 cups** plain (canned) **tomato sauce**, **1 cup water**, and **1 cup red wine**. Scrape up all the burned bits and when all is simmering, add to sauce pot.

5. Add **2 teaspoons fresh tarragon leaves**, minced (*or* **1 teaspoon dried** crumbled **leaves**) and **⅓ cup tamari**. Finally, chop enough straight leaf **Italian parsley** to make **½ cup** and add, together with fresh ground **black pepper** to taste. Cover and simmer 30 minutes.

6. To make polenta, bring **4 cups water** and ¾ **cup cornmeal** to a boil with **2 tablespoons olive oil** and **1½ teaspoons salt**. Use a small coffee grinder to grind **buckwheat groats** into flour—you will need **2 tablespoons**. Add buckwheat flour, whisk well, lower heat and cover. Simmer 15 to 20 minutes, stirring occasionally.

7. Prepare kale; clean and chop **1 bunch kale**. Add to a pot of boiling water and cook 30 seconds. Drain in colander.

8. When ready to serve, heat **olive oil** in a frying pan with a crushed unpeeled clove of **garlic**. Add chopped kale and stir over high heat until a little crispy. **Salt** to taste. Dip out polenta into dishes that are deep (such as shallow soup bowls) and top with mushroom ragoût. Pass more chopped **parsley** and serve the kale on the side.

8 servings

sauerbraten

From Denise Hackney, intern, September 1992.

1. Buy **6 cups seitan**, or, preferably, make your own (see index). Cut into ¼″ slices and set aside.

2. **Make miso gravy:** finely chop **2 tablespoons onion** and sauté in saucepan in **½ cup grapeseed oil** together with **2 cloves** crushed **garlic** and **6** minced **mushrooms**. While sautéing, add **½ teaspoon dried thyme** and **½ teaspoon dried basil**. Cook over medium heat, stirring frequently, until well browned. Add **½ cup unbleached white flour**. Cook several minutes, stirring. Add **6 oz. brown ale** such as Newcastle, and enough **water** to make gravy (vegetable cooking water is best if you have it). Add **3 tablespoons red** *or* **brown miso, 1 tablespoon tomato paste, 2 tablespoons dry sherry**, and **1 tablespoon tamari**. Simmer slowly ½ hour and correct seasoning.

3. **Make sauerbraten seasoning for miso gravy:** mix together **⅓ cup red wine vinegar, 1 cup dry red wine, 1 teaspoon dried ginger, 3 bay leaves**, and **6 whole cloves** tied in a strip of cheesecloth, and **2 tablespoons Sucanat** (*or* sugar). Add **1 tablespoon mustard** and **1 cup more water** to gravy pot and bring to a boil, stirring. Turn heat down and simmer 15 minutes. Remove cheesecloth bag and discard. Place seitan strips in sauerbraten gravy and set aside. Correct seasoning.

4. Prepare **sweet and sour red cabbage** (see following recipe).

5. Just before dinner, peel and quarter **6 potatoes**. Cook in adequate water until just done. Meanwhile, reheat sauerbraten and cabbage if necessary. When potatoes are done, serve potatoes, sauerbraten, and red cabbage. Sprinkle all generously with **fresh** chopped **dill**.

6. Note: **noodles** are good with sauerbraten and can substitute for potatoes in this recipe.

8 to 10 servings

THE MERMAID ROOM

sweet and sour red cabbage

Can be served hot or cold.

1. Quarter **1 large red cabbage**. Remove cores and shred. Thinly slice **2 large onions**. Turn onions into a pot large enough to hold them and the cabbage and sauté the onions in ⅓ **cup grapeseed oil**, stirring occasionally. When wilted and beginning to turn golden, add cabbage.

2. Flavor with ⅓ **cup Sucanat** *or* ¼ **cup organic sugar**, **1 cup red wine vinegar, 1 tablespoon caraway seeds** and **2 bay leaves**. Cover and cook one hour.

3. When cabbage is very well done, add **1½ tablespoons tamari** and lots of fresh ground **pepper**. Taste. Add **salt** if necessary.

makes 1½ quarts

arborio rice pilaf

1. Soak **4 cups dried porcini mushrooms** in **water** to cover.

2. Dice **1 cake** (8 oz.) **soy tempeh** and fry in **olive oil** in a large frying pan until crisp. Drain on a paper towel. Save pan with oil.

3. Squeeze porcini and set soaking liquid aside. Chop porcini coarsely. Chop **2 large onions** and **15 button mushrooms**.

4. First fry porcini, then add mushrooms and onions. Sauté over high heat, adding more olive oil if necessary, until mushrooms begin to brown, after they have given up all their liquid. Now add **4 cups Arborio rice** and stir over heat until translucent.

5. Combine ⅔ **cup dry white wine** and ⅓ **cup tomato paste**. Strain porcini soaking water though cheesecloth and add to wine mixture. Add **water** to make **6 cups** total liquid. Add liquid to frying pan with **2 teaspoons salt**. Lower heat and simmer until rice is soft. Add tempeh and toss all together.

6. Serve with **broccoli rabe**: blanch **1 bunch** in boiling **water**. Chop coarsely and sauté in olive oil with 2 crushed **garlic cloves** and ¼ **teaspoon red pepper flakes** until edges begin to crisp. Add **salt** to taste.

6 to 8 servings

WINTER

mushrooms madeira

1. Stem and slice 1½ pounds fresh shiitake mushrooms and 1½ pounds Portobello mushrooms. Set aside. Slice **2 frying peppers** (*or* **sweet green bell peppers**) and set aside in a separate container. Peel and slice **4 cloves garlic** and set aside. Peel, halve lengthwise, and thinly slice **2 cups yams**. Set aside.

2. Heat **grapeseed oil** in two frying pans or one large pan. Add most of the mushrooms and cook over highest heat to brown. As they shrink and brown, add rest of mushrooms. Add **oil** gradually if needed. When mushrooms are almost done (*very* well browned) add peppers and garlic and continue to fry, stirring well. When peppers are limp, add yams. Most likely, more **oil** will be needed. When most of the yams are browned, turn heat off.

3. Divide ½ **cup flour** between the pans, turn heat on low and stir to combine.

4. Measure ½ **cup madeira** and ½ **cup water** in a 2 cup measure. Deglaze pans with this mix. Scrape up and turn into a pot. You will need **3 cups** more **water** so use some to deglaze the pans thoroughly.

5. Add ½ cup diced **sun-dried tomatoes, 6 oz. cranberries**, ¼ **cup tamari**, and ¼ **cup balsamic vinegar**. Bring to a simmer until cranberries pop. Taste and correct seasoning.

6. Serve with **white rice** or steamed **broccoli** with **oil** and **vinegar**.

8 to 10 servings

spicy thai "chicken"

Chinese Buddhists have been making meat analogs for centuries. We are familiar with wheat gluten (seitan) and TVP (textured vegetable protein) and tempeh (fermented Indonesian style soy), but vegetarian Chinese restaurants have access to many other products. The one we like to use is frozen and is called "chicken strips."

1. Mince the soft parts of **1 stalk of lemongrass.** Dice **1 small red pepper.** In a sauce pan, gently sauté both in **2 tablespoons grapeseed oil.** When peppers begin to brown, add **2 to 3 tablespoons Thai red curry paste** (available in 4 oz. cans in Asian markets, we use Maesri brand) and **2 (14 oz.) cans Thai coconut milk.** Finally, add the contents of **3 packages "chicken strips,"** 7 to 8 oz. each.

2. Bring to a simmer. Add the **juice of ½ lime** and **2 tablespoons tamari**, or to taste. If you prefer a spicier flavor, add more red curry paste.

3. Serve with cooked **jasmine rice,** chopped roasted **peanuts,** minced **cilantro** and **scallions,** a wedge of **avocado,** and slices of **golden pineapple.**

6 servings

shepherd's pie

1. Dice **1 cake soy tempeh**. Cut **2 scraped carrots** into chunks, slice **2 celery stalks, 1 large onion, 1 leek**, and clean **2 cups mushrooms**. Set aside.

2. Barely cover **1 cup dried shiitake mushrooms** with warm water. Peel and slice **3 parsnips** and slice **½ head Napa cabbage.** Dice ¾ **cup yellow turnip** and parboil.*

3. Use **a few tablespoons grapeseed oil** and a heavy skillet to fry tempeh over high heat, turning often. When it is medium-brown, add mushrooms, squeezed and sliced shiitakes (reserve liquid) and all other vegetables except turnip. End with cabbage. Let each batch begin to brown before adding more vegetables. Meanwhile, season stew with **1 tablespoon ground coriander,** ¾ **tablespoon salt, 1 teaspoon cumin,** and **1 tablespoon** minced **fresh rosemary** (*or* **1 teaspoon dried**).

4. Stir in ½ **cup flour** and cook another 2 minutes. Now add: ½ **cup dry sherry, 1 cup dry white wine,** shiitake soaking liquid, ¼ **cup tamari, 1 cup cider,** and **1 to 2 cups miso gravy** (see index). Chop ¾ **cup parsley** and add.

5. Optional: soak **1½ cups soy protein chunks** in water 5 minutes. Drain and add to stew. Simmer all together (add turnips now) and add water if too thick. Set stew aside.

---

*Cover with water, bring to a simmer, and cook 5 to 10 minutes.

6. Make garlic-mashed potatoes: peel, dice, and boil **6 baking potatoes**. Peel **6 to 7 cloves garlic** and simmer, covered, in **2 to 3 tablespoons water** until very soft. When potatoes are very soft, drain. Turn into bowl. Use potato masher to mash. Add garlic and cooking liquid, **½ cup soy milk** and **⅓ cup olive oil**. Add **salt** and **pepper** to taste, together with **1½ teaspoons** minced fresh **rosemary**.

7. Turn shepherd's pie into a shallow casserole. Top with mashed potatoes. Heat in a 400°F. oven until potatoes brown a little.

6 servings

KRYSTYNA

estofado con chochoyotes

A Mexican stew with tiny dumplings. It is always preferable to presoak beans overnight rather than use canned ones. If you do so, presoak ½ cup black beans at least 5 hours. Rinse, cover with fresh water and cook until tender.

1. **Make vegetable stew:** coarsely chop **1 large onion,** dice **2 cups celery,** and **2 cups carrots.** Cut **1 large red pepper** and **1 large green pepper** into 1 to 2″ dice. Chop **3 to 4 jalapeño peppers.**

2. In a shallow, wide saucepot, sauté all vegetables in **½ cup grapeseed oil.** When onions begin to brown, add **3 cloves sliced garlic, 2 bay leaves, 1 teaspoon ground cumin, 2 teaspoons chili powder, 1 teaspoon ground black pepper, 2 teaspoons Kosher salt,** and **1½ teaspoons dried oregano.***

3. Stir all over high heat for a few minutes. Add **½ cup all-purpose flour** and cook to absorb the oil. Add **½ cup dry white wine, 2 cups water, 3 cups diced canned tomatoes** (15 to 16 oz). Bring to a simmer. Add **1 cup canned organic black beans,** rinsed, and **3 cups canned** *or* **frozen corn kernels.** Season with **¼ cup tamari.** Correct seasoning.

4. **Make chochoyotes:** the little dumplings: use a food processor to blend **1 cup masa harina** with **2 tablespoons coconut oil** and **1½ teaspoons salt, ¼ teaspoon** fresh ground **black pepper, 1½ tablespoons** finely minced **cilantro, 1½ tablespoons** finely minced **fresh epazote,** if available, and **2 tablespoons** finely minced **onion.** Gradually add

---

*Preferably Mexican rather than Mid-eastern oregano.

½ to 1 cup warm water. Add slowly, giving the mix time to absorb the liquid. The resulting dough mixture should be rather solid and not too soft, so don't add too much water. Turn machine off. Use your hands to form small balls slightly larger than marbles. Use a finger to make a depression in each one. You should have about 25 chochoyotes. Heat a pot of water with a splash of tamari. When boiling, add the dumplings. Lower heat and cool until they float to the top, 10 to 15 minutes.

5. Add cooked dumplings to the stew. Serve in bowls garnished with chopped cilantro and avocado slices.

6 servings

seitan with stir-fried vegetables

Wheat gluten is an ancient Asian use of wheat flour as a meat substitute. It is available in health food stores and Asian markets, or you can make your own (see following recipe). Our seitan comes from our tofu makers, The Bridge, Middletown, CT, where it is packed in a soy-ginger flavored broth.

1. Gently squeeze broth from **1 pound seitan**, using your hands, and reserve. Cut seitan into thin strips. Set aside. You will need **3½ cups liquid**, so add **water** and **2 tablespoons tamari** if necessary to make this amount.

2. Cut ¾ **pound carrots** into pieces, using the Chinese roll cut if you are familiar with that technique. By slicing diagonally through the carrots with your knife and then rolling the carrot part way, pieces come out in an asymmetric shape. Cut **2 large red peppers** into strips, and slice **3 cups mushrooms**. Peel and roll-cut enough **broccoli stems** to measure **4 cups**. This recipe uses usually discarded broccoli stems to good advantage.

3. In a wok or large frying pan heat **2 tablespoons grapeseed oil**. When hot, add vegetables. Turn vegetables constantly until edges begin to brown nicely. Add ½ **teaspoon dried ginger, 3 cloves crushed garlic**, and sprinkle lightly with **salt**. When browning is adequate, turn off the fire.

4. In a bowl, stir together the **3½ cups seitan liquid,
3 tablespoons cornstarch, 2 tablespoons tamari,
1 tablespoon Chinese (toasted) sesame oil,
⅓ teaspoon Chinese chili-paste-with-garlic**, and
1 teaspoon agave nectar. Pour over mixture in pan and
turn on heat. Stir until gravy is thickened and clear.
Add seitan strips and heat thoroughly before serving.

5. Serve over **brown rice** and garnish with sliced
scallions.

6 servings

SARAH

sake-steamed yukon gold potatoes

Adapted from *The Breakaway Japanese Kitchen*, by Eric Gower.
This is comfort food. Serve with **Roasted Gingered Beets** and
Fried Kale (see index).

1. Peel **3 Yukon Gold potatoes** and cut into thick
   wedges. Cook in boiling **water** until not quite done.
   Drain in a colander. Heat **grapeseed oil** in a large
   frying pan and sauté the potato pieces over high heat
   for 5 minutes or until they brown a little. Add
   1½ cups sake and continue cooking until sake almost
   disappears (it will splatter and be messy). Add
   2 tablespoons tamari and mix well. The potatoes
   should be coated with a delicious brown gravy.
   Serve immediately.

onion phyllo tart

These ingredients may not seem to be appropriate used together, but expect to be pleasantly surprised.

1. Peel and slice thinly **6 large onions**. A mix of red and Vidalias may be used, but any onions will do. Set aside. Grate the **zest of 3 limes**. Finely chop the tender part of a **stalk of lemongrass**, and chop **1 large jalapeño chile** (discard the seeds).

2. Heat **3 tablespoons grapeseed oil** in a large skillet (such as a 12″ cast iron pan). Sauté onions over moderate heat, stirring every now and then. After 5 minutes, add chile, lime zest, and lemongrass. Lower heat and cook about 10 minutes more, stirring occasionally. Add ¾ **cup unsweetened large-flake coconut**. Season with 1½ **teaspoons salt** and fresh ground **pepper** to taste.

3. Preheat oven to 400°F. You will need a baking pan, such as a 6″ x 12″ lasagne pan. Combine ⅓ **cup grapeseed oil** with **2 tablespoons tamari** in a cup. Use a pastry brush to coat the pan. Lay **14 sheets of phyllo pastry** in the pan. As you proceed, brush each with the tamari/oil mix, stirring it as best you can. Add onion mix to the pan. Place 14 more sheets on top, brushing each with the oil mix. When all sheets are in the pan, use a knife to score the tart into large diamonds. Bake 20 to 30 minutes, or until brown.

4. This tart is nice with steamed **asparagus** *or* **broccoli**, or with sliced steamed **beets** dressed with **dill** and **lemon** and a little **vinaigrette** (see glossary). Note that this onion tart reheats well.

6 to 8 servings

gnocchi
with tomato fondue

From Frank Tessier. We asked our friend Rachel Portnoy's French chef husband to make vegan gnocchis. This is Frank's answer. Time consuming to make, but the result is excellent. The tomato fondue is delicious and usable for other dishes as well.

1. **Make tomato fondue:** cut out stem end and cut an "X" in **15 plum tomatoes**. Bring a pot of **water** to a boil. Dip tomatoes in boiling water for a few seconds only, a few at a time. Remove to **ice water** and peel. Repeat until done. Halve tomatoes and scrape out seeds and discard. Dice tomatoes.

2. Chop **1 small onion, 3 peeled shallots** and **3 peeled garlic cloves**. Sauté in a **few tablespoons olive oil** over very low heat. Add a bouquet garni of **fresh thyme, rosemary,** and **tarragon**, wrapped in **leek leaves** and tied with cord. Add to pot with ½ **tablespoon salt, fresh grated pepper, 1 teaspoon sugar,** and **1 tablespoon tomato paste**. Cut a round of **parchment paper** and push it down to cover the fondue mix. Simmer over lowest heat 2 hours, until quite dry.

3. **Make gnocchi:** wrap **5 baking potatoes** in foil. Bake at 375°F until very soft. Peel. Push through a potato ricer. This should keep potatoes fluffy. The grater attachment on a food processor will work well also. Weigh potatoes and add approximately ⅓ of that **weight** of **all-purpose flour**. Add flour, **fresh grated nutmeg,** and **pepper,** and ½ **tablespoon salt** to potatoes. Mix well, but try not to compact potatoes. Roll into 1″ diameter ropes and cut quickly into 1″ pieces. Refrigerate.

4. **Make wild mushroom sauce:** soak **1 cup dried shiitakes** and ¾ **cup dried porcini mushrooms** in **hot water** to cover. Mince **1 clove garlic** and **1 to 2 shallots**. Squeeze mushrooms, retaining liquids separately, and slice into thin slivers. Use ¼ **cup olive oil** to sauté garlic and shallots with ¼ **teaspoon hot pepper flakes**. When softened, add mushrooms. Raise heat and stir until mushrooms are well browned. Add ¼ **cup flour** and mix well. Deglaze with **1 cup dry white wine** and the reserved **mushroom liquids**. Bring to a boil. Add **1 tablespoon tomato paste**, **3 tablespoons tamari**, and **2 cups water**, or as needed. Taste for **salt** and add if necessary.

5. Poach gnocchi in **simmering water**. They will float to the surface when done. They may be reheated in the wild mushroom sauce. Serve 6 to 8 in a shallow bowl. Center with tomato fondue, and garnish with chopped **parsley** and a few **fresh thyme leaves**.

8 servings

llapingachos
con salsa de mani

A traditional Ecuadorian potato and cheese croquette. In this recipe tofu replaces the cheese. From Ricardo Jennings of Tao-Fu, Quito, Ecuador.

1. Toast ½ **pound unsalted peanuts** in a 400°F oven until lightly browned, stirring every few minutes for 10 to 15 minutes total. Set aside.

2. **Make llapingachos:** wash **6 medium potatoes**, cut into large chunks, cover with water in a pot, and boil until just tender. Drain and set aside.

3. If available, gently heat **1 tablespoon annatto seed** (achiote) in **2 tablespoons grapeseed oil** until it is quite yellow. Discard the seeds.

4. Trim **3 scallions** and peel **3 cloves garlic**. Chop the scallions and add with crushed garlic to the annatto-colored oil. Sauté until golden.

5. Peel potatoes and put into a mixer. Beat well. Add ½ **pound tofu**, ½ **tablespoon salt**, sautéed garlic and scallions, and freshly ground **pepper**. Mix well again. Taste for salt and pepper, correct seasoning. Turn mixture into container and chill.

6. **Make salsa de mani (peanut sauce):** chop another **3 scallions** and crush another **2 cloves of garlic**. Sauté in frying pan with **1 tablespoon grapeseed oil** with ⅓ **teaspoon red pepper flakes**, ½ **teaspoon dried rosemary**, ½ **teaspoon dried oregano**, and ¾ **teaspoon ground cumin**. Use a blender or food processor to pulverize the peanuts with the sautéed vegetables and seasonings, adding ¼ **pound tofu**

and **2 to 3 cups water** as needed. Try to get the sauce as smooth and creamy as possible. Flavor with **2 to 3 tablespoons tamari** and ½ **tablespoon miso.** Mix again and correct seasonings. Add **Tabasco sauce** if not spicy enough for your taste. Turn sauce into a pot and bring to a simmer.

7. **To serve:** we like to garnish the llapingacho plate with cooked beets, so scrape **1 small bunch beets,** barely cover with **water** in a pot and cook until just done, about 20 minutes.

8. When ready to serve, heat a frying pan or griddle until hot. If potato mixture seems soft, shape 3 cakes per person on a flour-sprinkled sheet of waxed paper. Otherwise, use your hands to shape cakes. Add **grapeseed oil** to griddle or skillet and fry cakes over high heat until edges look brown and crusted. Use spatula to scrape up each cake, turn over and press down so that finished cakes are about ½″ to ¾″ thick. While second side browns, cut long vertical slices of **ripe plantain** to fry alongside potato cakes. Serve llapingachos with peanut sauce, plantain slices, shredded **lettuce,** and **avocado.** Slice **beets** for the side of the platter and top potato cakes with minced **scallions.**

6 to 8 servings

empanadas

1. **Make filling:** cut **1 package (8 oz.) tempeh** into dice. Set aside. Chop **1 onion, 2 to 3 frying peppers, 3 cloves of garlic,** and **2 seeded jalapeño peppers.** Sauté all in **olive oil** as needed in a large skillet, preferably cast iron. Take time to cook vegetables over moderate heat until they brown well.

2. Add ½ **cup dry soy protein,** crumbled. Stir all together well. Chop **1 cup olives stuffed with pimentos** and add with **2 tablespoons tomato paste** and **1 cup diced fresh tomatoes.** If available, add **2 canned Hatch chilies** (see glossary), diced. Finally, chop ¾ **cup fresh cilantro** and fold into mixture. Add **salt** and **pepper** to taste and correct seasoning. Let cool.

3. **Make coconut oil piecrust:** place **3 cups all-purpose flour** in a bowl. Add **1 tablespoon salt** and 2½ **tablespoons sugar.** Stir together. In a two-cup measuring cup, place ¾ **cup coconut oil** (melted if necessary), **2 tablespoons flax seed "eggs"*** and ⅓ **cup water.** Stir until blended with a fork. Add to flour mix, stirring with fork until dough forms a smooth mixture. Divide dough into thirds and divide each third into eighths. Keep at room temperature. Coconut oil piecrust is difficult to work with; however the flax seed "eggs" should help stabilize the dough. If you have trouble rolling out rounds with your rolling pin, use two squares of plastic wrap, dusting your hands with **flour** as needed. Fill round with heaping tablespoon of filling and use the plastic wrap to fold rounds in half. Pinch edges. Use a spatula to lift onto on

*See Glossary.

ungreased baking sheet. Repeat until 24 empanadas are completed.

4. Refrigerate shaped empanadas 15 minutes. Meanwhile, preheat oven to 375°F. Bake 20 to 30 minutes or until done.

5. Serve with wedges of thin-skinned **oranges** and **salad**, two to three empanadas per diner. These can be frozen or refrigerated, and reheat nicely.

8 to 10 servings

WINTER

seitan
vegetarian wheat meat or wheat gluten

This recipe is from Louise Griffin and Mary Ann Powers of *Something Special* in Miami. Homemade wheat gluten is delicious.

1. Mix together **8 cups whole-wheat flour** (intended for bread, not pastry) and **3 cups cool water** for 10 to 15 minutes. A dough hook is most efficient, if your mixer has one.

2. Place kneaded ball in a large bowl of cool water, enough to cover, and let sit 30 minutes.

3. Remove from bowl and knead under running water until all cloudiness disappears and the ball starts to feel like bubble gum. This will take about 20 minutes. The result is wheat gluten.

4. Bring **2 quarts water** to a boil in a large pot. When boiling, uncover. Slice or cube the gluten and drop into the boiling water. Stir once to prevent sticking.

5. Once pieces have floated to the top, reduce heat and simmer 30 minutes.

6. Remove to a container. Make a marinade of ½ **cup tamari, ½ cup water, 1 tablespoon lemon juice**, and **herbs** of your choice. Louise and Mary Ann use sage, thyme, and rosemary. Store in the refrigerator for up to one week, or freeze.

makes 2 pounds

persimmon sorbet
with winter fruits

We use the last of our ripe persimmons to make this. Then it is frozen to be served for dessert on New Year's Eve.

1. Purée enough **persimmons** in a food processor to yield **4 to 5 cups**.

2. In an ice cream maker, combine purée with **2½ tablespoons agave nectar, 4 teaspoons lemon juice, ¼ teaspoon salt, ¼ teaspoon dried powdered ginger, ¼ cup orange papaya** (or other similar) juice and **¼ cup grapeseed oil**.

3. Follow directions for making ice cream. When sorbet is done, freeze it.

4. For a winter dessert, serve a scoop of sorbet on overlapping slices of fresh **oranges, pineapple**, and **kiwi fruit**. Cookies make a good accompaniment as well. See recipe for **almond oat cookies**.

makes 2½ quarts

sourdough orange cake

1. Combine dry ingredients in a large bowl: **3⅓ cups unbleached all-purpose white flour, scant ⅔ cup sugar, 2 teaspoons baking soda, ½ teaspoon salt, ½ teaspoon turmeric** and **½ teaspoon ground cardamom.** Stir well with a dry whisk.

2. Preheat oven to 350°F. Use another, smaller bowl to combine wet ingredients: **1 tablespoon grated orange rind, ½ cup sourdough starter,* ⅔ cup orange juice, 1 tablespoon lemon juice, 1 cup coconut oil** (melted if necessary), **1 teaspoon vanilla extract,** and **2 tablespoons Grand Marnier** (*or* **½ teaspoon orange oil**).

3. Briefly combine wet and dry ingredients and turn into an ungreased removable-bottom tube pan. Bake until a tester comes out dry in the middle, 50 minutes to 1 hour and 15 minutes. Let cool on a rack, then use a knife to cut away the cake pan sides.

4. Make **orange raspberry glaze**. In a pot combine **1½ cups orange juice, 2 teaspoons lemon juice, ¼ teaspoon grated nutmeg, dash salt, scant ¼ cup maple syrup** and **2½ tablespoons cornstarch.** Stir all together over high heat until thickened. Add **1 package frozen raspberries**. Alternatively, make the frosting for **orange carrot cake** (see index).

one 9" to 10" cake

---

*See glossary for information on sourdough starter.

sourdough chocolate devastation cake

A very easy and delicious vegan cake. You will need good quality unsweetened cocoa and sourdough starter (see glossary) to make it.

1. Lightly oil two 9″ cake pans. Preheat oven to 325°F.

2. Combine dry ingredients in a bowl: **¾ cup unsweetened good quality cocoa powder,* 2 cups sugar, 3 cups unbleached white flour, 2 teaspoons baking soda, ¾ teaspoon salt, 2 tablespoons grain coffee,** and ½ teaspoon cinnamon.** Stir together with a dry whisk.

3. Combine wet ingredients in another bowl: **1 cup thick sourdough starter, 2¼ cups water, 2 tablespoons vinegar, ¾ cup grapeseed oil,** and **1½ teaspoons vanilla.** Stir well with a whisk.

4. Combine wet and dry mixtures with as few strokes as possible. Some lumps are not a problem. Turn into pans immediately and bake 25 to 30 minutes, or until cakes begin to pull away from the sides of the pans and a toothpick inserted into the center comes out clean. Remove and cool on racks.

---

*Such as Vahlrona.

**Such as Cafix.

chocolate frosting

This frosting sets up firm and protects the cake from becoming dry. Because of this, this cake will stay fresh about five days in the refrigerator if covered with plastic wrap. From Mary Préjean.

1. Chop good quality **semi-sweet chocolate*** to measure **1 cup**. Combine with **1 teaspoon vanilla**, **3 tablespoons maple syrup**, **¼ cup grapeseed oil**, and **3 tablespoons unsweetened cocoa powder**. Place over lowest heat or melt in double boiler (a pan of simmering water with a heatproof bowl set over it). Don't stir until chocolate is entirely melted. Alternatively, the pot of frosting mixture may be put in a warm place, such as on top of the stove, while the cake bakes. Once the chocolate melts, stir gently with a spoon until mixture thickens slightly. Frosting will be soft but will thicken as you stir it.

2. When cakes and frosting are cool, spread frosting over cake.

one 2-layer 9″ cake

---

*Such as Vahlrona.

bûche nöel

Bûche Nöel means Yule Log. It is a cake roll cut to resemble a log and used to celebrate the coldest time of a year—for us, the Winter Solstice. For years a cake was made to celebrate our Noel´s birthday. These days we make this vegan version.

1. Prepare the **chocolate devastation cake** (see index), but bake it in a 12″ x 17″ pan previously oiled and lined with waxed paper. Prepare a dish towel on a counter and sift **confectioner's sugar** over it. Turn baked cake (it will cook in a very short time) onto the towel. Peel waxed paper and discard. Roll towel and cake together and cool on a rack.

2. Make **coconut milk whipped cream** (see index), adding **2 tablespoons unsweetened powdered cocoa**, sifted, to it. Sweeten to taste with sugar or agave syrup.

3. Spread cooled and unrolled cake with fruit-only raspberry jam. Spread chilled whipped cream over cake. Carefully re-roll. Cake is quite fragile, so use caution.

4. Make 2 parallel cuts diagonally at each end of the cake 2 to 4 inches in. Use these short pieces to form short side branches on the log. Place log and branch stumps on a tray.

5. Cut up good quality **semi-sweet chocolate**, such as Valrhona, to measure **1 cup**. Turn into a pot. Add **1 teaspoon vanilla extract, 3 tablespoons maple syrup, ¼ cup grapeseed oil** and **3 tablespoons unsweetened cocoa powder**. Stir over lowest heat until dissolved. Set aside until cool. Whisk thoroughly.

6. Use a narrow-bladed spatula to spread frosting over the cake and the tines of a fork to make tree bark-like grooves.

10 to 12 servings

chocolate hazelnut torte

1. Roast **3½ cups** peeled **hazelnuts** at 350°F until light brown. Cool. Leave oven on.

2. Oil and line two 9″ cake pans with waxed paper. Set aside. Melt **½ pound bittersweet chocolate** (we use El Ray) in **½ cup brewed coffee** over low heat. Let cool, whisk. Set aside.

3. Use a food processor to grind hazelnuts. Add **½ cup all-purpose flour** to processor. Turn out into a bowl. Add **1 more cup all-purpose flour**, **½ cup sugar**, **¼ teaspoon salt**, **1 teaspoon baking soda**, **1½ teaspoons baking powder** to bowl. Use a dry whisk to stir all together.

4. In a separate bowl, stir together **1 cup sourdough starter** (see glossary), **1 cup water**, the cooled chocolate and **¾ teaspoon vanilla extract**.

5. Quickly combine wet ingredients and dry ingredients. Don't overmix. Turn into prepared pans and bake until center bounces back when pushed with your finger. Let cool 5 minutes. Run a knife around the edge, pushing gently on cake. Turn out and wait until very cool to frost.

6. **Make frosting:** heat **1 cup Sucanat** over low heat in a heavy pan until it melts and begins to caramelize. Add **¾ cup coconut milk** *or* **soy milk** and simmer until caramel is dissolved. Whisk in **4 oz.** cut up **semi-sweet chocolate.** Add dash **salt** and **½ teaspoon vanilla extract.** Frosting must be completely cool to be spreadable. Spread frosting between layers and onto top of cake. Alternatively, use frosting from the **chocolate devastation cake** (see index).

one 9″ two layer cake

black forest cake

This is not a tidy cake. Layers of chocolate cake are sandwiched with cherries and whipped "cream."

1. Defrost **1 cup frozen sweet cherries**. Preheat oven to 350°F.

2. **Make coconut milk whipped cream:** heat together in a small pot the contents of a **14 oz. can coconut milk, 2 tablespoons sugar, 1 tablespoon kudzu, ¼ teaspoon salt, 1 tablespoon coconut oil,** and **1 teaspoon instant agar-agar.*** Whisk until mixture comes to a boil and thickens slightly. Add **1 scant tablespoon balsamic vinegar, ½ tablespoon cognac** and **½ teaspoon vanilla extract.** Stir. Chill until solid in refrigerator.

3. **Make cherry filling:** in another small pot combine **½ cup apple cherry juice** with **⅓ cup dried sour cherries** and **¼ cup cherry preserves.** Add a **pinch of salt** and simmer until liquid is reduced to 1 to 2 tablespoons. Drain defrosted sweet cherries, saving juices. You will need **1 cup cherries,** each cut in half. Add **scant tablespoon cornstarch** and **2 teaspoons balsamic vinegar** to juices and stir. Add cut up cherries and cornstarch mix to pot. Stir. Simmer until thickened. Taste and add **sugar** if you like. Set aside.

---

*Available in Asian markets as Telephone brand.

4. **Make cake:** use **lecithin oil** (see glossary) to lightly grease three 8″ cake pans. Set aside. Use a dry whisk to combine **2 cups flour, 1¼ cups sugar, ⅓ cup unsweetened cocoa, 1 teaspoon baking soda,** and **½ teaspoon salt**. Melt (if solid) **½ cup coconut oil**. Add to it **1⅓ cups hot water, 4 teaspoons white vinegar, 2 teaspoons instant coffee** and **2 teaspoons vanilla extract**. Stir liquid ingredients together. Add to dry ingredients. Blend with spoon but do not overmix. Pour into the prepared pans. Cakes will seem thin. Bake 25 minutes or until centers are firm to the touch. Cool pans on racks 15 minutes before turning cakes out. Brush each layer with **Jamaican rum** *or* **brandy**.

5. **Assemble cake:** turn coconut whipped cream into a food processor. Blend until fluffy—about 5 minutes. Place 1 cake round on cake plate. Top with ⅓ of the whipped cream and then ⅓ of the cherry filling. Repeat with 2 more layers. Refrigerate cake.

one 3-layer 8″ cake

raspberry fool

From Maddie Sobel. The word "fool" originally came from an old English word which meant folded. Fools were fruit purées folded into whipped cream.

1. Pour **2 quarts apple-raspberry juice** or a similar organic fruit juice into a saucepot. Sprinkle ⅔ **cup agar-agar flakes** over the juice, cover and bring to a simmer over low heat until dissolved. Meanwhile stir **2 tablespoons kudzu** into ½ **cup water**. When agar is dissolved, stir kudzu once more and add to pot, stirring until mixture thickens. Raise heat slightly and cook 15 minutes with lid ajar.

2. Remove pot from stove. Add **4 cups fresh** *or* **frozen raspberries, pinch salt,** ¼ **cup lemon juice,** ⅓ **cup maple syrup.** Stir. Cool to room temperature and then chill in refrigerator until firm. This will take 1½ hours.

3. Meanwhile make **almond crème**. Begin by making 1½ cups almond milk: pulverize **2 cups almonds** in a processor. Add **2 cups hot water** and process again. At this point, a blender may make a finer mixture. Strain through cheesecloth and squeeze cloth to get **2 cups almond milk**. (Purchased almond milk is not as well-flavored as this.) Place almond milk in a pot. Add **2 tablespoons agar-agar**. Cover and use low heat to dissolve as above. When dissolved, add **1 cup water** with **1 tablespoon kudzu** stirred well together. Turn up heat till mixture simmers then turn into blender and purée. Add: **½ cup coconut oil**, **½ teaspoon salt**, **¼ to ⅓ cup agave syrup**, **1 tablespoon lemon juice**, **1 teaspoon vanilla**, and **½ teaspoon almond extract**. Purée and correct seasoning. Chill until solid.

4. When raspberry mix is cold and firm, purée in processor. Turn out into a bowl. Now process almond crème (no need to wash processor). Turn almond crème over raspberry mix and fold both together incompletely so that white swirls show. Serve in a stemmed glass with **slivered** toasted **almonds**.

5. This makes a pretty Valentine's Day dessert together with the **chocolate hazelnut cake** (see index) spread in a sheet pan and baked, then cut into heart shapes.

6 to 8 servings

sourdough lemon walnut cake

Also see index for other fruit toppings.

1. **Prepare cake:** you will need **sourdough starter** (see glossary). You will also need a 9″ to 10″ tube pan with removable bottom, ungreased.

2. Grate **rind of 2 lemons.** Stir together in a bowl: lemon rind, ⅓ **cup lemon juice, ⅓ cup thick sourdough starter, ½ cup coconut oil** (melted if solid), **1½ teaspoons vanilla,** and **1¼ cups coconut milk** (one can). Whisk all together. Set aside.

3. Preheat oven to 350°F. In a bowl stir together **2½ cups unbleached white flour, ⅔ cup organic sugar, ¾ teaspoon baking soda, 1 tablespoon baking powder, ½ teaspoon ground cardamom,** and **¼ teaspoon salt.** Chop **1 cup walnuts.**

4. Combine nuts, liquid, and dry ingredients, and pour into pan. Place in oven. Cake should bake about one hour and be golden brown and slightly withdrawn from the edges. Adjust your oven heat accordingly. When cake tests done, invert pan on a plate to cool completely. Then use a sharp knife to loosen sides of pan and finally the bottom to release the cake onto the plate. Sift **confectioner's sugar** over cake top.

5. **Prepare lemon raspberry glaze:** in a small pot combine ⅓ **cup agave nectar, 3 tablespoons cornstarch,** a grating of **nutmeg, pinch salt, 3½ tablespoons lemon juice,** and **1 cup water** and **10 oz. frozen raspberries.** Bring to a boil, stirring until sauce thickens and clears. Refrigerate to store.

one 9″ to 10″ cake

lagusta's lemon curd
lemon tart with hazelnut crust

1. Pour **1 bottle (1½ cups) lemon soda** into a pot. Add
   **¾ cup water, 1¼ cups sugar, 1½ tablespoons
   instant agar,*** **½ cup canned Thai coconut milk,
   1 tablespoon lemon zest, ⅓ cup cornstarch**, scant
   ¾ teaspoon salt, and **¾ cup lemon juice**.

2. Whisk all together and bring to a boil. When slightly
   thickened, remove from heat. Add **2 teaspoons
   vanilla extract**. Cool, chill until quite firm.

3. Turn mixture into a processor and blend long enough
   to fluff it up. Use as a cake filling, or for a pie, with a
   hazelnut pie crust (see index).

   8 to 10 servings, or enough for one pie

WINTER

---

*Telephone brand, from a Thai market.

orange carrot cake

This is a delicious carrot cake with a great texture. The frosting is reminiscent of whipped cream cheese.

1. Toast ½ **cup walnuts** in a 300°F toaster oven. When light brown, remove and chop coarsely. Set aside. Warm 1¼ **cups orange juice** to room temperature. Set aside.

2. **Optional:** heat ¼ **cup raisins** in **3 tablespoons Meyer's rum.** Cook about 5 minutes over low heat. Set aside. Preheat oven to 375°F.

3. Grate 1¾ **cups carrots.** Turn ½ **cup coconut oil** into food processor. In winter it is solid, so melt it first in a small pot. Add ⅔ **cup sugar.** Turn machine on until mix is fluffy. Turn off. Add ¼ **cup sourdough starter,** the orange juice and reserved carrots. Process briefly to just blend.

4. Use a dry whisk to stir together: **2 cups plus 2 tablespoons all-purpose flour, 1½ teaspoons baking soda, 1 teaspoon dry mustard, 1 teaspoon salt, ½ teaspoon** *each* **cinnamon, nutmeg** and **cardamom,** and ¼ **teaspoon ground cloves.** Stir together the contents of the food processor, the dry ingredients, the raisins, and the walnuts. Don't overmix. Turn into an ungreased 8 to 9″ springform pan and bake in the preheated oven for 40 to 50 minutes, or until cake pulls away from the sides of the pan. Cool completely on a rack.

5. Meanwhile, make the frosting: combine in a pot;
   1 cup orange juice, grated rind of 1 orange, ½ can
   (7 oz.) coconut milk, ½ cup sugar, dash salt, ⅓ cup
   powdered soy milk and 1½ teaspoons instant agar-
   agar.* Stir over high heat until mixture boils. Turn off
   heat and add 2 teaspoons vanilla extract and
   2 teaspoons balsamic vinegar. Cool; chill.

6. When frosting is very firm and stiff, use a food
   processor to beat it until very creamy. Turn the cake
   out onto a plate and frost. Serve cake with sliced
   pineapple.

one 8″ or 9″ cake

*Telephone brand, from an Asian market.

orange apricot tofu mousse

1. Make the tofu mousse base as described in the recipe for **cranberry tofu mousse** (see index).

2. Cut up and soak **1 cup dried apricots** in **1 cup water** for 2 hours. If still hard, bring gently to a boil. Cool. Peel and slice **2 oranges** and add to apricots. Taste this sauce and add **maple syrup** if it seems to need sweetening. Since the mousse itself is sweet, the fruit sauce which tops it should be somewhat tart. Finally, peel and slice **2 kiwi fruit**, if you like, to mix into the sauce. Chill and serve over mousse.

6 servings

tapioca pudding

1. **Make tapioca pudding:** combine in a large soup pot **1 cup medium tapioca, ¾ cup sugar, 2 cups soymilk, 2 cups water, 1 (14oz.) can Thai coconut milk** (or other unsweetened and no preservative coconut milk) and **½ teaspoon salt**. Bring to a boil, stirring often so that tapioca won't stick together. Cook until tapioca is soft (taste!).

2. Stir **2 tablespoons kudzu** (available in natural foods stores) in **½ cup water**. When dissolved, add to simmering tapioca, whisking vigorously. Remove from heat as soon as mixture thickens, and add **1 teaspoon vanilla extract**. Refrigerate. Mixture will be quite soft until cool. If it becomes too firm when cool, add water to reach desired consistency.

3. **Make caramel sauce:** in a small heavy pot place **¾ cup sugar** and **6 tablespoons water**. Heat, covered, until sugar dissolves. Remove cover and cook over high heat until mixture is light brown. Turn off heat. Add **¼ cup elderberry** or **damson plum jam** and stir until well mixed. If sauce is too stiff, add more water and boil up.

4. Serve tapioca pudding in stemmed glass bowls with caramel topping and **banana** or **pineapple slices**.

makes about 1½ quarts, serves 6 to 8

black cherry mousse

Sweetening-free.

1. In a pot combine **1 cup unsweetened dried Bing cherries**, **4 cups** good **fruit juice**, such as apple raspberry or organic, unsweetened grape juice. Add a dash **salt**, dash **cinnamon**, and sprinkle ¼ **cup agar-agar flakes** over the top. Do not stir in. Let mixture rest 30 minutes.

2. Meanwhile prepare almond milk by placing **2½ cups almonds** (with skins is okay) and **3 cups very hot tap water** in a blender. Pulverize. Squeeze almond milk through cheesecloth and set aside.

3. Place cherry mix over low heat, covered, and bring to a slow simmer until agar-agar dissolves.

4. In a separate pot, bring almond milk to a simmer. In a measuring cup, dissolve **4 tablespoons kudzu** in ⅓ **cup water**. Stir well and add to almond milk, stirring until thickened. Flavor with ½ **teaspoon vanilla extract** and ¼ **teaspoon almond extract**.

5. Combine cherry mix and almond milk. Fill stemmed dessert glasses and chill. Serve with slivered **toasted almonds**.

7 to 8 servings

chocolate silk pudding or pie filling

Comfort food.

1. Combine in a medium-sized pot: the contents of **1 (14 oz.) can coconut milk, 2 cups soy milk,** scant **½ cup sugar, 4 oz. bittersweet chocolate** such as El Ray or Vahlrona, **⅓ cup cornstarch, 2 tablespoons unsweetened cocoa powder, 2 tablespoons instant coffee powder, ½ teaspoon salt,** and **½ teaspoon grated orange rind.**

2. Use a whisk to stir all ingredients together over medium heat. Cook, stirring frequently, until mixture comes to a visible simmer and has thickened somewhat. This will take 10 minutes. Remove from heat. Add ½ **teaspoon vanilla extract** and stir well. Turn into individual custard cups, or into a large glass bowl.

3. Serve with slivered **toasted almonds** and **coconut milk** to pour over the top. This pudding may be poured into a prebaked pie crust such as the **hazelnut pie crust** (see index) and served with **coconut milk whipped cream** (see index) to make a chocolate pie.

8 servings

"key" lime pie

1. Preheat oven to 375°F. Roll out **hazelnut pie crust** (see index) and fit into a 10″ glass pie plate. Use foil and dried beans to weight crust. Bake until light brown. Remove foil and beans and let cool.

2. **Filling:** grate **zest of 2 limes** and squeeze **juice from 6 to 8 limes**. You will need ¾ cup of juice. Turn into a small pot. Add a dash **salt**, contents of **1 can of premium Thai coconut milk** and **2½ tablespoons agar-agar flakes**. Cover and dissolve agar without stirring, over low heat.

3. Stir together ⅓ **cup powdered soymilk**, ¼ **cup water**, ⅔ **cup light agave syrup** (*or* maple syrup), and **3 tablespoons kudzu**. Whisk into dissolved lime juice–agar mix and return to a simmer while stirring. When slightly thickened, remove from heat. Chill until solid.

4. Turn lime filling into a food processor. Turn machine on until filling becomes fluffy. Turn into pie crust. Garnish with **lime zest** curls and **coconut milk whipped cream** (see index), if desired.

one 10″ pie

our best almond oat cookies

1. Coarsely chop **2 cups almonds** in a food processor. Turn off and add: **1½ cups walnuts, 2 cups oats, 1 teaspoon baking powder,** ½ **teaspoon baking soda,** ¾ cup flour, and **1 cup date sugar** (*or* ¼ cup **maple sugar**). Process briefly.

2. Pour into a 2 cup measure: **1 cup grapeseed oil, 1 cup apple cider** (*or* other fruit juice, *or* water), and **2 teaspoons vanilla.** Turn machine on. Pour in liquids and ½ **cup currants.** Don't overmix.

3. Preheat oven to 350°F.

4. Drop batter by spoonfuls onto ungreased cookie sheet. Use a fork to pat them out. Bake till a little brown around the edges, approximately 10 minutes. If the underside seems to be getting done and the top is still soft, use a small spatula to flip each cookie over.

approximately 2 dozen

hazelnut oat cookies

From Steve Szost.

1. Preheat oven to 375°F. Coarsely chop 1¼ cups hazelnuts (filberts) *or* other nuts.

2. In a bowl mix together: **2 cups oat flakes, 1 cup unbleached white flour, ½ cup currants** (*or* raisins), **3 tablespoons Sucanat** (*or* sugar), **3 tablespoons dried unsweetened shredded coconut, 3 tablespoons potato starch,** and **1 teaspoon baking soda.** Add nuts also and mix together thoroughly to distribute the currants. Hands work best.

3. Pour ½ **cup grapeseed oil** into a measuring cup. Add ¼ **cup apple** (*or* other fruit) **concentrate** (*or* maple syrup) and ¼ **cup water** to the measuring pitcher. Flavor with **1 teaspoon vanilla extract.**

4. Stir wet mixture thoroughly into dry ingredients. Drop by spoonfuls onto a lightly oiled baking sheet. Bake until golden brown. Remove from cookie sheet immediately.

makes about 2 dozen cookies

gingersnaps

The pepper is essential.

WINTER

1. Preheat oven to 375°F. In a bowl whisk together 1½ cups flour, 1 cup whole wheat flour, 1 teaspoon baking soda, ⅓ cup maple sugar, 2½ teaspoons ground ginger, ¼ teaspoon ground nutmeg, ¼ teaspoon ground cloves, ¼ teaspoon salt, 1¾ teaspoons cinnamon, ½ teaspoon ground black pepper.

2. Mash ripe banana to yield ¼ cup. Combine with ¼ cup molasses, 1 teaspoon vanilla, ½ cup grapeseed oil, and ¼ cup maple syrup.

3. Mix wet and dry ingredients together and roll into balls. Place on a cookie sheet and flatten each ball with a fork. Bake in preheated oven for approximately 12 to 15 minutes. Let cool slightly. Remove with a spatula to a rack to cool.

makes about 3 dozen cookies

korova cookies

Adapted from a butter version in Dorie Greenspan's *Paris Sweets*.

1. Sift or whisk together **1¼ cups flour, ⅓ cup unsweetened cocoa powder,*** and **½ teaspoon baking soda**. Set aside. Chop **½ cup pecans**. Set aside.

2. Use a standing mixer to cream together **¾ cup coconut oil,**** ⅔ cup dark brown sugar, ¼ cup sugar, ½ teaspoon fleur de sel** (or Kosher salt) and **1 teaspoon vanilla extract**. Beat briefly on low speed until just combined.

3. Add flour mix and pecans. Beat on low speed until mixture forms a solid mass. Turn mixer off.

4. Turn cookie dough onto a counter. Divide in half. Shape each into a solid roll approximately 2″ in diameter. Wrap tightly in foil and refrigerate for 30 to 40 minutes, or until just firm enough to slice.

5. Preheat oven to 350°F. Slice each roll into ½″ rounds. Mix may be crumbly. Place cookies on an ungreased baking sheet, pushing broken bits back into the cookies.

6. Bake 12 to 14 minutes. Place pan on rack and don't move cookies until they are cool.

2 dozen rounds

---

*Use good quality cocoa, such as Vahlrona.

**We use Omega organic oil (see glossary and introductory material for more information). At room temperature, it is solid in the winter, and in summer it is liquid. For this recipe it must be firm, so chill it in the refrigerator if need be.

linzer cookies

1. Place **1 cup unblanched almonds** in a food processor. Turn on machine to grind almonds fine. Turn off.

2. Add to processor: **1 tablespoon** grated **lemon rind**, **½ cup flour, 3 tablespoons sugar, ¼ teaspoon salt, pinch cinnamon** and a **pinch cloves**. Turn machine on to blend. Add **½ cup coconut oil** and **2 rounded tablespoons flax seed "eggs"** (see glossary). Process until dough comes together into a moist ball. Turn out and divide in half. Use your floured hands to shape each into 2″ diameter rolls. Wrap in foil or plastic wrap and refrigerate 30 minutes.

3. Preheat oven to 350°F. Use a French chef's knife to slice ¼″ to ½″ cookies. Place them next to each other on an ungreased baking sheet. Use a fork or your fingers to flatten them somewhat. Bake 10 minutes. Carefully turn the fragile cookies, using a thin spatula, and bake 5 to 7 minutes more.

4. Let cool 5 minutes. Spread half the cookies with good quality **raspberry jam**. Loosen the rest of the cookies gently with the spatula and top the jam ones to make sandwiches.

makes about 2 dozen cookie sandwiches

SPRING

SOUPS

SALADS

ENTREES

fassoulada

A wonderful Greek soup that is quick to make and which reheats beautifully, from Hope Zachariades, a neighbor of many years ago, a wonderful and generous cook.

1. Soak **1 cup dried cannelini beans** in water overnight.*

2. Drain beans, add fresh water, and cook until tender.

3. Dice by hand **1½ carrots, 2 stalks celery with leaves, and 1 medium onion.** Vegetables should be chopped neatly and evenly. Heat **¼ cup olive oil** in soup kettle and begin frying carrots first. After 5 minutes add onions, then celery. When all vegetables are medium brown, add **1 teaspoon salt, pepper,** and **1 small (8 oz.) can Italian plum tomatoes,** chopped. Simmer, covered, 10 minutes.

4. Add **1 to 2 cups water** and cook another 10 minutes or until vegetables are tender. Add the cooked cannelini beans. More water may be added for best consistency. Chop a small bunch **Italian parsley** and add.

6 servings

---

*If beans cannot be soaked overnight, they can be brought to a boil in water, removed from heat for 1 hour and then returned to stove and cooked until tender. Or you may use canned cannelini beans.

split pea and carrot soup

1. In a large soup pot, simmer **1 pound split peas** in ample **water** to cover until just done. Do not add salt.

2. Chop **3 medium onions** and ½ **bunch celery** (including leaves) and sauté in **2 tablespoons grapeseed oil** in a frying pan. When medium brown, add **2 large cloves garlic**, crushed, ¾ **teaspoon marjoram**, and **2 bay leaves**. Stir until well browned.

3. Turn vegetables into kettle of cooked split peas. Deglaze frying pan by adding ½ **cup red wine**. Bring to a simmer, scrape up brown bits, and add to soup kettle.

4. Simmer soup at least ½ hour or until it seems done. Season with about **1 tablespoon salt** and lots of fresh ground **pepper**. Any lentil or dried bean soup must be salted after the beans are cooked to avoid toughness.

5. When soup is about done, peel, quarter, and dice **1 bunch of carrots**. Add to soup and continue cooking until carrots are just done.

6. Serve soup with a splash of **port wine** in each bowl.

8 to 10 servings

chickpea, potato, and carrot soup

1. Soak ¾ **cup dried chickpeas** overnight in **water** to cover. The next day, drain, discarding the soaking liquid. In a medium pot, bring the chickpeas to a boil in **2½ cups water** and simmer until the chickpeas are cooked. Set aside.

2. Chop **1 onion**. In a medium soup pot heat ¼ **cup olive oil**. Add onion and ½ **teaspoon dried thyme**, and fry over high heat until onions begin to brown. Meanwhile, thinly slice **2 large cloves garlic**. Add to pot and cook briefly.

3. Cut **1 large peeled potato** into cubes. Slice **1 carrot**. Add to soup pot with **2 cups canned tomatoes**, chopped. Add **1 cup liquid from the can** and the cooked chickpeas with their cooking water. Season with **1½ teaspoons salt** and a generous grating of **black pepper**. Simmer until vegetables are soft, about 20 minutes.

4. Check seasoning and serve with lots of chopped **straight leaf parsley**.

6 servings

spicy gingered carrot soup

1. Coarsely dice **1 Spanish onion** and **2 small seeded jalapeño peppers**. Peel and slice **⅓ cup fresh ginger**. Peel and slice **6 cloves garlic**.

2. Heat **3 tablespoons grapeseed oil** in a soup pot. Add **1 teaspoon turmeric** and sauté all vegetables, stirring until they begin to brown.

3. Peel **2 large potatoes** and cut into large dice. Peel **2 sweet potatoes** and do the same. Coarsely cut up **2 celery stalks**, and **6 peeled carrots**. Add all vegetables to soup pot together with **8 cups water** and **½ cup red lentils** (picked over first to remove any small stones). Bring to a boil over high heat, then turn fire lower and cover pot. Cook over low heat until vegetables are tender. Let cool 20 minutes.

4. Purée soup in batches in a blender. Return to soup pot. Finish with the juice of **3 to 4 limes**, **1½ tablespoons Bragg's Liquid Aminos**,* salt, **pepper**, and **tamari** to taste.

8 servings

---

*See index for information on Bragg's Liquid Aminos.

mulligatawny soup

Made from red lentils and coconut milk.

1. Wash **2 cups red lentils** and cover with water to
   soak for about 30 minutes. Red lentils are available in
   health food stores, Middle Eastern markets or Indian
   markets, where they are known as masur dahl.

2. Drain lentils and turn into a soup pot. Add **2 quarts
   water** and bring to a boil. Skim foam from surface.
   Tie a few whole **cloves, 2 bay leaves**, and a few
   whole **peppercorns** in cheesecloth, and add to pot
   along with **1 tablespoon turmeric, 4 peeled cloves
   garlic, 1 teaspoon whole cumin seed**, and
   1 small fresh hot chile pepper. Simmer, covered,
   1 to 1½ hours.

3. When lentils are cooked, remove cheesecloth
   and purée soup in several batches in blender or
   processor. Return to soup pot. Add **1 tablespoon
   salt, 2 tablespoons lime or lemon juice**, and **1 cup
   canned organic coconut milk**. Correct seasoning. If
   soup seems too thick, dilute with water. Garnish with
   a **slice of lime** *or* lemon in each bowl.

6 to 8 servings

SPRING

hot and sour soup

with wild daylily buds

1. Collect **1 quart wild daylily buds**. Be sure you know what they are. Snap off buds without the stems.

2. Soak ½ **cup dried "tree ears"** (a dried mushroom available in Chinese markets) in boiling water.

3. Shred ¼ **red cabbage** and quarter and slice **1 summer squash**. Stir-fry these vegetables in **2 tablespoons Chinese toasted sesame oil** in fry pan.

4. Meanwhile, in large soup pot, bring 2½ **quarts water** to a boil. Add ⅓ **cup tamari** and ¼ **cup rice wine vinegar** (or **2 tablespoons apple cider vinegar**). Add fried vegetables and oil to broth with the daylily buds. Rinse tree ears, squeeze, and tear apart. Pull off wood and dirt. When clean, add to soup pot. Simmer until vegetables taste done. Don't overcook.

5. Stir together ¼ **cup cornstarch** and ½ **cup water**. Add to simmering soup. Dice **1 pound of tofu** and add it. Taste for seasoning. Soup will need dilution with water if it tastes too strong or sour, and it may need more tamari or salt. To make it spicy, add **1 teaspoon chili-paste-with-garlic** (available in Chinese markets) and add **2 tablespoons Chinese toasted sesame oil**.

6. If you can get them, roast **2 tablespoons Szechuan peppercorns** in hot dry skillet and then grind with mortar and pestle or in blender. Garnish each serving with **1 teaspoon sesame oil**, **2 tablespoons chopped scallions**, and a sprinkle of the **Szechuan pepper**.

6 servings

okra gumbo

In the northeast, tender baby okra can be found in the Spring in Latina and African-American markets. Only small okra, no more than 3 inches long should be used; otherwise, they are tough and stringy. In other parts of the country small okra pods will be available at other times of the year.

1. With a small sharp knife scrape the skins of **1½ pounds baby okra** lightly to remove surface fuzz. Unless the okra is really dirty, do not wash it as it will become soggy. Cut off the stems of each okra and slice each pod into rounds. Set aside.

2. In a soup pot heat **3 tablespoons grapeseed oil** and add **1½ cups finely chopped onions.** Cook until soft but not brown. Stir in **2 teaspoons fresh hot peppers**, finely chopped, **6 cloves garlic**, crushed, **2 tablespoons green peppers**, chopped, and **2½ cups canned tomatoes**, chopped. Cook for 10 minutes.

3. Add **1½ quarts water**, bring to a boil and add **½ cup brown rice**. Cook the soup at a simmer for 15 minutes and then add the okra, **1 tablespoon salt**, and some fresh grated **pepper**. Let the okra and rice cook another 15 minutes or until the rice is done and okra is tender. You may need to add another cup of **water** at this time if the soup is too thick. Serve at once. This soup reheats well.

6 to 8 servings

SPRING

red lentil soup

1. Pick over **2 cups red lentils** to remove stones and dirt. Rinse in a colander and set aside.

2. Peel and slice **2 large onions**. Peel and slice **8 cloves garlic** and **3 tablespoons fresh ginger**. In a heavy frying pan heat ¼ **cup grapeseed oil** and sauté ginger together with **2 teaspoons ground cumin** and **2 teaspoons ground coriander**. Continue sautéing a minute or two, stirring well.

3. Turn vegetables into a soup pot. Add the lentils, **8 cups water**, and ⅓ **cup tamari**. Drain and discard liquid from **2 cups canned tomatoes** and add tomatoes to soup. Cover and bring to a boil. Simmer until lentils are tender, about half an hour.

4. Turn the soup, a few cups at a time, into a blender and purée. When all is smooth, return to pot and season with **salt** and **pepper**. You will likely need **2 teaspoons salt**. Correct seasoning.

5. To make a **spiced oil garnish**, heat **4 tablespoons grapeseed oil** in a small pan and add ½ **teaspoon dried red pepper flakes**, ½ **teaspoon whole cumin**, and ½ **teaspoon turmeric**, stirring for a few seconds.

6. To serve, ladle hot soup into bowls and drizzle a spoonful of sliced oil around in a spiral on top of each bowl. Garnish with chopped **cilantro**.

6 to 8 servings

lemon lima bean soup

1. Pick over **3½ cups dried baby lima beans** to remove stones and dirt. Cover with **water** and let soak 4 to 6 hours. Drain water, barely cover with **fresh water** and put up to cook.

2. Meanwhile, slice **3 large onions** and mince **3 cloves garlic**. Sauté the vegetables in a soup pot in ⅔ **cup olive oil** with ⅔ **teaspoon dried thyme**. When vegetables are golden, turn off heat and set aside.

3. When the lima beans are cooked, use a slotted spoon to dip out about ⅔ of them. Add to the soup pot. Mash the remaining beans and add with their cooking liquid.

4. Season soup with ⅓ **cup tamari**, **2 tablespoons tomato paste**, and **1½ tablespoons lemon juice**. Taste and correct seasoning. Serve with generous amounts of chopped **straight leaf parsley**.

6 to 8 servings

SPRING

meloukhiya

The green vegetable which is the base for this soup is, according to Claudia Roden in *A Book of Middle Eastern Food*, one of Egypt's national dishes. It is available dried in many Middle Eastern markets and tastes something like spinach with a texture like okra. It is in the mallow family.

1. Make a broth by simmering **4 quarts water** with **1 large unpeeled onion, 3 stalks of celery with leaves, 3 carrots**, cut into thirds, and some **sprigs of parsley**. Simmer 1 to 2 hours. Strain over a large container or bowl and press down on the vegetables to extract the juices. Discard vegetables.

2. Dice **1 medium onion** and **4 to 5 peeled cloves garlic**. In a soup pot heat **2 tablespoons olive oil**. Sauté onion and garlic until softened and golden. Add ¾ **teaspoon ground coriander**, ¼ **teaspoon cinnamon**, and ¼ **teaspoon allspice**. Continue stirring until slightly browned. Add ½ **cup white rice** and sauce, stirring, until rice becomes translucent.

3. Add strained broth, ¼ **cup tamari**, and 1½ **teaspoons salt**.

4. Turn **3 oz. dried meloukhiya** into a bowl. Add lukewarm **water** to come up halfway. Squeeze the greens with your hands to moisten. Remove any rough sticks. Add to pot and simmer at least 20 minutes more. Correct seasoning. More **salt** may be needed, and you may want a splash of **Tabasco**.

10 servings

shredded root vegetable salad

1. Use a shredder to grate **6 carrots**, **3** peeled **white turnips** *or* **1 small rutabaga**, and **2** or **3 small** scraped **beets**. Keep them in separate bowls. Chill.

2. When ready to serve, arrange the three vegetables in small mounds on beds of **Boston lettuce**. Top with **onion rings** and dress with **vinaigrette** (see glossary) and a dash of **gomashio** (see glossary).

6 to 8 servings

dandelion salad

This salad is only for the first couple weeks in April (in the Northeast) when **dandelions** make beautiful bouquets of leaves but there are no signs at all of flower buds. Don't bother with the few in your lawn that are trying to compete with the grass. Find a waste space that dandelions are making their own. Use a sharp knife to collect the cleaner central leaves. Wash thoroughly and dry well in a towel or salad spinner. Crisp in refrigerator and serve with **vinaigrette** (see glossary) and **onion slices**. This first salad of Spring is most welcome and not at all bitter if dandelion leaves are picked early enough.

spinach salad
with tamarind peanut dressing

1. Weigh 2½ oz. fresh ginger. Use a spoon to peel. Peel 4 cloves garlic. Place ginger and garlic in processor with 1½ teaspoons red pepper flakes, 3 heaping tablespoons tamarind concentrate, and ½ cup rice wine vinegar. Process, scrape down, and process again.

2. Add: 2½ cups peanut butter, 1½ cups grapeseed oil, ½ cup tamari, 3 tablespoons sugar, 1 tablespoon salt, and 1 can Thai coconut milk. Process again. Taste and correct seasoning. Thin with ¾ can (from the coconut milk) of water.

3. Serve dressing over spinach leaves with mung bean sprouts, cucumber slices, and radishes. Garnish with peanuts.

makes 6 cups of dressing

SPRING

hiziki or arame salad nest

Arame means "tough maiden," comparing this seaweed to the Japanese women who dive for pearls. You may find it less available than the more expensive hiziki.

1. To sort for little stones or shells, turn about **1 quart arame** or **hiziki** into a large bowl. Cover with **cold water**. Swish sea vegetable through the water and lift out into a colander. Check bottom of bowl for stones or shells and discard. Repeat three times, using fresh water each time. Washing also removes much of the fishy flavor. Turn drained sea vegetable into a soup pot, add **3 cups water** to barely cover, **2 tablespoons agave nectar**, **3 tablespoons tamari**, and bring to a boil. Simmer about 1 hour. Taste for flavor and add more **agave nectar** or **tamari** as needed. When sea vegetable is well fluffed, turn it and the cooking liquid into a container. Cool, cover, and chill.

2. Combine ½ **cup water**, ¼ **cup rice wine vinegar**, **2 tablespoons tamari**, and **1 tablespoon agave nectar** in a small pot. Bring to a boil. Cool, chill.

3. When marinade has cooled, peel, seed, and dice **1 cucumber**. Add to marinade and refrigerate.

4. When ready to serve, use a slotted spoon to lift sea vegetable onto each plate. Shape into a nest. Drain some cucumber and add to nest. Dice ½ **pound tofu** (soft tofu is preferred), and add some cubes to each nest. Surround sea vegetable with **watercress leaves**. You will need about **2 bunches** in all. Spoon marinade over cress, as well as a **few drops of Chinese toasted sesame oil**. Sprinkle tofu with **gomahsio** (see glossary).

6 servings

orange asparagus salad

1. Select **6 fat asparagus stalks** for each salad you wish to serve. Break off the base as low as it will snap. Using a small sharp knife, thinly peel each asparagus stalk.

2. Use a steamer to cook asparagus stalks briefly. Three to four minutes should be enough. Turn into container and spoon **vinaigrette** (see glossary) over asparagus while it is still hot.

3. Use a small sharp knife to peel **thin-skinned oranges** of their skin and pith simultaneously. One orange will make two salads. Slice oranges thinly and add to asparagus containers. Spoon vinaigrette over oranges. Chop about **1 tablespoon onion per salad** and sprinkle on top of asparagus and oranges. Chill until ready to serve.

4. Arrange Boston or red leaf **lettuce** on a plate. For each salad, arrange three overlapping orange slices in the center and three asparagus spears on each side. Drizzle **vinaigrette** over and add **onion rings** if desired.

SPRING

pasta primavera salad

For a taste of early Spring, you may hunt wild herbs to flavor this salad or use some domesticated ones from your garden or a farmer's market. Some cooks will have to depend on the sadder resource of the supermarket.

1. **Fresh cavatelli** has the best texture and the look of Spring fertility, though dried pasta shells, or other shapes may be substituted. Cavatelli is usually available in Italian neighborhoods. Put up a large pot of water to boil with **1 tablespoon salt**. When boiling, add **1 pound fresh cavatelli** *or* ¾ pound dried pasta. Cook until barely done, tasting pasta to be sure it is still "al dente." Drain in a colander and run cold water over until cooled. Shake colander vigorously and turn pasta into a bowl. Add **2 tablespoons** good quality imported **olive oil** and **2 scant tablespoons tamari**. Toss together.

2. Gather herbs. You will need ⅔ **cup sorrel**, finely chopped, to give the salad a tart taste, **1 tablespoon watercress**, minced, for a mustard flavor, **1 tablespoon garlic leaves**, and 1½ **tablespoons onion tops**, chopped. Turn the herbs into bowl with pasta and toss well.

3. Toast ⅓ **cup walnuts** in a toaster oven until they smell good and begin to change color. Let cool and chop coarsely. Drain and chop ½ **cup canned pitted olives**. Add nuts and olives to pasta. Mince ½ **small tabasco pepper** very fine, and stir into ¼ **cup vinaigrette** (see glossary). Add to pasta and toss well.

4. This salad is best served at room temperature, but must be chilled to preserve it. Serve on **lettuce** with a drizzle of **vinaigrette** (see glossary), garnished with a **slice of red onion**.

4 hearty servings

garden herb salad

This recipe can be made only if you have a garden of herbs—some in profusion—and fresh-picked lettuce available. If you do:

1. Gather a **generous bunch of garlic leaves**, a **couple of fronds of fennel, 8 or more comfrey leaves**, a **large handful of chives** and a small **bunch of soft tips of thyme** (you may add other favorites).

2. Pick enough **lettuce** to serve four people generously. Wash, tear into pieces and add to salad bowl.

3. Bundle the herbs together, slice thinly, then chop well. Toss with the lettuce.

4. Dress this salad with the best quality **olive oil**, **balsamic vinegar** and **salt** and **pepper**, all to taste.

4 servings

caesar's wife salad

A salad beyond reproach, as Caesar's wife was supposed
to be.

1. Place **1 pound tofu** in food processor. Add scant
    2½ tablespoons red miso, 4 small peeled **garlic
    cloves, 3½ tablespoons nutritional yeast** and
    3 tablespoons tamari. Process.

2. Combine **2 cups olive oil** and **1 cup grapeseed oil**.
    Squeeze **½ cup lemon juice**. Add lemon juice to
    processor, turn on machine, and gradually add oils,
    pouring slowly.

3. Season with **dash Tabasco** and fresh ground **pepper**.
    Thin with **½ cup water**, or as needed.

4. Tear **Romaine lettuce** leaves into pieces for each
    diner. Top with dressing and toasted **croutons**.

Makes about 1 quart dressing

jícama arugula salad

Jícama is available in Hispanic and Asian markets. It is an August crop, and arugula (roquette) is an Italian herb that grows best in the cool weather of spring. Nevertheless, both are available in their respective markets in early spring as well as autumn. The combination is felicitous.

1. Lay a few leaves of **loose leaf lettuce** on a salad plate. Add springs of **arugula** (roquette).

2. Peel **1 jícama** and slice into thin rounds. Cut into quarters or smaller as desired. Place on salad. Top with **red onion rings**.

3. Season **vinaigrette** (see glossary) with **coarse mustard** *or* a **mustard seasoned with horseradish**. Add dressing to salad just before serving.

wild rice salad

Since we do without meat, vegetarians can sometimes splurge on this precious and delicious fruit of the wild aquatic grass, Zizania aquatica. It is gathered by the Ojibwa (Chippewa) of the Great Lakes region who call themselves "Menominee" which means "wild rice people." Be sure to buy real, foraged wild rice, not that which is cultivated in managed paddies. Real wild rice has a heftier price tag and superior nutritive value than cultivated "wild" rice, which accounts for about 50% of "wild" rice on the market and is grown in California. Real wild rice will generally note its provenance on the package, and its harvesters are generally paid a fair wage.

1. Wash **2½ cups wild rice** and drain in strainer or colander. Bring **4 cups water** and **1½ teaspoons salt** to a boil. Add rice and cook, covered, over moderate heat for 35 minutes.

2. Scrape **carrots** and cut in thin ovals to measure **2½ cups**. Prepare **2½ cups asparagus** by cutting into ¾″ pieces, and cut **2 cups celery** in the same manner. Set aside in separate bowls.

3. In a stainless steel pot combine the following to make a marinade: **½ cup water, ½ cup wine vinegar, ½ cup apple juice, 1½ teaspoons salt, ½ teaspoon dried thyme, 2 bay leaves, 1 clove crushed garlic**, and **½ cup olive oil**.

4. Bring marinade to a boil and add carrots. Simmer 3 minutes. Add asparagus and celery, and simmer 2 more minutes. Add **1 teaspoon prepared mustard** to pot and stir well.

5. Immediately pour vegetables into a colander over a bowl so that they do not continue cooking.

6. Add marinade to wild rice when it is done cooking. Cool rice and vegetables separately. When cooled, combine, adding **1 tablespoon lemon juice** and **1 teaspoon salt**. Chill.

7. To serve, arrange rice on leaves of **Boston lettuce**. Top with slivered, toasted **almonds**, and garnish with **watercress**.

8 servings

wild rice crêpes
with shiitake mushrooms and
with spinach and pignoli nuts

Indian starches will produce egg-free crêpes that are easy to make, and delicious. A version using chapatti flour and semolina is listed as "Malpoora" in *The Art of Indian Vegetarian Cooking* by Yamuna Devi. This version uses chickpea flour, also known as gram flour or besan.

1. **Make crêpes:** in a blender, place **2 tablespoons potato starch**. Measure out **2½ cups water** and add a little water to the starch. Turn machine on, adding water as needed to make a thin paste. Add **1 teaspoon salt, 2 tablespoons grapeseed oil**, **½ teaspoon toasted sesame oil, ½ cup chickpea flour**, and **2 cups unbleached white flour**. Process, gradually adding as much water as the processor can conveniently hold. When very smooth, turn into a pitcher. Whisk in water as needed to make batter into a thin cream.

2. We cook our crêpes in 3 seasoned crêpe pans which are used only for that purpose. Heat your pans over a moderate flame; wipe out each with an **oiled** piece of absorbent paper, and pour batter in when pans are hot enough. Swirl batter to spread. When lightly browned on one side, carefully turn with a spatula to barely cook the other side. Slide crêpes out and stack neatly on a dish. Set aside.

3. **Cook wild rice mix:** we use a combination of **brown basmati rice** and **wild rice**, but you could use all of either one. Place **1⅓ cups (mixed) rice** in a pot, add **scant 1 teaspoon salt** and **2 cups water**. Cover and

cook over lowest heat about 40 minutes. Do not stir. Check to see whether rice is done or whether more water is required. When cooked, divide rice between two bowls with approximately one-third of it in one bowl and two-thirds in the other. Set both aside.

4. **Make mushroom sauce:** soak **10 dried shiitake mushrooms** in **2 cups very hot tap water**. Thinly slice **2½ cups button mushrooms**. Peel **2 cloves garlic** and **4 shallots**. Chop garlic and shallots together. Squeeze water out of shiitakes and reserve it. Cut off stems and slice shiitakes thinly.

5. In a frying pan heat **2 tablespoons olive oil**. Sauté the button mushrooms over very high heat. When they begin to brown, add shiitakes, shallots, and garlic. Stirring constantly, cook until very well browned. Stir in **2 tablespoons flour** and cook a minute more. Pour in ¼ **cup mirin** *or* **Chinese rice wine** (Shao Hsing), and add reserved shiitake liquid. To flavor this sauce, add **1½ tablespoons tomato paste, 2 tablespoons tamari, 1½ tablespoons nutritional yeast**, and **1 tablespoon white miso**. These ingredients should be available at your health food store. Bring sauce to a simmer and correct seasoning. We add **1 tablespoon balsamic vinegar** also. Set aside.

6. **Make spinach filling:** shred clean **spinach** and measure **6 cups**, packed, discarding thick stems. Set aside in a bowl. Peel and chop **2 shallots** and coarsely chop ¼ **cup pignoli nuts**. Heat **1 tablespoon olive oil** in a frying pan. Sauté the shallots and nuts until the former are wilted and the latter begin to brown. Now add the spinach and use a slotted spoon to stir

and turn the mixture until spinach wilts. Season with a **splash of tamari**. Add spinach to the bowl with the smaller amount of cooked rice. Add mushrooms and enough shiitake sauce to moisten the larger bowl of rice. Reserve remaining sauce (gravy).

7. **Form crêpes:** place a spoonful or two of filling on each crêpe and roll up. Then place on a lightly **oiled** cookie sheet. There should be twice as many mushroom crêpes as spinach crêpes. Cover with plastic wrap and refrigerate.

8. **To serve:** before serving, preheat oven to 375°F. Reheat remaining shiitake gravy. Steam **16 to 18 spears of asparagus**. Heat crêpes in the oven for about 10 minutes.

9. Arrange one spinach and two mushroom crêpes on each plate in the shape of a fan. Place asparagus spears in between the crêpes. Spoon gravy over the base of the fan.

8 to 9 servings

grilled greens-stuffed tofu pockets

This recipe depends on the special flavor of pumpkin seed oil. It is one of our most favorite meals.

1. Shred **4 cups greens**: a mixture of **Swiss chard, kale, mustard, mizuna** and/or **spinach**.

2. Mince **1 clove garlic**. Sliver **½″ fresh ginger root**. Seed and dice **1 small jalapeño pepper**.

3. Add garlic, ginger, and pepper to a large frying pan with **1 tablespoon olive oil**. Sauté until softened. Add greens and turn up heat. Cook, stirring, until greens begin to wilt. Add **1 tablespoon pumpkin seed oil** and sauté a few minutes more. Turn into a large bowl. Season with **1½ teaspoons tamari** and **1 teaspoon lime juice**. Mix, taste, and correct seasoning. Let cool.

4. Slice cakes of tofu horizontally in half. Then slit each half partway, and stuff with greens mixture. You will need **4 pounds tofu**.

5. **Make marinade:** combine **¼ cup tamari, 1½ tablespoons pumpkin seed oil, ¼ cup grapeseed oil, 1 crushed garlic clove, ½ small** seeded and minced **jalapeño, ½ teaspoon minced fresh ginger**, and **¼ cup chopped fresh cilantro**. Mix all together well and spoon over tofu pockets on a tray. Refrigerate, covered with plastic.

6. Soak **1 pound rice stick noodles** (from a Thai market) in water to cover 15 minutes or until softened. Now turn into a pot of boiling water. Cook until just done, drain, and cool in cold water. Drain and set aside. When ready to serve, reheat rice noodles in a steamer.

7. At serving time, grill or broil two marinade-brushed tofu pockets until browned. Serve with rice noodles and chopped **scallions**.

8 servings

LAGUSTA

tempeh-stuffed baked potatoes

This is an easy and delicious way to serve tempeh.

1. Scrub **6 large Idaho potatoes** and bake in a 400°F oven about 1 hour or until tender.

2. Meanwhile, cut **1 cake tempeh (8 oz.)** into thin matchstick lengths, then crosswise into dice. Set aside. Chop **1½ medium onions, 1 large stalk celery** with **leaves**, and **2½ cups mushrooms**. In a large frying pan heat **2 tablespoons grapeseed oil** and fry tempeh over high heat until crisp, then add vegetables and continue frying until all are crisp and browned a bit. Meanwhile, add ¾ **teaspoon ground coriander, 1 clove** crushed **garlic,** ½ **tablespoon salt**, and freshly ground **pepper**. When mixture is very well browned, turn off heat and stir in **3 tablespoons dry sherry, 1½ tablespoons lemon juice**, and ½ **cup** chopped **parsley**. Taste for seasoning. Set aside.

3. When potatoes are done, slice off ½″ of the skin on top. Use a pointed spoon to scoop out about ¾ of each potato. Turn the potato pulp into a mixer to mash until fluffy. Add **2 tablespoons grapeseed oil** and about ⅓ **to** ½ **cup soymilk** or enough to keep mixture soft and fluffy, but not too soft. Add **salt** and freshly ground **pepper** to taste. Briefly mix in cooled tempeh and vegetables. Don't over mix. Restuff potato shells. Sprinkle with **paprika** and refrigerate until serving time.

4. Through not essential, it is nice to serve these potatoes with **miso gravy** *or* **shiitake gravy** (see index).

5. When ready to serve, heat potatoes for 20 to 30 minutes in a preheated 400°F oven or toaster oven. Meanwhile, cut **8 carrots** into matchsticks and steam until just done, about 10 minutes. Divide **1 head of broccoli** into flowerets and steam until done, about 5 minutes. In a small pot heat ¼ **cup olive oil**. Peel **1 clove garlic** and lightly bruise it with the handle of a French chef's knife. Add to melted oil with **3 tablespoons bread crumbs**. Cook over moderate heat until crumbs are somewhat browned. Remove and discard garlic clove.

6. When potatoes are heated through and tops look well browned and crisped, remove to serving plate. Add gravy if you like, and serve with steamed broccoli and carrots, garnished with the bread crumb oil.

6 servings

sweet & sour tempeh

1. In a shallow container mix ⅔ cup white wine, ⅓ cup tamari, ⅓ cup water, 2 cloves crushed garlic, and ½ teaspoon freshly grated ginger. Marinate 2 cakes of tempeh (8 oz.) in this for several hours. Cut tempeh in half crosswise (each half will serve one person), and place in shallow frying pan with marinade. Stew, covered, for about 5 minutes. Cool. Place tempeh in covered container in refrigerator until time to serve, and reserve marinade separately.

2. **Prepare sweet and sour sauce**: combine in a bowl ¼ cup vinegar, 2½ tablespoons molasses, ⅞ cup water, 1 tablespoon tamari, ⅔ cup dry sherry, 2 tablespoons cornstarch, 3 tablespoons catsup, 1 tablespoon Chinese sesame oil, and 2 teaspoons freshly grated ginger. Dice pineapple from 1 small can unsweetened pineapple and add with juices. Set aside.

3. Cut 2 carrots, 1½ green peppers, and 3 scallions into matchstick-sized pieces. Peel and crush 3 cloves garlic. Heat 1½ tablespoons grapeseed oil in frying pan. First fry carrots over highest heat, then add peppers and scallions, garlic last. Sauté until browned but still crispy. Stir sauce mixture well and add, stirring. Bring to a boil and cook until thick and clear. Remove from heat and add reserved tempeh marinade. Cover to keep warm.

4. **Prepare brown rice:** bring 2 cups short grain brown rice and 3 cups water to a boil in a pot with scant teaspoon salt. Reduce heat to a simmer and cook about 40 minutes.

5. Preheat broiler. Place tempeh in oiled pan and brush tops with **oil**. Turn pieces until well browned/charcoal broiled. Slice each cake into matchstick pieces and place over rice. Top with **sweet and sour sauce** and sliced **scallions**. If available, serve with **kim chi** (see following recipe).

4 servings

kim chi

1. Cut **1 large Chinese cabbage** in quarters, then eighths, and finally into 1″ pieces. Put into a large bowl and sprinkle with **2 tablespoons sea salt**. Let stand 15 minutes.

2. Cut **1 bunch scallions** in half lengthwise then crosswise into 1″ pieces. Add **1 large clove** crushed **garlic, 1 large cucumber**, peeled and sliced, **1 tablespoon turmeric, 1½ tablespoons red pepper flakes**, and **1 teaspoon** freshly grated **ginger root**. Turn into a jar or crock.

3. Thoroughly rinse cabbage in cold running water by covering with fresh water and draining 3 times. Put drained cabbage into the jar or crock, pushing down on contents. Add **water** to barely cover, then add **1 tablespoon sea salt**. Stir as well as you can.

4. Cover and let ferment 3 to 5 days at room temperature, stirring at least once a day. When cabbage develops a typical sauerkraut flavor, refrigerate.

bibim bap

We received a gift of kim chee from a Korean customer, Barbara Yu, made by her mother, Hong Yu. Barbara suggested that we use it for Bibim Bap, a dish our Korean cookbooks call garnished rice. Both our customer and the book suggested serving the dish with more hot pepper sauce—Gochujang or Kochujang.* You can also adjust the heat of the dish by increasing the amount of kim chee used. We like serving it with sticky rice, but any rice may be used as the base.

1. **Make sticky rice:** soak **1½ cups sticky rice**** in water to cover or for at least 5 hours. Steam over boiling **water** until rice is chewy-tender. Set aside. (Or make any non-sticky rice.)

2. **Prepare and cook garnishes:** soak **3 to 4 dried shiitake mushrooms** in **hot tap water** 10 minutes. Meanwhile cut vegetables into matchstick sizes: **3 scallions, 1 carrot, 1 small zucchini** and **half a cucumber** may be used.

3. Blanch **3 cups mung bean sprouts**** in boiling **water** 1 minute. Drain and run cold water over sprouts.

4. Heat **2 to 3 tablespoons grapeseed oil** in a wok. Add thinly sliced, squeezed shiitakes. When they begin to brown, add the other vegetables in small batches, including mung bean sprouts. As each batch browns a little, scoop it out into a bowl.

5. Slice **2½ to 3 cups kim chee**** into thin slivers. Place in wok and stir fry, adding more **grapeseed oil** as needed.

---

*To make your own kochujang or gochujang, combine 2 tablespoons red pepper, 2 tablespoons tamari and 2 tablespoons Korean bean paste. Sweeten if you like.

**Available in Korean markets.

Return other vegetables to wok. Add **2 tablespoons toasted sesame oil** and **2 teaspoons salt**.

6. **Serve:** you can now stir all together and reheat briefly and serve with the sticky rice. Or, you can make individual bowls of rice, sprinkled with a little **sesame oil**. Place vegetables in separate piles of cucumber, bean sprouts, vegetables, kim chee in each bowl. Place a dollop of gochujang in the center. Or you can skip the rice altogether and serve the kim chee, bean sprouts and vegetable mixture cold, as a salad.

4 to 5 servings

SELMA

couscous

A North African dish usually made with meat. This long recipe is easier to make than it seems.

1. Soak 1½ **cups chickpeas** (garbanzos) overnight, or bring them to a boil in **water** to cover, turn off fire and leave 1 hour. In either case, simmer gently until cooked (2 or more hours).

2. **Prepare millet:** sauté **2 cups millet** in **2 tablespoons olive oil.** We use millet instead of the couscous grain, which is steamed semolina, because of its superior nutritional value and excellent flavor. When millet is toasted, add **4½ cups water, 2 teaspoons salt,** and ½ **teaspoon cinnamon** and simmer till steamed. Do not overcook. Stir in ⅓ **cup grapeseed oil.** Millet can be steamed in a couscousier, if you have one, while the vegetable stew cooks beneath in the couscousier base.

3. **Make gravy:** in couscousier base or large pot, sauté **1 large onion,** coarsely chopped, in **2 tablespoons olive oil.** Add **2 cloves** crushed **garlic,** ¾ **teaspoon turmeric, 2 teaspoons dried mint, 2 teaspoons dried oregano, 1½ teaspoons cumin seed,** dry-roasted and ground, ¾ **teaspoon ground ginger,** and ⅓ **teaspoon coriander.** Sauté until medium brown. Cut **1 small rutabaga** into 1″ pieces and add to pot with **water** to cover. Simmer about 10 minutes. Cut **2 carrots** into ½″ pieces and add to pot. Simmer 5 minutes. Peel **2 to 3 potatoes,** cut into 1″ chunks and add to carrots. Cook 10 minutes, adding water as necessary. Peel and cut **2 sweet potatoes** into chunks and add together with ½ **cup cabbage,** sliced, and **1 cup diced prunes.**

Continue simmering vegetables and adding water as needed. Add **2 cups** canned **tomatoes** or tomato sauce, and when chickpeas are done, drain them of their water and add. If you have **Chinese chili-paste-with-garlic**, add **1½ teaspoons**. If not, add **cayenne pepper** to make a spicy gravy. Add up to **2 tablespoons tamari, juice of 1 lemon**, and ¼ **cup hatcho (yellow)** *or* **aka (red) miso** (this gives the meat-like flavor). Simmer until vegetables are done and gravy tastes good. Adjust seasoning. Be sure there's enough water as you go along for there to be ample gravy.

4. **Make "harissa"** or hot sauce: remove about **1 cup gravy** from pot into a small bowl. Add **1 teaspoon cayenne, ½ teaspoon ground cumin, ½ teaspoon ground coriander, 1 teaspoon dried oregano**, and **1 tablespoon tamari** to make a very concentrated spicy sauce for individual seasoning.

5. When ready to serve, steam millet to reheat and also reheat stew. Just before serving, add **1 cup green peas**, fresh or frozen. Don't overcook them. For each plate make a ring of millet. Put several large serving spoons of vegetables and gravy in the center. Top with **slivered almonds**. Serve with **radish orange escarole salad** (see following recipe) and harissa on the side.

Note: other vegetables that could go into the stew include **turnips, zucchini,** *or* **Brussels sprouts.**

6 to 8 servings

radish orange escarole salad

1. Use a small sharp knife to peel **4 thin-skinned oranges**, removing white pith as well as rind. Slice thinly into a bowl. Also slice **10 large red radishes** into bowl.

2. Mix together **1 tablespoon sugar**, **⅛ teaspoon salt**, **⅓ cup lemon juice** and pour this dressing over the oranges and radishes.

3. Serve on beds of **escarole**. Drizzle a little **vinaigrette** (see glossary) over the escarole.

6 to 8 servings

rice noodles
with stir fried vegetables and tofu

1. **Prepare vegetables and tofu:** dice **1 cup firm tofu** and set aside. Shred **2½ cups bok choy.** Dice **1 large red pepper.** Cut **2 cups asparagus** in 1″ pieces. Set all aside.

2. **Make chili-vinegar sauce:** combine **½ cup rice vinegar, 2 tablespoons sugar** and **1 sliced hot jalapeño** or other hot chili. Set aside. Soak **½ pound rice noodles** in water to just cover for 15 minutes.

3. **Combine gravy ingredients: 1 tablespoon tamari, 1½ tablespoons rice wine vinegar, 1 teaspoon sugar, 1 tablespoon sweet white miso** and **1 tablespoon red miso.** In a separate measuring cup combine **1 tablespoon cornstarch** and **3 tablespoons water.** Set aside.

4. **Stir-fry:** mince **2 tablespoons garlic.** Use a wok to heat **2 tablespoons grapeseed oil.** Sauté garlic for just a minute, then add vegetables and turn heat up. Cook until they begin to brown. Add gravy ingredients and well-stirred cornstarch mix. Bring to a boil, stirring. Turn off heat and transfer vegetables to a bowl you can keep warm.

5. Add a little more **oil** to the wok and heat. Add drained noodles and tofu. Fry until well cooked (it will splatter!) and noodles are tender. Combine with vegetables. Grate **black pepper** over and serve with chili vinegar sauce.

4 to 6 servings

SPRING

yam and ground-nut stew

Of North African inspiration.

1. At least six hours before dinner or the night before, prepare the following mixture of seasonings in a measuring cup. Combine: **⅔ teaspoon red pepper flakes, 1 teaspoon ground dried ginger root, 1½ teaspoons ground cardamom, 1½ teaspoons ground coriander, ¼ teaspoon nutmeg, ¼ teaspoon cloves, ¼ teaspoon cinnamon**, and a **dash of allspice**. Stir all together. Estimate half the mixture and set it aside. Place the remainder in a shallow container and add the **juice of 1½ lemons and 1½ limes**. Cut **8 oz. soy tempeh** (one package) into thin strips. Place in container with seasonings, toss gently, cover and refrigerate.

2. When marination is complete, heat **grapeseed oil** in a frying pan until quite hot, and then fry the tempeh strips until crisp. Drain on paper towels and set aside.

3. Peel and dice **2 to 3 large yams**, cutting them into 1″ pieces. Also slice **2 parsnips** and coarsely chop **1 large onion**. Heat ¼ **cup grapeseed oil** in a large saucepot and sauté onion first, adding the reserved mixture of spices. Also add ⅔ **cup raw peanuts** (available at health food stores) and **2 cloves** chopped **garlic**. Then add parsnips and yams and continue sautéing until vegetables are lightly browned.

4. In a bowl combine: ⅓ **cup organic peanut butter,** ¼ **cup tamari, 1⅔ cups water,** and **2 teaspoons lemon juice.** Add to saucepot together with **3 plum tomatoes,** fresh or canned, cut into dice. Cover and simmer 15 minutes or until done. Correct seasoning.

5. Before serving, prepare **okra-cornmeal pudding** (see following recipe), and cook **brown rice.** Serve the stew with the rice. Sprinkle the tempeh on top and offer the pudding on the side.

5 to 6 servings

okra-cornmeal pudding

A Caribbean dish known as fungi or coo-coo.

1. Mince **2 tablespoons onion.** Sauté in a **splash of olive oil** in a saucepot. When wilted, add **2½ cups water** and **1½ teaspoons salt** and bring to a boil. Meanwhile, thinly slice **2 cups okra** and add to the simmering liquid. Cook, covered, 10 minutes.

2. Stir together **1 cup cornmeal** and ½ **cup cold water.** Add to okra, stirring well. Cook until cornmeal thickens. Stir in **1 tablespoon olive oil** and cover until ready to serve. This pudding will reheat with a little added water.

5 to 6 side dish servings

spinach and eggplant lasagne

A satisfying dairy-free version of this classic dish.

1. **Prepare tomato sauce first**: coarsely chop **2 medium onions** and slice **3 cloves garlic**. In a pot add **¼ cup olive oil** and sauté vegetables with **1 teaspoon oregano** and **1 teaspoon basil**. When onions are wilted and golden, add a **6 oz. can of tomato paste**. Stir for a few minutes then add **6 oz. water** and a **splash of red wine** if desired. Cook until sauce thickens, stirring often. Add the contents of a **28 oz. can plum tomatoes**. Break up the tomatoes. Season with **1 tablespoon salt, 1 teaspoon pepper**, and **3 tablespoons pesto**, if available. Let sauce simmer for another ½ hour.

2. **Prepare vegetables and pasta**: peel **2 medium eggplants.** Cut lengthwise into ½″ thick large slices. Heat a large frying pan or griddle so that the seared eggplant slices will be seared on both sides. If you use a cast-iron skillet, this can be done with no oil whatsoever. Otherwise, use a little olive oil. Turn seared eggplant into a shallow baking pan. Add **¾ cup water** mixed with **2 tablespoons tamari** and **2 tablespoons dry sherry**. Cover with foil and bake at 350°F for ½ hour.

3. Cook **1 package lasagne** until done, 5 to 8 minutes. Turn gently into a colander and rinse under cold water. Set aside.

4. Wash **24 oz. spinach**. Remove stems and chop coarsely. Mince a **small peeled onion**. Sauté onion in **2 tablespoons olive oil**. When softened, add spinach and stir over high heat until wilted. Grate **nutmeg** and **pepper** over the spinach and **salt** lightly. Turn into a bowl and set aside.

5. **Assemble and bake lasagne**: use a large rectangular baking pan. Spoon some tomato sauce over the bottom. Cover with ¼ of the lasagne noodles. Use a fork to arrange ½ the eggplant slices over the pasta. Add a little more tomato sauce, then another quarter of the pasta. Cover it with all the spinach, and top that with a third layer of pasta, then more tomato sauce and the rest of the eggplant, more sauce, and a top layer of pasta. A few more spoons of sauce and a foil cover will make the lasagne ready to bake in a 350°F oven for 25 to 45 minutes.

6. Reheat if necessary, and serve with extra tomato sauce on the side.

8 to 10 servings

iddlis

Iddlis are Indian dumplings, usually served for breakfast.

1. Soak **1 cup urad dal*** (a kind of lentil available in Indian groceries) in **water** to cover 6 to 8 hours or until very soft.

2. Drain dahl. Blend with ¾ **to 1 cup water.** When foamy and creamy, pour into a large container. Add **2 cups "cream of rice"** (from the Indian market) and **scant 1 cup more water.** Also add **2 teaspoons salt.** Chop **1½ cups cashews,** mince **1** seeded **jalapeño pepper,** chop **½ cup cilantro.** Mix these together with **1 tablespoon black mustard seed.** Add to dahl-rice mix. Stir well. Cover with plastic wrap and a lid. Put in a warm place (such as above the refrigerator) overnight or until fermented and foamy.

3. You will need an iddli steamer. Use a mixture of **lecithin** and **oil**** to oil each depression. Without stirring, dip out a spoonful of iddli mix to half fill each depression. Lower iddli steamer into a pot with ½" boiling water. Cover and lower heat. Steam 12 to 15 minutes or until iddlis are firm to the touch. Let cool a few minutes. Use a small flexible spatula to remove iddlis. **Oil** steamer again and repeat until all are cooked (about 5 batches). Iddlis may be reheated in an ordinary steamer. We serve 5 iddlis per diner with **dry roasted okra, rasam,** and **cilantro chutney** (see following recipes).

8 servings

---

*Most pulses should be fresh (no more than a year old) to soften properly when cooked. Use fresh urad dahl.

**See glossary.

rasam

A thin spicy gravy served with South Indian food. From Abhilasha Sandeep.

1. Wash **2 cups oily toor dahl*** very thoroughly in hot water. Bring **6 cups water** to a boil with **4 teaspoons salt** and add dahl and cook covered 20 minutes until very soft. Add **4 cups more water** and cook covered 15 minutes. Whisk to make a thin sauce.

2. Add ½ **teaspoon turmeric**, ¼ **cup dried coconut**, **2 teaspoons tamarind paste**** and **4** diced **plum tomatoes**. Stir well over low heat. Set aside.

3. Heat **1 tablespoon oil** in a small frying pan. Add **2 teaspoons black mustard seed**, **1 tablespoon hot pepper flakes**, and **4** fresh **jalapeño chiles**, seeded and minced. Sauté until mustard seeds begin to pop and chiles have softened. Add **3 tablespoons rasam powder*** and stir well.

4. Pour contents of frying pan into rasam.

makes approximately 2½ quarts

SPRING

---

*Available in Indian markets.

**Lemon juice may be substituted for tamarind.

223

dry roasted okra

The long cooking and large amount of spices make this okra delicious (Selma says, like candy!).

1. Cut both ends off **3 pounds baby okra**—tip and stem end. Slice thinly. Heat **2 tablespoons grapeseed oil** and ½ **teaspoon toasted sesame oil** in a large frying pan and sauté okra over moderate to low heat for 20 minutes.

2. Meanwhile, mix together **3 tablespoons ground coriander, 1 teaspoon ground cumin,** ½ **teaspoon cayenne, 1 teaspoon garam masala, 1 teaspoon turmeric,** and 1¾ **teaspoons salt.** Add these seasonings to the okra, stir well and cook 5 minutes more. Okra may be reheated in the oven, uncovered.

cilantro chutney

In food processor place **1 bunch cilantro** (remove stems first), **3 to 4 tablespoon sesame seeds, 1 to 2 slices fresh ginger,** ⅓ **cup dried coconut, 1 to 2 fresh jalapeño chilies** (seeded), **1 tablespoon Sucanat, 1 teaspoon salt, 3 tablespoons water,** and ½ **teaspoon lemon juice.** Process. Add **soy milk** as needed.

stir-fried bok choy

with mushrooms and tofu

Boy choy is an easy vegetable to grow, with fine flavor best suited
to stir-frying.

1. Put up **1 cup short grain brown rice** to cook slowly
   in **1¾ cup water** and **½ teaspoon salt**. Rice will need
   about 40 minutes to cook.

2. Soak **2 oz. dried Chinese mushrooms** (*or* dried
   shiitakes) in **warm water**. Set aside.

3. In a four-cup measure combine **¼ cup tamari**, **¼ cup
   dry sherry**, **¼ cup cornstarch**, and **3 cups water**.
   Add a **scant ½ teaspoon Chinese chili-paste-with-
   garlic**. Set aside.

4. Chop **1 large onion**. Mince **4 cloves garlic**. Wash
   and cut **1½ quarts bok choy** in thin diagonal slices.
   Lift mushrooms from liquid, squeeze gently and slice,
   discarding any tough stems. Reserve soaking water.

5. Heat a wok or frying pan and add **2 tablespoons
   grapeseed oil**. Add onion, bok choy, and mushrooms.
   Stir fry, lifting and turning vegetables. Add garlic and
   continue to cook vegetables until softened and golden
   brown. This will take 10 to 15 minutes.

6. Stir the tamari-cornstarch mixture well, adding the
   reserved mushroom soaking liquid. Pour into hot
   wok or frying pan and continue stirring until sauce is
   simmering and thickened.

7. Dice **½ pound of tofu** and add to wok. Taste to see
   if any **salt** is needed. Serve over cooked brown rice.
   Garnish with chopped **scallions**.

4 servings

japanese soba noodles

Soba noodles are made of buckwheat flour. Some kinds also contain jimenju, wild mountain sweet potato. We find them delicious. To make a complete dinner, serve with **Sea Vegetable Salad** and **Makizushi** (see following recipes).

1. **Prepare side dishes before cooking soba:** bake **1 sheet of nori** in a 325°F oven until crisp. Cut into small squares. Slice **2 bunches scallions** into rounds. Shred **1 large daikon** (Japanese radish) if available, *or* **1 bunch icicle radishes.** You will need **wasabi**, a dried Japanese herb similar to horseradish, which is mixed to a soft paste with cold water just before eating. It is sharp, so each diner needs a very small dab of it.

2. **Make Soba Tsuyu,** the sauce: flame ½ **cup dry sherry** by heating it and then tipping the pot so the wine catches fire. Add ¾ **cup tamari** and **3 cups water.** Add a **1″ square of kombu** and bring to a boil, covered. Once it has boiled, set the sauce aside and remove the kombu and discard.

3. **Cook soba:** when ready to serve, bring a large pot of **water** to a boil. Add **3 (8 oz.) packages soba noodles** and boil no more than 5 minutes, or till just done. Drain and serve immediately, or drain and run **cold water** over soba and reheat in a steamer.

4. Serve soba in shallow bowls. Add the soba tsuyu sauce to each bowl and serve extra pitchers of sauce on the table. Top each serving with scallions and nori squares. Side dishes of wasabi, daikon, **makizushi**, and **sea vegetable salad** are served with the soba. Stir daikon and wasabi into your soba dish as you eat.

9 servings

sea vegetable salad

1. Rinse thoroughly and soak ½ **package** (2 oz. or so) **arame** seaweed and ½ **package** rinsed **wakame** seaweed separately in **cold water** for about 5 minutes or until freshened. Don't let seaweed soak too long. Remove from water, squeezing slightly. Cut off tough stems from wakame and cut into smaller squares. Arame will probably not need cutting. Arrange the seaweeds in rows on a large platter.

2. Shred or grate **6 carrots** and **4 medium white turnips.** Arrange them on the platter with the seaweed.

3. In a cup, mix together ¼ **cup rice wine vinegar, 4 teaspoons agave nectar,** and ¼ to ⅓ **cup tamari.** Pour this dressing over the sea vegetables and over the carrots and turnips. Sprinkle **gomahsio** (see glossary) over the salad. Cover and refrigerate until ready to serve.

4. Simmer ½ **pound tofu** in water for 5 minutes. Blend tofu in a blender with **2 tablespoons** of the **water** it simmered in, **1 tablespoon rice wine vinegar,** ½ **teaspoon agave nectar, dash cayenne pepper,** and **2 tablespoons gomahsio.** Purée the tofu until smooth. Add more water if necessary. It should have the consistency of thin mayonnaise. Add more rice wine vinegar if you think it should be more sour.

5. Serve each diner small portions of carrot, turnip, and each sea vegetable. Sprinkle this salad with chopped **scallions** and place a tablespoon of the tofu sauce in the middle of each small salad plate. More **gomahsio** can be sprinkled on top.

9 servings

makizushi

A vinegared rice appetizer rolled in seaweed. This is our version of nori rolls, which we have been making for almost 30 years.

1. Soak **5 large dried shiitake mushrooms** in just enough **water** to cover for ½ hour.

2. Remove from liquid, cut off and discard tough stems and slice mushrooms. Put mushroom slices and their soaking liquid in a small pot. Add **2 tablespoons tamari** and **1 tablespoon agave nectar** *or* **1½ tablespoons sugar**. Simmer until the liquid has reduced to less than a tablespoon.

3. Wash **2 cups Kokuho Japanese rice** under running water and drain. Place in a pot with **2½ cups water** and a **1″ square of kombu** (kelp). Let soak 20 minutes. Bring to a boil and simmer 10 to 15 minutes. Let rest off heat 5 minutes, covered.

4. In a pot, mix **⅓ cup rice wine vinegar, 2 tablespoons agave nectar** *or* **3 tablespoons sugar, 1¼ teaspoons salt**, and **2 tablespoons dry sherry**. Bring to a boil and then cool. Use a fork or chopsticks to mix rice and vinegar together in a bowl.*

5. Prepare **8 or 9 leaves of fresh spinach** by steaming them until barely done. Grate **2 carrots**. Peel **1 cucumber**, cut into quarters lengthwise, remove seeds and cut each quarter into 3 long strips. If available, cut very thin strips of **beni shoga** (Japanese pickled ginger). It will also help if you have a placemat made of reeds to roll the makizushi.

---

*Be sure to use freshly made Kokuho rice, which will be sticky and will hold together when makizushi is rolled and cut.

6. You will need **6 sheets of nori**. Pass 1 sheet at a time over a flame on one side only to enhance its flavor and place it on your placemat or on a dish towel. Place a thick layer of vinegared rice over the nori, leaving 1″ bare at the edge facing you and ½″ bare at the other end. In the center place a cucumber strip, a couple of spinach leaves, a thin line of grated carrot, a row of shiitake mushrooms, and beni shoga strips. Carefully roll up the nori in the mat and squeeze gently to firm up the makizushi roll. Remove from mat or towel, let rest a few minutes, and then use a very sharp knife to cut into 9 rounds. Chill, covered, until ready to serve. Repeat with remaining nori.

6 to 8 servings

chinese bean curd skin rolls

There is an Eastern tradition of boiling soy milk and removing the skin that forms on top. It is rich and delicious. The Japanese call their version "yuba." We buy the Chinese kind in a Chinese market. The large rounds (30″ diameter) come in a plastic package, and may be stored in a freezer.

1. Defrost **bean curd skins** if frozen.

2. **Make filling:** soak **1½ cups dried shiitake mushrooms** in ¾ **cup water.** Dice **1¼ cups wheat gluten** (seitan) and reserve liquid from it. Set aside. Shred enough **Chinese cabbage** to yield **6 cups.** Dice **onion** to yield **3½ cups.** Cut in half, and then sliver cut **1 to 2 carrots,** to yield 1¼ **cups.** Combine cabbage, onion, and carrots in a bowl. Set aside.

3. Thinly slice **2 cloves garlic;** chop **2 tablespoons fresh cilantro,** and combine wheat gluten with both. Set aside.

4. Remove tough stems from softened shiitakes and discard. Slice thinly. Save soaking liquid.

5. Heat **3 to 4 tablespoons grapeseed oil** in a large frying pan. When quite hot, add cabbage mixture and shiitakes. Fry over high heat, turning often with a slotted spoon, until very well browned. Add wheat gluten and cook a few minutes more. Turn off heat.

6. Combine liquids from mushrooms and wheat gluten in a measuring cup. You should have about ¾ cup. Add to it: **1½ tablespoons rice wine vinegar, 2 tablespoons tamari, ¾ teaspoon salt, grating black pepper, 1 tablespoon sesame oil, 1¼ tablespoons cornstarch,** and **1½ teaspoons sugar.** Stir well together.

7. Add liquid seasonings to frying pan, and stir over high heat until mixture thickens. Turn out into a bowl to cool.

8. **Make dipping sauce:** combine **⅓ cup tamari, 1½ tablespoons sugar, 1½ tablespoons sesame oil, ¾ teaspoon salt,** and **1½ cups water.** Set aside.

9. **Form rolls:** cut 3 circles of bean curd skin in half. Then divide the halves into thirds. These will look like large triangles. Brush each lightly with dipping sauce to soften. Place a finger of filling on the circular edge. Fold end over, sides in, and roll. Place on a tray and repeat, until filling is used up. You should have 16 to 18 rolls. Cover with plastic wrap and refrigerate.

10. **To serve:** make steamed **white rice. Oil** a baking sheet, and preheat the oven to 400°F. When oven is hot, carefully place rolls on baking sheet. Brush tops lightly with **oil** and bake until crisp and brown. Serve 3 rolls per diner with rice and dipping sauce, topping each plate with sliced **scallions** and chopped **cilantro.**

5 to 6 servings

broiled ma-po tofu and rice

1. Soak **5 dried shiitake mushrooms** in hot water to cover. Separately soak **1 tablespoon fermented black beans** in water for a few minutes. Drain and chop. Cut **1 large green pepper** in thin slivers. Also cut **4 scallions** in half and then into ¾" pieces. Peel **3 cloves garlic**. Drain mushrooms, reserving liquid, discard tough stems and slice.

2. Use **1 tablespoon grapeseed oil** and **1 teaspoon toasted sesame oil** to stir fry mushrooms, peppers, crushed garlic, and scallions. When light brown, turn off heat and add fermented black beans, **2½ tablespoons tamari**, **1 tablespoon miso**, **1 tablespoon hoisin sauce**, **2 teaspoons chile-paste**, **2 tablespoons dry sherry**, **1½ tablespoons tomato paste** and the reserved mushroom liquid. (Be careful not to add any grit from the bottom of the bowl.) Simmer until slightly thickened and then add **1½ tablespoons rice wine vinegar** and enough **water** until consistency seems right.

3. Prepare brown rice: simmer **2½ cups brown rice** (we prefer short grain) in **4½ cups water** for about one hour or until tender. Add more water if necessary if rice seems too hard and liquid is all gone; add **salt** to taste.

4. You will need ¼ to ½ **pound tofu** for each diner. Split 4 large pieces of tofu in half diagonally, making a large triangle; then cut each triangle in half horizontally, making a thinner triangle. Put **1 tablespoon sesame oil** in a pan and turn tofu pieces in the oil to coat. Slice **4 scallions** thinly. Set aside.

5. Preheat broiler. Broil tofu pieces until bubbly on one side only. Make a ring of brown rice on a dish. Lift out 2 pieces of grilled tofu and place at center of dish, point to point, resembling a butterfly in shape. Spoon some sauce over the top, sprinkle with scallions and **gomahsio** (see glossary), if desired.

8 servings

KATE

risotto
with arborio rice and porcini

We serve this with **Eggplant Caponata** (see following recipe) and
Broccoli Rabe.

1. **Make risotto:** the special taste of this recipe depends
   on finding the right ingredients. Dried *Boletus edulis*
   (porcini) and the plump grains of Arborio rice make
   this risotto delicious. Soak **2 cups porcini** in **water**
   to cover.

2. Dice ¼ **pound** (½ cake) of **tempeh**. Heat
   2 tablespoons olive oil quite hot and fry the tempeh
   until crisp. Turn off heat and remove tempeh from pan.

3. Squeeze porcini to remove liquid and chop coarsely.
   Reserve liquid. Chop **2 medium onions** and **8 to 9
   button mushrooms**. Turn heat on under frying pan;
   add more **olive oil** if necessary, and begin to fry
   porcini first, then add mushrooms and onions. Fry
   over very high heat, stirring constantly.

4. When vegetables are lightly browned, add **2 cups
   Arborio rice**. Stir over heat until grains become
   translucent. Then add ⅓ **cup dry white wine** and
   3 tablespoons tomato paste. Turn off heat. Strain
   porcini soaking liquid through cheesecloth to remove
   grit, then measure—you will need 3 cups liquid, so
   add **water** as needed. Add liquid to pan with
   2 teaspoons salt, stir well, cover, and simmer until
   rice is just tender. Don't overcook. Taste and correct
   seasoning. More salt may be necessary, and perhaps
   another splash of white wine will improve flavor. Add
   tempeh to risotto and stir lightly together.

5. **Prepare broccoli rabe:** cut off and discard stem end of **2 bunches broccoli rabe**. Cut into 2″ lengths. Heat **water** to boiling in a pot and blanch broccoli rabe briefly. Drain.

6. When ready to serve, heat **2 tablespoons olive oil** in a frying pan. Sauté the rabe until it begins to brown. Add a minced **clove garlic** and sauté one minute more. Add **salt** to taste.

7. Risotto will reheat well in a steamer. Add a **handful of frozen peas** to the risotto. Be sure to fry the broccoli rabe at the last minute.

8. Serve risotto with **broccoli rabe** and **caponata** (see following recipe).

6 to 8 servings

ALISON

caponata

A superb recipe from Linda Kraus.

1. Wash **2 medium eggplants** and dry. Cut into 1″ cubes, but do not peel. Fry in ¼ **cup best-quality cold-pressed extra virgin olive oil** over very high heat until light brown. Be sure oil is hot before eggplant is added to pan. Use a slotted spoon to remove eggplant to a large pot.

2. Slice **2 medium onions**, dice **2 medium peppers** and **1 stalk celery**. Fry the onion in remaining oil a few minutes to soften (add more oil if necessary) and then add peppers. When light brown, add these vegetables and the uncooked celery to the eggplant. Add **2½ cups** diced **fresh tomatoes** *or* **puréed, canned plum tomatoes**. Cover and simmer 15 minutes.

3. Meanwhile, rinse **3 oz. capers**, either brine or salted. Chop coarsely if they are large. Mix together **2 teaspoons agave nectar** and **3 tablespoons wine vinegar**. Add capers and vinegar mix to eggplant with **4 tablespoons pignoli nuts, salt**, and freshly ground **pepper** to taste. Finally add ½ **cup** chopped **pitted black olives**. Reheat mixture briefly. Cool and then chill. Once Caponata is cold, you will need to taste again for seasoning. Cold foods will often need more salt.

6 to 8 appetizer servings

sun-dried tomato, shiitake, and artichoke heart sauce for pasta

1. Soak **1 cup dried shiitake mushrooms** in **2 cups hot tap water**. When soft, slice thinly. Reserve soaking liquid.

2. Measure **2 cups sun-dried tomatoes**. Place in a pot with **2 cups water**. Bring to a simmer. Remove from pot and chop coarsely.

3. Meanwhile mince **4 cloves garlic** and **3 shallots**. Set aside.

4. Slice the contents of a **package of frozen artichoke hearts** (about **2 cups**) in half-inch pieces. Heat ¼ **cup olive oil** in a frying pan and sauté the artichoke hearts and the shiitake mushrooms over high heat until they begin to brown a little. Add ½ **teaspoon hot pepper flakes** and reduce heat. Add garlic and shallots and sauté until wilted. Add **2 tablespoons fresh basil**, chopped, or **1 teaspoon dried basil**. Turn into a saucepot.

5. Add mushroom soaking liquid, the sun-dried tomatoes with their liquid, if any, **3 tablespoons tomato paste**, **2 teaspoons salt**, and **4 cups canned plum tomatoes**, cut up. Bring sauce to a simmer and cook 10 minutes. Taste and correct seasoning. This is nice served on a tubular pasta such as **penne** *or* with **shell shapes**. Be sure to garnish with fresh chopped **parsley**.

about 2 quarts sauce

dominican picadillo
with lime-flavored rice and twice-fried plaintains

Picadillo is a Latina stew served over rice or as a stuffing. It usually contains small amounts of ground meat. Seitan or tempeh are good substitutes.

1. **Make picadillo:** chop **4 medium onions** and **6 cloves garlic.** Set aside. Dice **1 cake tempeh** (8 oz.). In a frying pan, heat ¼ **cup olive oil.** First fry the tempeh, and when it becomes brown and a little crisp, add the onions and garlic together with **1 teaspoon hot pepper flakes, 1 teaspoon dried oregano, ½ teaspoon allspice,** and **1 teaspoon ground cumin.** Fry, stirring until mixture is golden brown. Add more oil if needed. When browned, lower heat.

2. Dice **seitan** (wheat gluten) to make **1½ cups.** Add to frying pan together with **2 bay leaves, 2 cups diced tomatoes, fresh** or **canned, ½ cup raisins,** and **½ cup green olives,** chopped. You will also need **1½ tablespoons capers** which should be rinsed and chopped coarsely if they are large. Add to pan along with **2 tablespoons tamari** and cover loosely. Stew the mixture for about 30 minutes, adding **½ cup water** whenever it seems dry. You may need a total of **2 cups water.** Season with **2 teaspoons salt,** freshly ground **pepper** and **2 tablespoons cilantro,** chopped.

3. Serve picadillo with lime rice and twice-fried plantains. **Make lime rice:** cook **3 cups white rice** in **5 cups water** with **4 tablespoons lime juice, 2 tablespoons olive oil,** and **1 tablespoon salt.**

4. **Make twice-fried green plantains** (recipe from Rose Lauture): cut the ends off and peel **2 green plantains** (save the skins). Cut the plantain into ½″ pieces and soak in a bowl of **salted water**. Meanwhile heat **grapeseed oil** in a frying pan and fry the plantain pieces until light brown.

5. Remove pieces from the oil and place them, one at a time inside the plantain skin. Use the heel of your hand against the skin to flatten each slice.

6   Dip again in the salty water and re-fry until golden brown. Drain on a paper towel-lined plate and, if desired, squeeze a little **lime juice** over all.

8 servings

SPRING

seitan apanada

Seitan is wheat gluten. On a trip to Ecuador, one of us had it in a vegetarian restaurant prepared "apanada"—breaded and fried. Using sourdough starter makes this into an exceptionally tasty "cutlet."

1. Prepare **mustard-pepper gravy** to serve with the **seitan** (see index).

2. **Prepare rice and pigeon peas:** we serve this meal with **white rice** and **pigeon peas** (available in Latina markets). Soak **1 pound pigeon peas** in **water** to cover for several hours. Drain, cover with **fresh water** and bring to a boil. Add **1** diced **onion** and simmer for an hour or more until tender. Drain. Return to pot adding ¼ **cup olive oil, 1 tablespoon dried basil**, crumbled, and **2 teaspoons dried oregano**. Use a potato masher to partially crush pigeon peas. Add **salt** to taste and reheat to blend flavors. Set aside. Steam **2 cups white rice** in **3 cups water** and set aside.

3. **Prepare apanada:** slice **1 pound seitan** (from your local health food store) into thin "cutlets." Whisk ½ **cup sourdough starter** with ¼ **cup flour** and ½ **to** ¾ **cup water**, or until it is a consistency that is softer than pancake batter but thicker than crêpe batter.

4. Be sure rice, beans, and gravy are hot.

5. Heat **3 to 4 tablespoons grapeseed oil** in a frying pan. When hot, dip seitan slices in the sourdough batter and fry in hot oil. Turn pieces to be sure both sides are brown and crisp. You will find that very little oil is absorbed.

6. Serve with rice, pigeon peas, and gravy. A **papaya slice** makes a nice garnish, if available.

6 to 8 servings

mustard and pepper gravy
with mushrooms

A simple gravy.

1. Slice **2 cups mushrooms**. Heat ⅓ **cup grapeseed oil** in a wide-bottomed pot until quite hot. Fry mushrooms until crisp and brown over high heat. Add ⅓ **cup unbleached white flour** and **3 tablespoons whole wheat flour**. Lower heat and stir mixture for a couple of minutes.

2. Gradually add **2½ to 3 cups water**, stirring constantly as mixture thickens. Season with **1 to 2 tablespoons coarse Dijon mustard**, lots of **fresh ground black pepper**, **1 tablespoon red** *or* **brown miso**, and **1½ to 2 tablespoons tamari**. Whisk all together and taste. Add **salt** if necessary. Correct seasoning.

3. Finely chop ¼ **cup parsley** and add to gravy. Reheat as needed. This is good over mashed potatoes or with seitan.

makes approximately 3 cups gravy

platanos rellenos

Fried stuffed plantains, a Cuban dish from Rosario Menocal.

1. Choose **ripe plantains** in a Latina market. Regardless of the color, ripe ones yield to finger pressure. You will need **5** of them.

2. **Make filling:** finely dice ½ **cake** (4 oz.) of **tempeh**. Chop **1 small onion** and crush a **small clove** of **garlic**. Dice **1 small frying pepper** and **1 hot pepper**. Set all aside. Heat **2 tablespoons olive oil** in a frying pan and add tempeh. Fry over high heat, until the tempeh is well browned. Add all the vegetables and continue frying until they have wilted and turned golden. Turn off heat.

3. Chop **4 pitted green olives** and add to filling. Chop **1 tablespoon** fresh **cilantro** and add. Season to taste with **salt** and **pepper**. Stir in ½ **tablespoon tomato paste** and **1 small** diced fresh **plum tomato**. Taste and correct seasoning.

4. **Form plantains:** use a knife to cut plantains in half and then peel them. They don't peel as readily as bananas do. Simmer plantains in **boiling water** 5 minutes. Drain and mash thoroughly, using a potato masher. Let cool.

5. Shape well-mashed plantain into cup shapes. Fill each with tempeh mixture. Close and roll between hands into an oval shape. Stir together **2 tablespoons water** and **1 tablespoon kudzu**. Dip plantain ovals into this mixture then roll in **breadcrumbs** until well coated. Refrigerate on a tray until dinnertime.

6. Before dinner, prepare **rice and beans** to accompany the Plantanos Rellenos: pick over **1½ cups black "turtle" beans** and then soak in water to cover 4 to 5 hours. Or bring to a boil and let sit one hour. Either way, drain beans and cover with fresh water. Add sprigs of **epazote** (an herb that supposedly counteracts the gassy effects of beans and adds good flavor), if you have it. Simmer until beans are done. Then season with **salt** and ground **cumin**. Dice **1 small onion** and **1 garlic clove**. Sauté in **2 tablespoons olive oil**. When golden, combine with drained beans. Mash beans somewhat. Correct seasoning.

7. **Prepare rice:** heat **¼ cup olive oil** in pan and add **1½ teaspoons achiote seed**. Heat gently until oil is quite yellow. Use a slotted spoon to discard seeds. Chop **1 green pepper, 1 small jalapeño pepper, ½ small onion** and **1 small clove garlic**. Add to frying pan and sauté. Then add **1½ cups white rice** and sauté until rice is translucent. Add **1 teaspoon salt, ½ teaspoon dried oregano,** and **2½ cups water**. Cover and simmer until rice is done.

8. At dinnertime, heat **oil** in a wok or large pot. Deep fry the platanos, a few at a time. Drain on absorbent paper.

9. Serve 3 platanos per diner, with rice and beans. Garnish with fresh **cilantro**.

8 to 10 servings

banana cream pie

1. Heat oven to 375°F. Use **hazelnut pie crust** recipe (see index). Roll out and completely bake crust for a 9″ to 10″ pie. (You will need to use foil and beans to weight the crust for 10 minutes. Remove foil and beans and bake crust until light brown. Set aside to cool.)

2. Turn contents of **2 (14 oz.) cans of coconut milk** into an appropriate-sized pot. Tie **1 tablespoon annatto seed*** in a scrap of cheesecloth and add to pot. Add **3 tablespoons agave nectar** (*or* **4 tablespoons organic sugar**), **3 tablespoons coconut oil**, **¼ teaspoon salt**, **1 teaspoon grated lemon rind**, **1½ tablespoons lemon juice**, **2 teaspoons vanilla extract**, **¼ teaspoon almond extract**, and **2 teaspoons instant agar-agar** (see glossary). Bring all to a determined simmer, stirring constantly. Cool. Remove cheesecloth with annatto and discard seeds. Chill mixture.

3. Slice bananas to cover bottom of crust. You will need **4 to 5 bananas** in all, including those to be puréed below.

4. Turn the solid chilled mix from the refrigerator into a food processor together with 1½ bananas. Process thoroughly, for as long as 4 to 5 minutes, or until mixture is very creamy. Taste and adjust for sweetness and saltiness. Add a dash of **balsamic vinegar** if you like. When just right, turn into pie shell and chill. Garnish pieces of pie with banana slices.

one 10″ pie

*Optional. It will color the pie filling a pale yellow.

better brownies

These are cakey, not overly sweet, and utterly delicious.

1. Make brownies: heat oven to 300°F. Spread ¾ **cup walnuts or pecans** (or a combination) on a cookie sheet and toast for 15 minutes. Remove from oven, let cool, and chop coarsely. Raise oven heat to 375°F.

2. Measure ¾ **cup semisweet** good quality **chocolate** (such as Vahlrona) into a small pot. Add ¾ **cup brewed coffee**, ¾ **cup soy milk**, ½ to ⅔ **cup coconut oil**, and a scant ¼ **cup flax seed "eggs."*** Cover and place over very low heat.

3. In a bowl combine: **1½ cups all-purpose flour, 1½ teaspoons baking powder, ¾ teaspoon baking soda, ½ teaspoon salt, 1 cup organic sugar**, and ½ **cup unsweetened cocoa**. Stir all together with a dry whisk. Add chopped nuts and mix.

4. Use same whisk to stir chocolate mix until well blended. Turn chocolate into dry ingredients and blend both together. Don't overmix. Turn into an ungreased 8″ x 8″ Pyrex pan. Bake in a preheated oven until a toothpick in the center comes out clean. Remove from oven and cool on a rack.

5. Make frosting: measure **1 cup semisweet chocolate pieces**. Turn into a small pot. Add **3 tablespoons maple syrup**, ¼ **cup grapeseed oil**, **3 tablespoons cocoa powder** and **1 teaspoon vanilla extract**.

---

*Flax seed eggs: Adapted from *The Candle Café Cookbook*, by Joy Pierson and Bart Potenza, Clarkson Potter, New York, 2003. Soak ⅓ cup flax seeds in ⅔ cup hot water in a blender for 15 minutes. Blend until whole seeds are no longer visible. You may need to add another ⅓ cup hot water. 1 tablespoon equals replacement for 1 egg. Store covered in the refrigerator.

Cover and let sit on top of the warm stove until melted, or use a double boiler. Don't stir until chocolate has melted. Then whisk. It will thicken as you stir vigorously. Spread over cooled brownies.

one 8″ x 8″ pan

dried fruit compote

1. You will need to shop for dried fruits, preferably organic. Cut the tips off **1 cup dried figs** and then cut in half. Quarter **2 cups prunes**, halve **2 cups dried apricots**, and remove any cores from **2 cups dried apple slices**.

2. Place all the dried fruits in a stainless steel pot. Barely cover with approximately **5 cups water**, and bring to a boil. Meanwhile, **slice 2 lemons** (preferably organically grown). Discard pits and slices that have no juice sections. Add lemon to pot together with **2 large pieces of stick cinnamon**.

3. When fruits and lemons are soft, remove cinnamon sticks and add ⅓ cup agave nectar, ½ cup dried currants, and ½ teaspoon powdered cardamom. Thin with apple juice if necessary. Chill or plan to serve at room temperature.

4. Toast **slivered almonds** and **Brazil nut slices**.

5. Prepare **almond oat cookies** (see index). Serve compote with cookie and toasted nuts. **Coconut milk whipped cream** (see index) is delightful with compote.

6 to 8 servings

gingered rhubarb fool

Fool is an old word which meant folded. It applied to fruit folded into whipped cream. We use almond cream instead. We make a raspberry one also—see index.

1. Cut **4 cups rhubarb** into fine slices. Turn into a pot with **2 cups** good **organic fruit juice** of your choice. Grate **1 tablespoon fresh ginger** and add to pot together with ⅓ **cup maple syrup** *or* **agave nectar**, and ⅓ **teaspoon salt**. Cover and stew until rhubarb is tender.

2. In a separate pot, slowly heat another **2 cups of fruit juice** with ⅓ **cup agar-agar flakes**, covered. Stir **1½ tablespoons kudzu** in a cup containing ¼ **cup water**. Stir well, and turn into the barely simmering agar-agar mix when flakes have dissolved. Stir until thickened. Add **1 to 2 teaspoons lemon juice** and combine contents of both pots. Cool and refrigerate until quite cold and rather solid.

3. Make **almond cream** (*or*, alternatively, make **coconut milk whipped cream**, see index): pulverize 1¼ **cups almonds** in a food processor. When very fine, add 1¼ **cups hot water** and process again. Strain, using cheesecloth. Squeeze to get maximum almond cream. Heat slowly in a covered pot with 1½ **tablespoons agar-agar flakes**. When dissolved, thicken as above with ½ **tablespoon kudzu** dissolved in ½ **cup water**. Sweeten with ¼ **cup maple syrup** or agave. Add ¾ **tablespoon lemon juice**, ½ **teaspoon vanilla**, ¼ **teaspoon almond extract** and ¼ **cup coconut oil** and chill.

4. When both are cold and firm, purée separately in a food processor. Keep the machine on until each mixture is quite fluffy. Fold together, leaving mixture streaky. Turn into stemmed glasses. Top with slivered **toasted almonds**.

6 servings

rhubarb compote

1. Slice enough **rhubarb stems** to yield **16 cups**. Turn into a nonreactive pot with **2 cups apple raspberry** (or other) fruit juice, cover and simmer until rhubarb is soft.

2. Sweeten with **1½ to 1¾ cups maple syrup** (to taste) and chill.

3. Serve with **almond crème topping** (see index) or **coconut milk whipped cream** (see index) and **slivered**, toasted **almonds**.

8 to 10 servings

maple rhubarb tofu mousse

1. In a stainless steel pot, mix together **2 tablespoons agar-agar flakes** and **2 cups** good quality **fruit juice** (apple-strawberry or apple-raspberry from a health food store are preferred). Bring to a simmer, add ½ **pound tofu** and cook gently 10 minutes. Lift tofu out and set it and the liquid aside.

2. Pulverize ¾ **cup sunflower seeds** or a mixture of **dried coconut** and **walnuts** very finely in a coffee grinder or food processor. Use processor to combine the finely ground seeds or nuts with ⅓ **cup maple syrup**, adding ¾ **cup grapeseed oil** very slowly, alternately with pieces of the drained tofu. The mixture should thicken like a mayonnaise if oil is added slowly enough. When well mixed and smooth, scrape down, add **1 teaspoon lemon juice**, ¾ **teaspoon salt**, and **1 teaspoon vanilla extract**. Turn machine on again and add the agar-agar and juice to the mixture. Taste for salt and sweet.

3. Lightly oil a ring mold or 7 individual custard cups or tea cups. Individual molds work quite well. Fill molds and refrigerate.

4. Dice **2 cups rhubarb** and put into a pot with ¼ **cup maple syrup** and ¼ **cup apple strawberry juice**. Let stand half an hour and then simmer until rhubarb is done, about 15 minutes. Cool, refrigerate.

5. Use a knife to loosen edges of mousse. Turn out ring mold onto a serving plate or turn out individual molds onto saucers. Top with **rhubarb sauce**.

7 servings

strawberry shortcake

1. Fill blender ⅔ full of **decapped strawberries**, about **1½ pints**. Add good **fruit juice** to come a third of the way up the height of the berries. Purée. Add **2 tablespoons Kirsch** and purée again. Add **sugar** only if needed. Turn out into a container and slice **2 cups fresh strawberries** into the sauce. Refrigerate.

2. Make **sourdough biscuits** (see index).

3. Make **coconut milk whipped cream** (see index).

4. Warm biscuits before serving. Spoon on berry sauce and top with cream.

6 to 8 servings

SPRING

fresh strawberry tart

1. Make **coconut oil pie crust** (see index). If you like, sprinkle crust with ½ **cup almonds**, toasted at 300°F until light brown and then chopped very fine in a food processor. Sprinkle almonds over crust, line with foil, weight with beans, and bake at 375°F until edges are brown. Remove foil and beans; let cool.

2. Pull stem ends off of **1 quart locally grown, organic June strawberries**. Arrange them pointed side up in baked crust, as close to each other as possible.

3. Heat **1 cup currant jelly** until it dissolves. Brush generously over berries. Chill pie.

4. Make **crème fraîche** (see following recipe).

5. Serve each piece of pie with a dollop of the "crème," or spread the "crème" over the pie and refrigerate.

one 9″ pie

crème fraîche

Salty and sour, like the dairy version.

In a small pot, combine: contents of **1 (14 oz.) can coconut milk, 2½ tablespoons sugar, 1 tablespoon grated lemon rind, 1½ tablespoons lemon juice, 1 teaspoon instant agar-agar,* ½ teaspoon almond extract, ½ teaspoon vanilla extract,** and **½ teaspoon salt**. Use a small whisk to stir constantly while you bring the mix to a boil. Cool, chill. When quite cold and solid, turn into a food processor and purée until the "crème" becomes silky. Refrigerate, and use within two days.

makes 1½ cups

---

*Telephone brand, available in Thai markets. For more on agar-agar, see glossary.

puerto rican sweet rice

From Justina Robledo.

1. Finely chop a **2-inch piece of ginger**. Boil the ginger in **2½ cups water** with a **stick** of **cinnamon**. Turn heat down to simmer, and cook for half an hour. Strain; save liquid.

2. Meanwhile wash **1½ cups of rice**—Goya* or Canilla* or other Latina brand. Soak rice in water to cover 15 minutes.

3. Drain rice. Turn into pot and add spiced liquid, the contents of a **14 oz. can of organic coconut milk, 2 to 3 tablespoons piloncillo**** (*or brown sugar*), and **¾ teaspoon salt**. Bring to a boil and stir. Lower heat and loosely cover pot.

4. Rice should be almost soft after 10 minutes. Add **⅓ cup raisins** and turn off heat. Cover pot tightly so that pudding will finish cooking.

5. Spread the still warm rice into a smoothed round on a serving plate. Sprinkle with **ground cinnamon** and **1 tablespoon lime juice**.

6. If you like, make a coconut cream sauce: heat the contents of a **can of organic coconut milk** with **3 tablespoons white sugar** until it comes to a boil. Turn off heat. Add **2 tablespoons Meyer's Rum**. Serve this cream in a pitcher. Slices of **papaya** or **pineapple** can be served as well. This pudding is best at room temperature.

8 servings

---

*Available in Latina markets.

**A brown sugar cake available in Latina markets.

HARVEST FEAST

EGGPLANTS FOR BABA GHANOUJ

MAITAKE MUSHROOM

ONION PHYLLO TART

MUSHROOM WALNUT PÂTÉ

OATMEAL SUNFLOWER SEED BREAD

Spicy Thai "Chicken"

Sancocho

ESTOFADO CON CHOCHOYOTES

SWEET POTATO CAKES, MAITAKE MUSHROOMS
AND SOBA NOODLES

ORANGE CARROT CAKE

CHOCOLATE DEVASTATION CAKE

LAGUSTA'S LEMON CURD TART & FRESH STRAWBERRY TART

COFFEE ALMOND ICE CREAM WITH GINGERSNAP

ASSORTED VEGAN COOKIES

STRAWBERRY ICE CREAM

black sticky rice pudding
with mango

An Asian market is necessary to obtain the ingredients for this simple and wonderful dessert.

1. Combine **2½ cups white sticky rice*** and ½ **cup black sticky rice*** and soak in **water** to cover overnight or for 10 hours.

2. Pour out excess water and turn into a pot. Add fresh water to cover rice by 1 inch. Bring to a boil, then cook over very low heat until quite well done (very soft). Add more water as needed.

3. Turn the contents of **4 (14 oz.) cans Thai coconut milk** into a pot. Add **2 cups brown sugar**: a mix of the **coarse dark brown sugar** called panela in Latina groceries or jaggery in Indian stores and North American brown sugar is best. Add **4 teaspoons salt** and **1 teaspoon** fresh ground **pepper**. Heat to dissolve.

4. Pour half the coconut-sugar mix over the rice and stir. Serve warm, with more coconut sugar sauce in a pitcher on the side, and with slices of **fresh mango**.

6 to 8 servings

---

*From a Thai or Asian market.

crème brûlée

Coconut milk, thickened, makes a credible facsimile of this famous delicate pudding. The vanilla bean is essential to its quality.

1. Use a small electric spice or coffee grinder to pulverize ½ **a vanilla bean in** ¼ **cup sugar.**

2. Combine in a pot: **1 (14 oz.) can Thai coconut milk, 1 can water,** pinch of **salt, 1 teaspoon instant agar-agar,* 1 tablespoon kudzu, 1 teaspoon annatto seed,**** grated **rind of** ½ **lemon, 2 whole star anise, 1 to 2 teaspoons lemon juice,** and ½ **teaspoon dried powdered ginger.**

3. Add the pulverized vanilla sugar and bring to a boil, stirring constantly. It will thicken only a little. Remove from heat and taste for lemon juice, salt, and sugar. Remember that there will be a caramelized sugar topping. Add **1 tablespoon balsamic vinegar** and **1 tablespoon brandy.**

4. Strain into 5 to 6 individual shallow ramekins. Chill.

5. Put ¼ **cup sugar** and ½ **cup brown sugar** in a shallow pan. Place in a 300°F oven ten minutes, or until brown sugar is quite dry. Turn mixture into a processor and pulverize. Set aside.

6. Before serving, the sugar should be sprinkled generously over the custards and caramelized. You can use a butane torch to do this, but it is easier to do it under

---

*Instant (powdered) agar-agar is extremely easy to use. Buy "Telephone" brand in a Thai or Asian market. Regular agar-agar (flakes or bars) would require a different procedure.

**Annato seeds should lend a delicate yellow cast to the pudding, and are optional. Turmeric should not be used as it turns the crème green.

a preheated broiler. The sugar must melt and turn brown, but not burn. Watch carefully! You don't have to serve these desserts immediately, however they must be served within several hours or else the crispy crust will go limp.

Serve with **hazelnut pie crust cookies** (see index).

5 to 6 servings

malaysian banana tapioca pudding

1. Soften **1½ tablespoons small pearl tapioca** in **warm water** 1 hour. Don't use quick-cooking tapioca.

2. Use a small pot to combine the contents of a **14 oz. can of light unsweetened coconut milk, 2 tablespoons chopped crystallized ginger** and **¼ cup sugar**. Bring to a simmer. Set aside for at least 30 minutes.

3. Peel, quarter and cut **3 firm bananas** into ½″ dice. Add bananas and drained tapioca to coconut milk pot. Cook, stirring gently for 5 minutes. Cool. Turn pudding into 6 small "pots de crème" containers and chill.

4. Serve with **hazelnut pie crust cookies** (see index).

6 servings

chinese sticky rice balls

This is Chinese snack food. We like it for dessert. You will need Asian red beans, labeled as such in Thai or Chinese markets, as well as glutinous rice flour, from the same sources.

1. **Sweet red bean paste** is available canned. Since it is the hard part of this recipe, you can buy the canned version if you don't mind it being a little overly sweet. Be sure the brand you buy contains no lard. If you decide to make your own paste, weigh **4 oz. red beans**. Cook in ample **water** to cover until very soft—at least 1 to 2 hours. Drain. Place in processor to pulverize. Push paste through a fine sieve and discard skins which remain.

2. Sweeten red bean paste with **3 tablespoons sugar** and add **2 tablespoons coconut oil**. Add **½ teaspoon salt**. Turn into a pot and cook over lowest heat to dry and thicken mixture. This takes at least 45 minutes and is very messy, since the beans will spit hot drops on everything nearby. A somewhat ajar lid will help contain the messiness. When it seems thick and dry, turn heat off. Cool. Refrigerate.

3. Stir together **2 cups glutinous rice flour, 3 tablespoons sugar** and ⅔ **cup warm water**. Stir vigorously and knead until silky. Dough should be soft like your earlobe. Turn dough onto an **oiled** counter. Roll into a rope and cut into 24 pieces.

4. Use your slightly **oiled** hands to flatten a piece of dough. Fill it with a marble-sized piece of chilled red bean paste. Cover bean paste with glutinous rice skin and roll balls between your palms. Set each aside until all are done.

5. The sticky rice balls may be boiled or fried. Try them both ways to see which you like best. Chop ½ **cup peanuts** and stir together with ½ **cup flaked coconut**. Roll the balls to be fried in a bowl of **sesame seeds**. Deep fry in a small pot in **2 to 3″ grapeseed oil**. They will have to be turned, but will puff up nicely. When they are brown, remove and sprinkle heavily with chopped peanuts and coconut.

6. Put the balls to be boiled in a pot of simmering **water** and cook 5 minutes. Add ¼ **cup sesame seeds** to the remaining peanuts and coconut and roll cooked balls in this mix. Serve hot or at room temperature. Serve 3 to 4 rice balls each to 6 to 7 diners.

6 to 7 servings

arroz con coco

From Ana Pilar Velasquez.

1. Two pots are necessary for this recipe. In one place
   1½ cups Arborio rice, ½ teaspoon salt and 3 cups
   water. Bring to a simmer.

2. In a second pot heat contents of 1 can unsweetened
   coconut milk and a small container frozen coconut
   cream or 1 can coconut cream with 1 can of water.

3. When rice has almost absorbed the water, add
   dippers of coconut liquid, a little at a time. Also add
   1 cinnamon stick and 2 cloves. Continue simmering
   and adding small amounts of liquid for 1 hour.

4. When cooked, stir in ¼ cup sugar, 1½ teaspoons
   vanilla and 2 tablespoons Meyer's Rum. Taste for
   sweet and add water if pudding is stiff—up to 1 cup
   more water.

5. Refrigerate. Serve in custard cups sprinkled with
   cinnamon.

6 to 8 servings

SUMMER

SOUPS

SALADS

ENTREES

sesame celery soup

1. Coarsely chop stalks and upper leaves to measure **4 cups celery**. Slice **2 cups onions**. Turn both into soup pot with **2 tablespoons grapeseed oil** and **1 tablespoon Chinese toasted sesame oil**. Fry over high heat until vegetables begin to brown slightly.

2. Add **⅓ teaspoon dried ginger** and **3 tablespoons flour**. Cook, stirring well, for a few minutes.

3. Add **2 quarts water, 3 tablespoons dry sherry, ¼ cup tahini** (sesame paste), **½ cup chopped canned tomatoes, ⅓ cup tamari** and (optional) **1 to 2 teaspoons Chinese chili-paste-with-garlic** (available at Chinese markets). Bring to a boil and taste for seasoning. The soup may need a little **salt** and freshly ground **pepper**.

4. Serve garnished with fresh **cilantro**.

8 servings

swiss chard and lentil soup

1. Pick over 1½ **cups French lentils** to remove any stones. Put in a pot, cover with **2 cups water**, and bring to a boil. Simmer until tender. Set aside.

2. Meanwhile finely chop **1 medium onion**. In a soup pot, add ⅓ **cup olive oil** and sauté the onion. Add **2 bay leaves**, ½ **teaspoon sweet Hungarian paprika**, and ½ **teaspoon hot Hungarian paprika**. When onions are soft and golden, add **2 cloves chopped garlic**. Cook briefly, then turn off heat and set aside.

3. Peel and dice **2 Idaho potatoes**. Add to soup pot with **2 quarts water** and bring to a boil. Cook until potatoes are almost done.

4. Meanwhile shred **1 bunch of Swiss chard**. Add Swiss chard and lentils to the soup pot. When the chard and potatoes are quite cooked, season with **2 tablespoons tamari**. Add **salt** and **pepper** to taste.

8 to 10 servings

SUMMER

chilled lemon zucchini soup
with leeks and herbs

1. Slit **3 large leeks** and wash out sand and dirt. Chop coarsely. Peel and chop **1 small onion** and **2 cloves garlic**. Turn vegetables into a frying pan with **2 tablespoons olive oil**. Sauté over high heat until slightly browned.

2. Collect garden herbs: we like **½ cup fresh basil**, chopped, **2 tablespoons summer savory** stripped of the hard stems, and **1 tablespoon thyme leaves**, similarly stripped. Add to frying pan while vegetables brown. Turn off heat. Now turn into a soup pot, deglazing the pan with a few tablespoons of **water** to salvage all the vegetable flavor.

3. Coarsely cut up enough **zucchini** to yield **5 cups**. Add to pot with **1 quart water**, the **grated rind of two lemons, 2 tablespoons tamari**, **½ teaspoon salt** and **fresh ground pepper**. Bring to a boil and simmer for 5 minutes.

4. Turn soup into a blender in several batches. Purée. Season with **¼ cup lemon juice** and taste to correct flavor. Chilling will dull the flavors of salt and lemon. Chill soup and taste again.

5. Garnish with chopped **fresh mint leaves** and slivered **toasted almonds**.

6 servings

summer three sisters soup

The Native American three sisters are corn, beans, and squash. This soup is best made from garden vegetables.

1. Make a broth by cutting the kernels off **4 ears of corn** (reserve kernels) and put the cobs into a soup pot. Barely cover with **water**. Bring to a boil and let cook ½ hour. Remove cobs and discard. Save the broth. Add **water** to make **10 cups**.

2. Cut up and peel a **medium Hubbard squash,** *or* **3 to 4 acorn** *or* **butternut squashes,** *or* a **small pumpkin.** You will need **8 cups squash**. Cut into cubes and cook in the corn broth.

3. Meanwhile, cut **4 cups fresh green beans** into 1 to 2 inch pieces. When squash is almost done, add the beans with a sprig or two of **fresh savory**. When beans are almost tender, add corn kernels. Turn off heat.

4. Season with **1 tablespoon salt** and **2 tablespoons cider vinegar**. Correct seasoning. If available, garnish with **fresh ripe elderberries**.

8 to 10 servings

gazpacho

An excellent soup to be made only when local tomatoes are in season. It's not worth eating otherwise.

1. Using a sharp knife, finely chop **4 medium tomatoes, 1 small cucumber, 1 small green pepper, 3 scallions, 4 tablespoons straight leaf parsley,** and **4 small stalks celery hearts.** Mince **1 small jalapeño chile** very fine. Put these vegetables into a container which can be refrigerated later.

2. Add to the container: **2⅔ cups best quality organic tomato juice, ¼ cup olive oil,** and **2 tablespoons lemon juice.** Season to taste with **salt** and **pepper.** Stir and chill thoroughly.

3. Rub soup bowls, preferably glass, with a cut **clove of garlic.** Add gazpacho to bowls and place an ice cube in each bowl before serving.

6 servings

callaloo

Callaloo is a Caribbean soup made variously from different Island greens. We make it from amaranth.

1. Wash and coarsely shred **12 cups amaranth** leaves. Wash **6 cups kale leaves** and strip off from stems. Set aside. If **okra** is available, slice **2 cups** and set aside.

2. Slice **1 large onion**. Peel and slice **4 cloves garlic**. Seed and mince **3 jalapeño peppers**.

3. Sauté onion, garlic, and pepper in ¼ **cup olive oil** in a large frying pan. When softened and beginning to brown, add kale and amaranth leaves. Fry over high heat. When greens collapse, add okra.

4. Peel and dice **1 batata** (available in Puerto Rican markets. It is white, but tastes like sweet potato. It is a good foil for the slightly bitter amaranth.) Simmer in **water** to cover until tender. Set aside.

5. Turn cooked vegetables into a pot. Add **6 cups water**, to barely cover. Add **2 (14 oz.) cans unsweetened, organic coconut milk**. Bring to a simmer and cook 10 minutes. Add batata and cooking liquid. Season generously with **salt** and **pepper** and the **juice of 1 lime**. Serve with **lime wedges**.

6 to 8 servings

SUMMER

sancocho

This is a soup-stew to be found in many Caribbean and Latin-American countries. It is usually garnished with pork; we substitute frozen tofu. You will find the root vegetables and seasonings in Latina markets.

1. A day or so before you want to make Sancocho, freeze **1 pound tofu** wrapped in foil. Defrost it before you begin to make the soup. Sometimes we find ourselves with more tofu than we can use fresh, and we freeze it in separate blocks, so it is always available for this kind of soup garnish.

2. **Make sofrito (seasoning base for soup):** gently heat a few **achiote seeds in ¼ cup grapeseed oil** until yellow color is suffused into the oil. Scoop seeds out and discard. Dice **2 green sweet peppers,** **½ small jalapeño pepper,** and **1 large onion.** Finely chop **2 cloves garlic** and sauté with other vegetables in the yellow oil with **2 teaspoons oregano** and **1 tablespoon ground cumin** until vegetables begin to brown. Set frying pan aside.

3. Set a large soup pot on the stove and put **1½ cups water** and **1 cup white rice** into it. Cook gently until rice is done. Turn heat off. Meanwhile, use smaller pot to separately cook the following vegetables. First peel and slice **1 medium yucca**, barely cover with water and simmer until tender. Turn into soup pot with cooking liquid. Repeat with **1 small yautia**, **2 carrots**, **1 yam**, **1 batata**, and **1 green plantain**. Unless you know the cooking time of these vegetables, it is best to cook them individually, preparing each as the last one is done. Peel and cut into chunks **½ small calabaza squash** and cook. Husk and cut **2 ears of fresh corn** into 2″ lengths and steam until done. Add to soup pot.

4. Dice the tofu into ½″ pieces and fry until crispy in the sofrito. Turn sofrito with tofu into soup pot and add **1 ripe plantain**, peeled and sliced, **⅓ cup tamari**, and **2 teaspoons salt**. Bring to a simmer and taste for seasoning. Add water if necessary.

5. Serve hot, garnished with slices of **avocado** and freshly **chopped cilantro**.

8 servings

SUMMER

roasted green chile corn chowder

From Anne Arkin. The essential ingredient for this superb soup is canned Hatch green chilies from New Mexico. They are available hot or mild; we use the mild.

1. Cook **6 to 8 ears of fresh corn** in a frying pan in ½ **cup water**, covered. When corn is tender, let cool. Use a knife to cut kernels off cobs. You will need **5 cups kernels**. Alternatively, you may use an equal amount of canned corn. Reserve cooking liquid, and turn cobs into a pot with the liquid plus **3 cups water**. Boil to make a stock.

2. Chop **onions** to yield **2½ cups**. Mince **1 to 2 jalapeño chilies**. Slice **3 to 4 cloves garlic**. Dice **carrots** to yield **1 cup**. Sauté these vegetables in ⅓ **cup grapeseed oil** in a soup pot. Meanwhile, dice **3 cups red potatoes**, scrubbed but not peeled. Add potatoes to pot together with **2 cups corn cob stock**. Cook until potatoes are tender.

3. Coarsely purée half the corn kernels in a food processor and add whole and chopped corn to pot together with the contents of **2 (14 oz.) cans coconut milk**. Dice **2½ cups Hatch chilies**. Mince ½ **cup cilantro leaves**. Add chilies and cilantro to soup and bring to a simmer. Add **salt** and **fresh ground pepper** to taste, and thin as needed with corn broth or water.

8 servings

tofu eggless salad

1. Dice **2 stalks celery with leaves**. Finely chop
   1 tablespoon chives *or* **garlic leaves** and
   2 tablespoons parsley.

2. Place **1½ pounds tofu** (reserve another **½ pound of
   tofu** for the "whites"), broken into large pieces, into a
   bowl or food processor with the chopped vegetables
   and herbs. Add **¼ cup grapeseed oil**, **¼ teaspoon
   turmeric**, **¼ teaspoon cumin**, **scant ¼ cup tamari**,
   1 tablespoon nutritional yeast, **1 tablespoon
   lemon juice**, **2 tablespoons sunflower seeds**, and
   freshly ground **pepper** to taste. Mash all ingredients
   together by hand with a potato masher or turn
   processor on and off quickly two or three times. The
   resulting salad should be well mixed with a somewhat
   lumpy texture like egg salad. Cut remaining ½ pound
   tofu into small pieces and fold it in. Taste for salt and
   lemon. Add a **dash of Tabasco** if desired.

3. Serve on a bed of **Boston lettuce** with **new pickles**
   and **avocado slices** for garnish. Top with **alfalfa
   sprouts** *or* **thinly sliced onion** and a **sprinkling of
   gomahsio** (see glossary). **Whole wheat toast** is a
   good accompaniment for this salad.

4 to 6 servings

bulgur and lentil salad
with tarragon and toasted walnuts

This salad is to tarragon as tabbouleh is to parsley: something to make when you have a lot of fresh tarragon.

1. Cover ½ **cup French lentils** with water in a pot and simmer until tender but not mushy. Uncover and let cool.

2. In another pot combine **1½ cups water, 1 cup bulgur,** and **1 teaspoon salt.** Cook covered until water is absorbed. Turn into a bowl to cool. Stir occasionally.

3. Meanwhile, mince ½ **cup shallots.** Add **3 tablespoons white wine vinegar** and **1 tablespoon fresh tarragon,** minced, to the shallots. Drain water from cooled lentils and discard. Combine lentils with shallot mixture.

4. Lightly toast ½ **cup walnuts** in a 300°F toaster oven. Cool. Chop. Set aside.

5. Shred ½ **cup carrots.** Dice ½ **cup celery,** choosing inside stalks and hearts, and chop enough **fresh tarragon leaves** to yield **3 tablespoons,** packed.

6. Add lentil mix to bulgur together with walnuts, carrots, celery, and tarragon. Season with ¼ **cup extra virgin olive oil, salt** and **fresh ground pepper.** Be assertive with the seasoning to counteract loss of flavor due to refrigeration. Chill.

7. Serve on lettuce with a drizzle of **vinaigrette** (see glossary) and thinly sliced **red onion.**

4 to 6 servings

pasta salad
with spinach pesto

Pesto is a traditional Italian flavoring made of pulverized garlic, basil leaves, ground nuts, Parmesan cheese, and olive oil. It is stored in jars (or frozen) for year-round use. We have omitted the cheese in this variation, and use ingredients fresh from the summer garden.

1. Bring a large pot of **water** to a boil with **1 tablespoon salt**. Clean a **10 oz. package** *or* **bunch of spinach leaves** and drop in the boiling water for a few seconds only. Lift spinach out with tongs or a slotted spoon. Drain over a pot, then remove to a food processor. Turn the contents of a **1 pound** box of **rotini** (spiral-shaped) or other pasta into the pot of water, and cook until just done. Drain in a colander and run cold water over the pasta to stop the cooking.

2. Meanwhile, add **1 large clove garlic** to the processor and **7 sprigs** of **fresh basil**. Turn processor on. Add **½ cup olive oil** and **3 tablespoons tamari**. Purée, then turn machine off.

3. We like to add **sun-dried tomatoes** to this salad. We use **⅓ cup**. Cook them in a few tablespoons of water to soften, then add a few tablespoons **olive oil**. Or buy them already prepared this way. Chop coarsely. Heat **½ cup pignoli nuts** in a 300°F toaster oven until light brown. Chop coarsely.

4. Turn pasta into a large bowl. Pour the spinach pesto over it and toss well. The spiral shape of the rotini holds the pesto sauce best. Add pignoli nuts and the sun-dried tomatoes. Grind **fresh pepper** over and mix again. Taste. More tamari may be necessary. Obviously this dish could be served hot as a dinner, but we prefer it at room temperature, spooned over chilled **lettuce leaves** that have been drizzled with **vinaigrette** (see glossary).

10 servings

chickpea salad

1. Soak **2 cups dried chickpeas** overnight in water. Rinse and cook chickpeas in fresh water until soft. Drain and cool. Cover with water in bowl and rub chickpeas lightly between your palms to release their skins. Skim skins from surface of water. You won't be able to remove all of them. Drain chickpeas and turn into bowl.

2. Shred 1½ **carrots**. Finely chop 1½ **stalks of celery** (hearts of celery are best), **1 sweet pepper**, ½ **small onion** and **2 leaves of comfrey**. Comfrey is an easy-to-grow plant whose long hairy green leaves are high in vitamin B12 for those who are interested. It adds a wonderful cucumber-like taste to the salad. The leaves of borage or burnet can be substituted or, if none of these are available, some diced cucumber can be added to the finished salad. However, comfrey has healing properties, especially for bones.

3. Make vinaigrette: in a small bowl, **combine 1 tablespoon tamari, 1 teaspoon lemon juice, 1 small clove garlic**, crushed, **1 teaspoon chili-paste-with-garlic** (found in Chinese markets, or substitute cayenne pepper or Tabasco), **salt** and **pepper** to taste. The vinaigrette should be fairly concentrated in taste.

4. Add vinaigrette to chickpeas. Toss and refrigerate. Serve cold on a bed of Boston **lettuce** with **avocado slices, slivers of red onion**, and **alfalfa sprouts**. Sprinkle with **gomahsio** (see glossary).

8 to 10 servings

soba noodle salad

Japanese buckwheat noodles—a satisfying meal for a hot night.

1. Combine ¼ **cup rice wine vinegar, 3 tablespoons tamari**, and **1 tablespoon fresh ginger**, grated. Set aside.

2. Combine **2 teaspoons wasabi powder,*** ½ **teaspoon sugar**, ¼ **teaspoon salt**. Add **1 tablespoon warm water** and stir, adding a little more water until syrupy. Now add **1 tablespoon toasted sesame seed oil** and **1 tablespoon grapeseed oil**. Set aside.

3. Toast **3 to 4 tablespoons unhulled sesame seeds** in a toaster oven at 300°F *or* in a dry skillet over low heat. When light brown, set aside to cool.

4. Bring a large pot of water to a boil. Cook **12 oz. (1 package) soba noodles** for only a few minutes until barely tender. Drain in a large colander. Cut up **2½ cups garlic chives** into 1″ lengths. Add to colander and mix with the hot noodles.

5. Rinse ¾ **pound mung bean sprouts**. Shake dry. Combine with the soba noodles.

6. Turn soba mixture into a serving bowl. Add both sauces and sesame seeds and mix together. Chill.

6 servings

---

*See glossary.

tabbouleh

We serve tabbouleh with hummus and baba ghanouj as a summer platter. See the following recipes.

1. Briefly rinse **1 cup fine bulgur** under running water in a colander. Let drain.

2. Squeeze **lemon juice** to yield **1½ cups**. Combine lemon juice and bulgur in a bowl, fork mixing them, and set aside for 30 minutes.

3. Measure ¾ cup good quality **olive oil**. Add **1 teaspoon salt** and ¼ **teaspoon cayenne** to the oil. Set aside.

4. Finely chop **1¾ cups parsley**, preferably homegrown flat leaf. **Dice 4 tomatoes** fine. **Finely chop 6 scallions**, and **mince ¼ cup fresh mint**.

5. Combine vegetables and herbs with the bulgur and the seasoned oil. Toss well. Refrigerate.

6. Serve with whole leaves of **romaine lettuce** and **pita bread**.

makes 2 quarts

hummus bi tahini

1. Soak **1 cup dried chickpeas** overnight. Drain off the water and put the chickpeas in a pot. To cook, add new water to cover the beans and cook till soft, about 1 hour.

2. Drain the chickpeas and put into a food processor or blender with ½ **cup olive oil**, 1½ **teaspoons salt**, **1 cup water**, **3 cloves garlic**, **2 tablespoons fresh mint leaves**, finely chopped, the **juice of 2 lemons**, and **1 cup tahini**. Good quality tahini is important in this recipe.

3. Purée the mixture till smooth, about 5 to 10 minutes. It should not be too stiff. Traditionally it is spread flat on a shallow dish and topped with a drizzle of **olive oil**. If the mixture is too thick, add more **water** to thin. It may also require more tahini and lemon juice to suit taste. Refrigerate and serve with **pita bread**.

makes 4 cups

SUMMER

baba ghanouj

While you can make baba ghanouj in the oven by baking the eggplant, the best way to do it is on a gas flame. An electric stove can be used if the burner is preheated until red hot.

1. Prop **1 eggplant** directly on your burner over high heat so it is vertical, stem up, for a few minutes. Then lay it on its side, turning every few minutes or so until the outside of the eggplant is charred and black and the inside soft.

2. Immediately remove the eggplant from the stove. Slit it open and scoop out the white soft flesh with a spoon and put it in a bowl, being careful to keep charred pieces out. You should know that cooking the eggplant this way makes a mess of the stove and you may choose to bake it in the oven; however, the smoky smell and taste will be absent.

3. Add **2 cloves** crushed **garlic**, **2 tablespoons** fresh chopped **Italian parsley**, the **juice** of **1 lemon**, **3 tablespoons tahini**, **salt**, and **pepper** to taste.

4. Refrigerate. When cool, serve with **pita bread**.

lentil salad

1. Prepare **lentil sprouts** 3 days in advance.*

2. Finely chop **1 cup carrots** and **1 small onion**. Bring to a boil **2½ cups water** and add the carrots, onion, **1 cup lentils**, **½ teaspoon dried thyme**, and **1 teaspoon salt**. Simmer ½ hour until tender. Drain if any liquid remains.

3. Spread out in a bowl and add **¼ cup olive oil** and **1½ teaspoons lemon juice**. Toss and let cool.

4. When cool, mix in **1 or 2 small fresh tomatoes**, diced. Taste for salt and add **fresh ground pepper**.

5. To serve, pile lentil salad on bed of lettuce and sprinkle generously with lentil sprouts, **red onion rings**, and **avocado slices**, if desired.

6. Drizzle the **vinaigrette** over the salad.

6 to 7 servings

SUMMER

---

*Lentil sprouts: (this procedure can be applied to any sprouts). Put 2 to 3 tablespoons lentils in a good sprouting jar. Canning jars are ideal, however, any jar which can be covered with plastic screening and turned upside down is okay. Cover with water. Let soak an hour or more and then drain. Find suitable dark spot which will allow air, and place jar upside down. Sprouts should be rinsed with water twice a day and returned to their dark spot to drain and grow. When sprouted (after 3 days), they should be refrigerated.

tomato salad

At last. We serve tomatoes only when they are vine-ripened and locally grown, so as much as we love them, they appear in salads only in August, September, and early October.

1. Slice **tomatoes** thickly and place on a bed of **lettuce** with sliced **onions** and **vinaigrette** (see glossary) on top.

   Or, alternate tomato slices, home grown **cucumber slices** (which, of course, don't need to be peeled or seeded) and very thin slices of **sweet onion**. Chop **fresh basil** and **oregano** *or* **thyme leaves** and sprinkle over the top. In a jar shake together a dressing of **2 parts olive oil** and **1 part balsamic vinegar**. Pour over salad, salt lightly and grind fresh **pepper** over. Don't refrigerate. Cold tomatoes lose their fresh flavor.

sabra salad
with tahini dressing

From Batya Bauman.

1. Dice **2 cups fresh, vine-ripened tomatoes**. Dice
   1½ cups thin, unwaxed cucumbers, if you don't
   grow your own, use Kirbys. Thinly slice **2 to 3 scallions**.
   Finely chop ¼ **cup straight leaf parsley**. Combine in
   a bowl. Drizzle with **olive oil**, and squeeze the **juice
   of ½ lemon** over all. Add **salt and pepper** to taste.

2. In a small bowl stir ½ **cup tahini** with a spoon, slowly
   adding cold water. Tahini will thicken at first. Keep
   adding water until sauce is creamy. Add about
   3 tablespoons lemon juice, 3 cloves crushed garlic,
   and **salt** to taste.

3. Serve salad in individual dishes and let each diner
   add tahini dressing as desired.

4 servings

SUMMER

ginger curried green bean and tofu salad

From Jacqui Alexander. This is a Caribbean curry which Jacqui serves hot. It would be fine with rice, but we also like it cold as a salad.

1. Cut **1½ pounds fresh green beans** in halves. Set aside. Cut **1½ pounds tofu** into dice and place in a bowl. Grate **1 tablespoon fresh ginger** and add to bowl. Pour ⅓ **cup tamari** over tofu and ginger and gently mix together. Set aside. Sliver **1 red bell pepper**. Set aside.

2. Heat **3 tablespoons grapeseed oil** in a frying pan. Add **1½ teaspoons whole cumin seed** (called girrah in Trinidad) and cook over moderate heat until the seeds pop a little, but don't let them brown. Now add **4 to 5** crushed **cloves garlic** and **2½ tablespoons curry powder**. Add the slivered red pepper. Let bubble until it all becomes dark yellow, but don't let the mixture brown or burn. Now add reserved green beans with a **grating** of **black pepper**. Turn beans in the sauce and fry for a minute or two, then add ¼ **cup water**, reduce heat and cover. Cook until beans are almost done but still crisp. Now add tofu with the marinade together with ½ **teaspoon garam masala** if you have it. Gently mix all together and cover again. Cook a minute or two more. Don't overcook. Let cool. Refrigerate.

3. Lay **lettuce leaves** on a plate. Spoon out green beans and tofu. Add some **sliced onions** and a few **cherry tomatoes,** if you like. Spoon a little **vinaigrette** (see glossary) over the lettuce and serve.

4. Jacqui likes **Patak brand mango chutney** with this dish when served hot. You may like it on the salad as well.

8 to 10 servings

broccoli, yellow squash, and shiitake mushrooms in black bean sauce
with thai rice noodles

1. Cut **broccoli** into small flowerets and peel and slice the stems thinly. You should have **5 cups**. Thinly slice **yellow squash** *or* **zucchini** to make **2½ cups**. Set both aside.

2. Soak **2 tablespoons fermented black beans** (available in Asian markets) in **water** to cover for 5 minutes. Soak **4 large dried shiitake mushrooms** in **warm water** until soft.

3. Put the fermented beans in a processor (or in a mortar and crush with a pestle) and process, adding enough water to make a coarse paste.

4. Peel and mince **2 cloves garlic**. Grate **¾ teaspoon fresh ginger**. Set aside.

5. Pour **2 tablespoons grapeseed oil** in a frying pan and add **1 tablespoon toasted sesame oil**. Begin frying broccoli over high heat. Stir until crisp and brown. Remove to a bowl. Fry squash the same way and turn into bowl. Turn off heat.

6. Squeeze liquid from mushrooms and reserve it. Slice shiitakes and fry in same pan. Remove to bowl once browned. Turn heat lower to sauté garlic and ginger gently, adding more of both oils if necessary. Turn off heat.

7. **Mix together:** 3 tablespoons dry sherry, 3 tablespoons tamari, and reserved shiitake soaking liquid. Measure and add **water** to make a total of ⅔ **cup** liquid. Separately stir together **2 tablespoons water** and ¾ **tablespoon cornstarch.** Add ½ **tablespoon maple syrup** *or* **agave nectar.** Add sherry mixture to frying pan together with black bean purée. Bring to a boil. Add cornstarch mix and stir until sauce thickens and clears. Pour ⅔ of the sauce (reserve the rest) over vegetable in bowl. Taste mixture and correct seasoning.

8. **Prepare rice noodles:** soak ½ **pound rice noodles** in water to cover for 15 minutes. Meanwhile, heat a pot of water to boiling. Add the drained noodles and boil until almost tender, about 5 minutes. Drain and run cold water over noodles until they are quite cool. Add ½ **to 1 cup water** to the reserved sauce, and pour over noodles. They will stick together if there is not enough liquid to keep them separate.

9. Serve at room temperature or chilled, rice noodles on one side of the plate, and sauced vegetables on the other. Garnish with toasted **sesame seeds** and sliced **scallions**.

4 to 5 servings

chilled thai rice paper spring rolls
with spicy peanut sauce

You will have to find a market which sells Thai and Chinese ingredients. Note that we substitute a thick Chinese sauce called soy paste for Thai fish sauce. Try to choose fresh-looking, unbroken rice papers for best results.

1. Soak **1 cup** of the dried fungus called **tree ears** in **water** to cover for 5 minutes. Clean the tree ears of dirt and wood, and chop coarsely.

2. Bring **1½ cups water** to a boil in a medium-sized pot and add **1 oz. cellophane noodles** and the tree ears. Simmer 3 minutes. Drain and season with **3 tablespoons soy paste** and fresh ground **pepper**. Combine with **1½ cups diced wheat gluten** (seitan) and set aside to cool.

3. Prepare ¼ cup chopped **cilantro, 2 tablespoons** minced **Thai basil** *or* **fresh mint** and ¼ cup chopped **red onion**. Combine in a bowl and set aside. Shred enough **carrots** to yield ¾ cup and set aside.

4. Pour water on a dinner plate or pie plate and dip **rice paper rounds** *or* **wedge shapes** into the water to soften, one at a time. Lift out onto the work surface and spread with wheat gluten-fungus mix. Top with shredded carrots, a **dribble** of **soy paste**, and a pinch of the herb-onion mix. Roll up, tuck in ends, and place on tray. Cover with plastic wrap and refrigerate.

5. Make **spicy peanut sauce** (see following recipe). Toast ½ **cup peanuts** and chop. Toast ¼ **cup sesame seeds** also.

6. Shred **lettuce** to serve as a bed under the spring rolls. Lay 3 rolls on top. Spoon a band of peanut sauce over the rolls. Garnish with **mung bean sprouts**, and the sesame seeds and peanuts. Slices of **cucumber** and **red onion** complete the plate.

10 servings

spicy peanut sauce

1. Chop **1 teaspoon lemongrass** very fine. Combine **1 tablespoon tamarind juice** *or* **1 tablespoon lime juice** with **1 teaspoon chili-paste-with-garlic** (available in jars in Chinese markets), **2 tablespoons minced garlic, 1½ cups creamy peanut butter** (preferably unsweetened, from a health food store), **2 cups coconut milk, 1 tablespoon maple syrup** *or* **agave nectar, 2 teaspoons salt,** and ½ **cup shallots,** minced. Refrigerate.

makes 3½ cups

SUMMER

koshari
egyptian lentils and rice

Mid-eastern recipes like this one require a lot of onions and generous amounts of good quality olive oil.

1. Rinse 1¼ **cups basmati rice**. Cover with **water** in a bowl and let soak while preparing other ingredients.

2. Pick over and wash 1¼ **cups organic French lentils**. Cover with 2½ **cups water** and cook until tender.

3. Thinly slice **2 large Spanish onions**. Cook in a frying pan over moderate heat in ⅓ **cup olive oil**. A cast iron skillet works best. When onions are transparent, add ½ **teaspoon red pepper flakes** and **3 cloves garlic**, sliced. Continue cooking, stirring occasionally, until onions just begin to caramelize. Use a slotted spoon to remove most of the onions to a bowl.

4. Crumple **2 cups** of **very fine vermicelli noodles** (called fides or shehriah*) into frying pan and sauté in remaining oil until brown and crisp. Turn off heat and set aside.

5. When lentils are soft, add drained rice to the pot and continue cooking until rice is fluffy. Add onions and vermicelli and turn off heat. Add **Kosher salt** to taste, at least ½ **tablespoon**.

6. Dice 1½ **cups fresh tomatoes** (or use good quality canned, such as Muir Glen). Combine with lentils and rice. Be sure salt is adequate. Serve hot or at room temperature.

---

*Available in Greek or Arabic stores.

7. Serve with **roasted beets** (see following recipe) and **cucumber salad** (see index), or fresh cooked asparagus.

6 servings

roasted gingered beets

1. Cut tops and roots off a dozen medium-sized beets. Rinse briefly. Place close together in a shallow pan. Drizzle with oil. Cover with foil. Roast at 400°F for one hour or until a knife-pierced beet indicates tenderness.

2. Use a paper towel to push skins off beets while they are still hot. Slice into a pot and add pan juices, if any. Add ½ cup water and 2½ tablespoons diced candied ginger (the kind which comes in syrup). Also add ½ teaspoon dried thyme, 1 teaspoon salt, and ½ teaspoon fresh ground pepper. Simmer all together to blend flavors. Add 1 to 2 tablespoons lemon juice and taste to adjust seasoning.

3. Top with ¼ cup chopped fresh dill. Serve at room temperature.

6 servings

grilled skirt "steak"
with pan-roasted peppers

This "steak" is made with seitan.

1. **Make marinade:** combine in a bowl juice of **2 limes, 2 tablespoons tomato paste, 2 large cloves garlic**, chopped, **½ teaspoon cayenne, 2 teaspoons ground cumin, 2 tablespoons chopped cilantro, 2 tablespoons olive oil**, and **½ cup añejo tequila**. Stir all together.

2. Thinly slice **2½ pounds seitan**. Sprinkle with **Kosher salt** and lay slices in bowl or container. Pour marinade over each layer. Refrigerate for at least two hours.

3. Slice **4 to 5 green frying peppers** and **2 to 3 jalapeños**. Discard seeds. Sauté in **¼ cup olive oil** over medium to low heat for about ½ hour, stirring on occasion. Peppers should begin to brown.

4. We like to serve this with Indian Harvest's **Jasmine Rice Blend**,* which contains lentils and radish seeds. Prepare whatever rice you prefer.

5. When ready for dinner, preheat broiler. Spread out seitan in a single layer and drizzle with **olive oil**. Broil until edges curl and brown. Serve with chopped **cilantro**, some marinade spooned over, the peppers and wedges of fresh **tomatoes**.

5 servings

---

*See glossary.

roasted summer vegetables
with pasta and pesto

From the August garden.

1. Quarter **8 large frying peppers** and discard seeds. Slice **4 medium zucchini**. Cut **1½ small eggplants** (unpeeled) into 2-inch wedges. Roast all in a large rectangular pan in **extra virgin olive oil** in a 350°F oven for 45 minutes. Stir occasionally. Sprinkle with **coarse salt** and fresh ground **pepper**.

2. Meanwhile crush **6 cloves garlic** and gather and chop **1 to 2 tablespoons fresh herbs** such as sage, rosemary, fennel, or thyme. Pick only 2 or 3. Add to roasted vegetables and stir well.

3. Cut **5 small tomatoes** in half. Add to pan and roast 30 minutes more, raising the heat the last 15 minutes to 450°F to glaze vegetables.

4. Make pesto in food processor: grind ½ **cup basil**, add **2 tablespoons extra virgin olive oil**, **2 tablespoons pignoli nuts**, and **2 cloves garlic**.

5. Cook **pasta** of your choice. Toss with pesto. Serve roasted vegetables over the pasta. Sprinkle with **tamari** and a **splash** of **balsamic vinegar.**

6 to 8 servings

SUMMER

seitan barbecue
with cole slaw and
Alison Dunn's chili-spiced oven-roasted potatoes

1. **Make almond mayonnaise** for cole slaw first: cover
   ½ **cup whole organic almonds** with water. Bring
   to a boil. Pour cold water into pot, and slip skins off
   almonds. Turn into a blender. Add **2 tablespoons
   lemon juice** and turn blender on. Add ½ **cup water**
   through the top and then ½ **cup grapeseed oil.**
   Blend until mixture becomes mayonnaise. You will
   have to scrape the sides down, and you may have
   to add a little more water. When the mixture is very
   creamy, season it with ½ **teaspoon salt**, ½ **teaspoon
   mustard**, and **hot pepper sauce.** Taste and correct
   seasoning. Set aside.

2. **Make cole slaw:** thinly slice **1 small cabbage.** Sliver
   a **small red pepper** and grate **1 carrot.** Thinly slice a
   small red onion. Combine almond mayonnaise with
   cabbage and vegetables. Taste and add salt and more
   hot sauce if you like. Refrigerate.

3. **Prepare barbecue sauce:** sauté **2 to 3 cloves**
   chopped **garlic**, **1 tablespoon diced ginger**, and
   ½ **teaspoon red pepper flakes** in a little **grapeseed
   oil.** Add **1 cup catsup**, **2 tablespoons molasses**,
   ⅓ **cup red wine**, **1 tablespoon tamari**, **1 tablespoon
   mustard**, ½ **tablespoon horseradish**, and
   1½ **tablespoons chili powder.** Dilute with **brewed
   coffee** to make a thick sauce.

4. **At dinner time, make chili-spiced oven-roasted potatoes:** wash but do not peel **3 to 4 russet potatoes**. Cut into 2″ pieces. Turn into a bowl. Heat oven to 500°F. Add to bowl: **3 tablespoons olive oil, 1½ tablespoons chili powder, 1½ tablespoons ground cumin seed**, and **2 crushed garlic cloves**. Use a slotted spoon to mix all together well. Spread potatoes out on a cookie sheet. Sprinkle with **Kosher salt**, and **fresh ground pepper**. Roast 15 minutes, turn, roast 5 minutes or until crisp and brown.

5. Meanwhile, thinly slice **2 pounds** purchased **seitan**, or make your own (see index). Marinate the slices in the barbecue sauce for 30 minutes to 2 hours before dinner. Drain seitan slices, dip in **water-diluted sourdough starter** (see index), and fry in a large skillet in ⅓ **cup hot grapeseed oil**. Fry until brown and crisp.

6. Serve seitan with extra barbecue sauce on the side. The cole slaw and chili-spiced potatoes complete the meal.

4 servings

thai rice noodle summer salad-supper

1. **Make dressing:** peel **3 cloves of garlic** and place in a blender. Remove seeds from **1 jalapeño chile.** Add to blender with **½ cup water.** Blend to crush garlic and chile. Now add **½ cup brown sugar, ½ cup lime juice,** and **½ cup rice vinegar.** Thai food is an intense balance of hot, sour, sweet, and salt. The classic salt is nuoc nam, a distillation of anchovies. Instead we add **¼ cup tamari, 2 teaspoons Kosher salt,** and **1 tablespoon tamarind concentrate.** Finally, to give the sauce some body or thickness, add **⅓ cup organic peanut butter.** Blend well. Be sure to taste to correct the seasoning. Refrigerate.

2. **Prepare the noodles:** place **1 pound thin rice noodles**—linguine sized—in a large bowl. Cover with **3 to 4 quarts boiling water.** Let stand 5 minutes or until soft. Drain; rinse with cold water; drain. Turn onto a large serving platter.

3. **Prepare vegetables and/or fruits:** shred **8 leaves** of **Napa cabbage.** Roll up a **dozen spinach leaves** and shred. Thickly shred **1 to 2 carrots.** Slice **5 to 6 scallions.** Peel and dice **1½ cups jicama.** Chop **½ cup cilantro** (*or* **basil,** for cilantro haters). Slice **1 to 2 kirby cucumbers.** Rinse **2 cups bean sprouts.** If available, slice an unpeeled seeded **pear, apple,** *or* **½** an **unripe papaya.** You will also need **1 cup salted peanuts.**

4. **To serve:** arrange fruit, vegetables and peanuts in discrete piles on the same platter as the noodles, or, if it is too small, on a separate platter. Sprinkle **scallions** and **cilantro** (*or* basil) over the noodles. Pass the dressing separately.

8 servings

CONNIE

pizza

The flavors of this pizza are more bright and clear with a drizzle of olive oil and no cheese. This is not a quick and easy recipe, but the results are worth the effort.

1. Make a **marinara sauce**, or defrost **slow roasted tomato sauce** (see index). You will need approximately **2 cups.**

2. Make green topping: blanch **8 cups** sliced **broccoli rabe** in boiling water for a minute. Drain. Finely slice **1 cup broccoli tops.** Shred **4 cups packed spinach leaves**. If you like, cut **1 cup frozen artichoke hearts** into 1″ pieces. Sauté all over high heat in **olive oil**, until greens begin to brown. Add **2** crushed **garlic cloves** and **salt** to taste. Turn off heat and turn out into a bowl. Set aside.

3. Place **3 large poblano chilies** under a broiler. Turn until skin blackens on all sides. Remove from oven and place in a paper bag. After 5 minutes, pull off skins, discard stems and seeds and cut into thin strips. Coat lightly with **olive oil** and drizzle with a few drops **balsamic vinegar.** Set aside.

4. Slice **3 to 4 narrow Asian eggplants** (unpeeled) thinly. Fry over high heat in olive oil, turning slices, until eggplant begins to brown. Add **1 clove crushed garlic, salt** and **pepper.** Turn out into a bowl. Add a few drops **balsamic vinegar.** Set aside. Sauté **2 cups oyster mushrooms** in the same pan. **Salt** and **pepper,** and when browned, add to eggplant. Mix both together. Set aside.

5. Pit **1 cup kalamata olives** and chop coarsely. Set aside.

6. **Make crust:** use a mixer with a dough hook to blend **4 cups all-purpose flour** and **2 teaspoons salt**. Add **1 teaspoon dry yeast** and **1 cup sourdough starter** (see glossary). Turn machine on. Add **3 tablespoons olive oil** and gradually, **1 cup warm water**. The dough will take between 5 and 10 minutes to form a ball which cleans the sides of the bowl. Be cautious adding the water; use just enough to form a silky ball. Set aside for 20 minutes.

7. Meanwhile, thinly slice **6 to 8 Roma tomatoes** and separate **fresh basil leaves**. You will need 1 leaf for every tomato slice.

8. Lightly **oil** two long baking pans and sprinkle with **coarse cornmeal**. Heat oven to 400°F.

9. Pat out and use a rolling pin to shape dough into two rectangles 6″ to 7″ wide and 22″ long. Coat with **tomato sauce**. Place a long thin band of eggplant-mushroom mixture on one long side. Place a similar band of greens at the other. In the middle, overlap tomato and basil slices. **Salt** and **pepper** tomatoes. Accentuate the three wide stripes with narrow stripes of chopped olives. Use the pepper strips to make diagonal X shapes to mark 10 servings. Drizzle olive oil over all and fold edges up on all four sides. Bake 30 to 40 minutes, or until pizza begins to brown.

10 servings

ratatouille niçoise

1. Choose **4 small to medium eggplants**. Slice in half lengthwise. Each half will be a serving casserole for one person, so consider how each eggplant will be cut to make it sit on the plate as level as possible.

2. Peel **4 large onions** and slice. Using a large sharp-edged spoon, scoop out the eggplant flesh. Chop it coarsely. Put eggplant halves together while mixture cooks.

3. Heat **3 tablespoons olive oil** in large heavy fry pan. You may be more comfortable using 2 fry pans, if you have them. If you are using 2 pans, **3 tablespoons oil** will be necessary in the second one as well. Add **1 teaspoon dried oregano** to pan with sliced onions. Sauté a few minutes. Add eggplant and turn heat high. Eggplant should brown and stick and be scraped up with a spatula. Scrape often.

4. Meanwhile, wash **8 small zucchini (*or* 4 to 6 medium)**. Slice in half lengthwise, then slice in half circles. When eggplant is browned, add the zucchini and continue turning the vegetables in the hot pan often.

5. Core and slice **12 small Italian frying peppers** and add to pan. If pan is too full, dump vegetables into a pot, for they now need to simmer covered 45 minutes to one hour. Season generously first with **salt** and **pepper**.

6. Meanwhile, peel (optional) **10 small fresh tomatoes** by quickly dipping in a pot of boiling water and then running them under cold water. Chop the tomatoes coarsely and turn into a large bowl with their juice. Mix cooked ratatouille with tomatoes in the bowl and taste for **salt** and **pepper**. Set reserved eggplant halves in shallow baking pan and fill each one with ratatouille mix. There will probably be some mix leftover. If you like, serve cold on toast like pâté.

7. Bake eggplants at 375°F for ½ hour uncovered until top is browned and glazed. Serve with **brown rice**.

8 servings

SUMMER

grilled summer vegetables
with balsamic vinegar and herbs

1. For each diner, cut a **wedge of radicchio**, ½ **green pepper**, **3 thick slices** of zucchini, and **3 thick slices yellow squash**. Don't peel **a large Spanish onion**, cut it into 8 wedges first (one each per diner) and then peel. You will need **tomatoes** and **Japanese** *or* **baby eggplants** as well, but these should not be cut until serving time, ½ of each per person. Place all vegetables on a tray, cover with plastic wrap, and refrigerate.

2. Mince ⅔ **cup shallots**. Mince ½ **cup fresh basil**, ⅓ **cup fresh thyme leaves** stripped from stems, and mix herbs together. Set aside.

3. Prepare brown rice: in a pot put **3 cups short grain brown rice**. Add **5 cups water**. Cover. Bring to a boil, then simmer 40 minutes or until done. Don't stir until water is absorbed. Add **1 teaspoon salt**. Set aside.

4. Combine ½ **cup balsamic vinegar** and 1¼ **cups water** in a pitcher and set aside.

5. When ready to serve, preheat broiler or outdoor grill. Cut eggplants in half lengthwise, then score the flesh in a cross-hatch pattern with a sharp knife. Arrange all vegetables, except radicchio, on pans or racks. Drizzle good quality **olive oil** over the vegetables. Sprinkle them with **coarse salt** and the herb-shallot mixture, 1 tablespoon for each diner. Once vegetables begin to brown, add oiled and salted radicchio. Remove pan from broiler when all vegetables are

browned and crisp, and arrange around a cone of cooked brown rice.

6. Pour a little of the water/vinegar mix into pan, and bring to a boil on top of the stove. Pour over vegetables and rice and serve. There should be enough herbs and vinegar mix to serve 8.

8 servings

FRIDAY NIGHT ANIMAL RIGHTS GROUP

palestinian musaqa

A lot of frying, but a beautiful and delicious dish.

1. Choose **3 medium-sized firm eggplants**. Peel and slice lengthwise very thin. Place in a large bowl, sprinkling each layer with **salt**. Cover with **water**; weight with a plate and set aside.

2. Slice **4 to 5 large yellow onions**. Turn into a large cast iron skillet. Add **olive oil** as needed and sauté over medium low heat, stirring on occasion, until onions melt and caramelize. Thinly slice **2 large garlic cloves** and chop a **large bunch of cilantro**. Add to onions and sauté five minutes more. Turn onions out into a bowl.

3. While onions are cooking, use a toaster oven set at 300°F to lightly brown **½ cup sliced almonds** and **½ cup pignoli nuts**. Set aside. Use a coffee grinder to pulverize: **1 teaspoon whole cumin, 1 teaspoon coriander, 1 tablespoon black peppercorns**, and **½ teaspoon whole allspice**. Grind finely. Turn out into a small bowl and hand grate **½ teaspoon nutmeg** to add to the spice mix.

4. Peel **3 large Yukon Gold potatoes** and slice thinly. Place in the unwashed pan adding **olive oil** as needed and fry potatoes on both sides until light brown. Line the bottom of a large shallow baking dish with the potatoes. Sprinkle then with 1 teaspoon of the spice mix and **salt** to taste.

5. Rinse and pat dry the eggplant slices. Fry them in the same unwashed skillet, adding **olive oil as needed**. When half the eggplant slices have browned lightly, place them on top of the potatoes. Distribute ⅓ of the caramelized onions over the eggplant, **salt** lightly. Fry the rest of the eggplant and set slices aside on a plate.

6. Now slice **4 medium-small zucchinis** lengthwise in thin strips. Fry them and arrange on top of eggplant in casserole. Add ⅓ of the onion mix, **salt** to taste and the spice mixture. Sprinkle the browned nuts over all. Top with rest of the eggplant and the remaining onion mix. Heat oven to 375°F.

7. Finally, dice **1 large yellow** *or* **red pepper**. Slice **3 to 4 plum tomatoes** thinly and arrange both on top of the casserole. Sprinkle with **salt** and with the **juice** of **2 lemons**. Boil **1 cup water** and dribble it over the casserole. Bake 20-30 minutes or until brown and glazed.

8. Use the same (still unwashed) fry pan to cook a **rice pilaf**: dice ½ **onion** and sauté for a few minutes in **olive oil**. When soft, add ¼ **cup pignolis** and, optional, ½ **cup shehriah** *or* **fides** (very fine noodles available in Greek or Arab markets). Sauté until light brown. Add **1½ cups long grain rice, 2½ cups water, 2 tablespoons tamari** and ⅓ **cup currants**. Cover and turn heat to very low, until pilaf is done.

9. Serve musaqa and pilaf together.

8 servings

tempura

The green shiso are especially delicious.

1. **First prepare dipping sauces:** boil **1 or 2 dried shiitakes**, a **piece of kombu** (seaweed) and some **daikon slices** in **1½ cups water** for 5 minutes. Strain, reserving the liquid (dashi) and set aside. Combine **1 tablespoon fresh** grated **ginger, ¼ cup tamari, 2 teaspoons brown sugar, 1 teaspoon toasted sesame seeds, 1 teaspoon hot chile oil, juice** of **½ lime** (*or* **lemon**) and **2** chopped **scallions**. Finish this sauce with **3 tablespoons** of the prepared **dashi**. Set aside. There should be 1¼ cups dashi remaining. Add **5 tablespoons tamari** and **2 teaspoons mirin** (rice wine) to it. Set aside. Correct seasoning of both dipping sauces. It is nice to have **½ cup** fresh grated **daikon, ¼ cup grated ginger** and **2 tablespoons toasted sesame seeds** to add as each diner would like.

2. **Make sticky rice:** the Japanese brand Nishiki is preferred—Cook **1½ cups** of **rice** to **2 cups water**. Set aside. Chill a **bottle of club soda** to add to the batter later.

3. **Prepare vegetables:** use **6 fresh shiitakes**, stemmed, slices of **2 baby eggplants, 1 sweet potato**, wedges of **1 or 2 onions**, each wedge held together with a toothpick, **green pepper pieces, 8 to 10 green beans, 1 lotus root**, sliced, and **1 dozen green shiso leaves**. Place all on a paper towel-covered tray.

4. **Make batter:** stir together **1 cup flour,** ⅓ **cup cornstarch, 1 teaspoon baking powder, 1 teaspoon salt** and ¼ **teaspoon cayenne.** Heat **2 to 3 cups grapeseed oil** in a wok. Choose an assortment of vegetables for each diner. At the last minute, add **1¼ cups cold club soda** into the flour mix and stir well. Dip each vegetable in batter and then into hot oil. Shiso leaves should be batter-covered on one side only. Don't crowd vegetables in wok. Drain each portion in a paper towel-lined basket and serve.

5. Diners have 2 dipping sauces and rice to eat, with daikon, ginger, and sesame seeds for garnish. Beer or sake are good accompaniments.

4 to 6 servings

slow-roasted tomato sauce

We wait for garden ripe tomatoes all year. Once they come, we are grateful for "Fourth of July," the earliest variety. But when the Brandywines are available, we choose them first for salads embellished with their complex flavor. What to do with all the other varieties of tomatoes we were tempted to try, and all the cherry tomatoes? Here's a delicious, simple solution.

1. In a large shallow baking pan, such as a lasagne pan, place enough unpeeled cut up **tomatoes** to come **halfway up** the sides of the pan. Small tomatoes may be quartered, cherries go in whole, and large tomatoes cut into pieces. Peel the cloves of **1 large head of garlic** and add to pan together with **1 to 2** whole **hot peppers**. *Optional:* cut up **baby eggplants** may be added also. Drizzle generously with **olive oil**, and place in the oven at 300°F for 3 hours. Tomato juices will rise in the pan, and slowly roast and dry. Edges of the tomatoes will caramelize when cooking is done. Stir every half hour, to mix in darker cooked pieces.

2. If the sauce has not begun browning at the edges after 3 hours, raise heat to 350°F for another hour. (Doesn't it smell delicious?) Twenty minutes before it seems done, add a **whole bunch** of **basil**.

3. Remove the pan from the oven. If you don't want the
   sauce to be too spicy, remove and discard the hot
   peppers. Use a potato masher to cream the garlic into
   the sauce, as well as to blend larger pieces of tomato.
   Many of the skins will have dissolved; however,
   if you like, you can pull some out and discard.
   Season to taste with **salt** and **pepper**. If you *still*
   have excess tomatoes, cut some up. Turn sauce and
   fresh tomatoes into a pot and bring to a boil, stirring.
   Texture and flavor are enhanced by using both slow-
   roasted and barely cooked tomatoes. If you have
   used too much olive oil, skim it off to use for other
   cooking purposes, and if sauce is too dry, add water
   as needed.

We freeze this sauce in small containers for
reminders of August in January.

eggplant pilaf

Best made with August garden abundance.

1. Thinly slice (do not peel) enough **Asian** *or* **baby Italian eggplants** to yield **12 cups**. Also slice **6 frying peppers** and **1 medium onion**. Set aside.

2. Pour **¼ cup olive oil** into a frying pan. Over high heat fry the onion, adding **1½ tablespoons fresh oregano** (*or* 1½ teaspoons dried). When onion wilts, add peppers. Gradually add slices of eggplant, stirring and frying.

3. Slice **2 to 3 small zucchini** *or* **yellow squash** to yield **3 cups**.

4. Add squash to frying pan and fry 2 to 3 minutes longer. If available in your garden, you can also add **3 cups** shredded **kale** *or* **Chinese cabbage**. Now add **¾ cup long grain white rice** and continue frying and turning vegetables and rice until the latter is opaque and the vegetables begin to brown. Turn off heat.

5. Season pilaf with **½ cup fresh basil leaves** (we prefer Thai basil), **⅔ teaspoon chili-paste-with-garlic** (available in small jars in Asian markets), and **1 teaspoon salt**. In a measuring pitcher combine **1⅓ cups water**, **¼ cup tamari**, and **1 cup dry sherry**. Add this stock to pan, cover, and simmer until pilaf is just done. Correct seasoning.

6. This is nice served with a small salad of fresh sliced tomatoes, cucumbers *or* summer squash, and mung bean sprouts. Dress with a mix of ½ **cup rice wine vinegar, ¼ cup tamari, scant 1 tablespoon sesame oil**, and a **dash mirin** (Japanese rice wine), if available. Sprinkle top with chopped **Thai basil.**

5 to 6 servings

pan-seared japanese baby eggplant

Simple treatment for homegrown vegetables.

1. Cook brown rice to go with the eggplants: wash **1 cup short grain brown rice** and cover with **1¾ cups water**. Simmer 40 minutes or until done.

2. Prepare **Dashi** (broth) for eggplant: in a small pot combine **1 cup water**, **¼ cup tamari**, and **¼ cup sake** *or* **dry sherry**. Add a piece of washed **kombu** if available. Bring to a simmer, remove from heat.

3. Combine **⅓ cup white (shiro) miso**, **1 tablespoon sake**, **1 tablespoon rice wine vinegar**, **1½ teaspoons agave nectar** and **¼** of the dashi (above).

4. Add **½ teaspoon** freshly grated **ginger root** to the remaining dashi.

5. Slice unpeeled **small, thin eggplants** in half lengthwise. Depending on how small they are, plan for 1 or 2 eggplants per diner. Use a sharp knife to cut cross-hatch marks in each eggplant half. Cut deeply but not through the skin. Heat **1 tablespoon grapeseed oil** in a frying pan until very hot. Add eggplants, cut side down, adding only the number which fit in one layer. Lower heat to moderate and cover pan. Cook 3 to 4 minutes. Turn eggplants over and cook, covered, 3 to 4 more minutes. Finally, uncover pan and be sure each eggplant half is browned and puffed. Repeat for remaining eggplants.

6. Pour a little dashi over eggplant and top with miso mixture, if you are using it. Serve with brown rice and **sesame green beans** (see following recipe).

sauce makes 5 to 6 servings

sesame green beans

1. Toast ½ cup **sesame seeds** in a heavy, dry frying pan, stirring constantly. Remove to a heatproof bowl.

2. Trim **5 cups green beans** and cut in half. Steam in ½ **cup water** and **1 teaspoon salt** until not quite done.

3. Meanwhile, in a small pot, heat **3 tablespoons sake** (*or* **dry sherry**). Add **1 teaspoon agave nectar** and **2 tablespoons tamari**.

4. Add sauce and sesame seeds to green beans and heat all together.

5 to 6 servings

baby eggplants
stuffed with sun-dried tomatoes, garlic,
parsley and cracked wheat

A hybrid of Greek and Italian cuisines.

1. **Prepare stuffing:** use kitchen scissors to coarsely cut up enough **sun-dried tomatoes** to yield **1 cup**, tightly packed. Coarsely chop **½ cup straight leaf parsley**. Peel **6 cloves garlic**. Turn all into container of a food processor and set aside.

2. Peel and coarsely chop **1 large onion**. Turn into frying pan, add **2 to 3 tablespoons olive oil** and fry over high heat, stirring constantly until onion is wilted. Turn into processor.

3. Turn processor on until mixture becomes a coarse paste. Turn off. Add **½ cup medium cracked wheat** (bulgur—available in Greek or Middle-Eastern stores) and **1½ teaspoons salt**. Process briefly again to mix.

4. **Stuff and bake eggplants:** you will need **1 to 2 dozen baby eggplants**, each 4 to 5″ long. Your own garden eggplants or Japanese eggplants will work well, or very small Italian eggplants. Cut off stem end. Make a long slit the length of the eggplant. When all have been trimmed and slit, use your fingers to stuff each one with the tomato-cracked wheat mixture. You may have more stuffing than you can use. Lay in a baking pan. Drizzle **olive oil** generously over the eggplants. Extra stuffing may fill space in the pan. Cover pan tightly with foil.

5. Bake in a 400°F oven for one hour. Serve with rice pilaf, plain rice or with pasta, as you like. A drizzle of **spicy tomato sauce** (see following recipe) is a desirable garnish.

6 to 8 servings

spicy tomato sauce

This goes well with stuffed vegetable dishes, especially stuffed eggplants.

1. Chop **1 small onion** finely. Sauté in **2 tablespoons olive oil** with **2** crushed **cloves garlic, 2 teaspoons oregano**, and **1 teaspoon basil**. When golden brown, add **15 oz. canned** plain **tomato sauce**. Rinse out can with **¼ cup red wine** and add to sauce. Finally, mince **1 tablespoon jalapeño peppers** and add to the simmering sauce. Cook about 10 minutes and taste, particularly for salt.

blue corn enchiladas
with potato and bean filling

1. Pick over **1 cup kidney beans**, carefully removing any stones or debris. Cover with **water** to soak overnight or for a minimum of 4 to 6 hours.

2. Drain beans. Cover with fresh **water** and cook until tender. If available, add a **sprig of epazote** to beans.

3. Peel and quarter **2 to 3 Idaho potatoes**. Cover with **water** and boil until tender. Set aside potatoes and water, do not drain.

4. Peel **1 medium onion** and slice thinly. Sliver **2 frying peppers** and **1 hot pepper**. Heat ¼ **cup olive oil** in a frying pan, and sauté these vegetables over moderate heat, meanwhile seasoning them with ¾ **teaspoon oregano**, ½ **teaspoon basil**, ¾ **teaspoon cumin**, **1 clove garlic**, minced, and **2 tablespoons** chopped **fresh cilantro**. When medium brown, use a slotted spoon to lift cooked beans into frying pan, reserving cooking liquid. Use a potato masher to crush beans, turning mixture as you do. Add **oil** if it seems necessary. Now add potatoes and mash, but don't make mixture too smooth. Add as much potato and/ or bean cooking liquid as seems necessary to make this filling into a soft mix. Season with **1½ teaspoons salt** and taste to correct seasoning. Set aside to cool.

5. Heat **1 pound blue corn tortillas**, 2 or 3 at a time, in a heated (dry) skillet or on a griddle, turning to warm and soften both sides. Pan or griddle will need to be quite hot to make tortillas flexible. Spoon a finger of filling on each tortillas, roll up, put into a tray or pan, cover with plastic wrap and refrigerate until serving time.

6. When ready to serve, heat 2 enchiladas per diner in a covered pan in the oven. Fry **ripe plantain slices** in a little **oil**. Serve the enchiladas with **spanish rice** and **salsa** (see following recipes), slices of **avocado**, **raw onion**, the plantain, and **jalapeño chiles**.

8 servings

spanish rice

1. Bring to a boil **2 cups white rice** and **3 cups water** in a covered pot. As soon as the water boils, turn the heat down, cover, and cook rice slowly until water is absorbed. Do not overcook.

2. Meanwhile, finely chop **1 medium onion** and mince **2 cloves garlic**. In a large frying pan sauté onion, garlic, and ½ **teaspoon cumin** in **3 tablespoons olive oil** until slightly browned. Add ⅔ **cup chopped canned tomatoes** and continue cooking until most of the liquid has evaporated.

3. Turn the cooked rice into the frying pan. Add **2 tablespoons tamari** and fry, stirring continuously, until all the seasonings are thoroughly blended with rice. Cover and set aside until ready to serve.

6 to 7 servings

salsa for enchiladas

1. Finely dice **5 plum tomatoes, half** of a **small jalapeño pepper,** ½ **small onion,** and **1 frying pepper.** Combine with **1½ cups canned tomato sauce** and ½ **teaspoon salt.** Set aside.

2. If available, cook and process a dried chile pepper as follows: you will need **half** of an **ancho, pasilla,** *or* **mulatto chile pepper.** Discard the seeds and tear into pieces. Place pieces in a small pot, add ½ **cup water,** cover and bring to a simmer. Cook 5 minutes. Turn into a food processor and purée.

3. Combine chile purée and the rest of the salsa. (If dried chiles are unavailable, ¾ **teaspoon good quality chili powder** may be substituted). Dilute salsa with **water** if too thick. Refrigerate until serving time, but take sauce out early enough so that it will be close to room temperature. Taste and correct seasoning.

makes 3 to 4 cups

okra beignets
fritters

Inspired by a recipe from South Carolina which included eggs and shrimp.

1. Slice **2 cups okra** ½″ thick. Turn into a bowl. Chop ½ **cup onion, 2 seeded jalapeños,** ½ **cup sweet pepper** and **3 cloves** of **garlic**. Add to okra with **1½ teaspoons salt**. Stir to combine. Leave at room temperature for at least 20 minutes or for up to 3 hours. The okra should yield a gelatinous juice.

2. Prepare **rice** and a moderately spicy **tomato salsa** *or* other piquant sauce *or* **chutney** (see index) to accompany the beignets.

3. Just before dinner, stir together ¼ **cup flour,** ½ **teaspoon salt, 1 teaspoon baking soda, 1 teaspoon baking powder,** ¾ **cup fine cornmeal,** and **3 tablespoons toasted sesame seeds**. Finely chop ¼ **cup cilantro** (*or* **basil,** for cilantro haters), and add the herb and dry ingredients to the okra.

4. Heat **grapeseed oil** in a pot big enough to fry the beignets. Add **sourdough starter** (see glossary) to the okra. You will need between **1 to 2 cups** of sourdough to make a rather thick batter. Use two spoons to scoop up batter and release into the hot oil. Cook until brown, turning once or as necessary. Remove to absorbent paper.

5. Serve beignets with **rice** and **salsa,** and **lime wedges** to squeeze over the fritters.

4 servings

SUMMER

southwest chili corn enchiladas

1. Peel **8 ears of fresh corn**. One at a time, stand each ear of corn on a counter and use a sturdy French chef's knife to cut kernels off the cob. Turn kernels into a bowl. Draw the knife along the cob to extract remaining corn milk, and let fall into the bowl. Set aside.

2. Heat your broiler quite hot and place **4 bell peppers** under the flame. Turn so that the skin becomes evenly charred all around. Add **2 fresh jalapeño peppers** and char in the same way. As each pepper is done, place it in a paper bag and close the bag. When peppers have cooled a few minutes, peel them, cut out stem and seeds and discard. Dice the pepper, turn into a bowl, and set aside.

3. Finely chop **3 large onions** and **4 cloves garlic**. Sauté both in **3 tablespoons grapeseed oil** in a frying pan. When golden brown, turn off heat and set aside.

4. Roast ⅔ **cup sunflower seeds** in a toaster oven. When light brown, let cool a few minutes and then crush in a food processor or with a mortar and pestle. Set aside in a bowl.

5. Use the processor to purée about ¾ of the corn kernels, adding a little water if needed.

6. Finally, dice **2 medium zucchini**. Add to the frying pan with **1 teaspoon salt** and sauté a few minutes more. When squash begins to brown a little, add the sunflower seeds, peppers, corn purée, and whole kernels. Let this mixture cook together a minute or two while you stir it. Correct seasoning, adding **Tabasco** if you like it hotter.

7. Let chili corn cool about ½ hour. Heat **2 dozen flour tortillas** on a hot griddle or in a cast-iron skillet, one at a time, to soften. Add a finger of chili corn and roll up. When all are filled, cover with plastic wrap and refrigerate.

8. Prepare **refried beans** and **spanish rice**. A **spicy tomato sauce** is an optional topping. See index for these recipes.

9. Reheat enchiladas in a covered pan. Serve with beans, rice, tomato sauce, and **jalapeño peppers** from a jar, if you like.

8 to 12 servings

SUMMER

summer ice creams

Ice creams made from premium organic coconut milk are surprisingly rich and delicious, and very satisfying.* A number of recipes follow. The use of alcohol tends to keep the mixture creamy rather than icy. The inexpensive home ice cream makers (wherein the bowl is kept in the freezer) work well; our favorite brand is the Girmi. It is most quiet. It's good to have a spare chilled bowl since the ice cream grows in volume as the machine freezes it, so you cannot fill the bowl to the top. On occasion, you may need to do a partial second batch if you have too large a mixture. That's when the spare bowl comes in handy. Otherwise, keep the extra mix chilled and process it in the cold bowl the next day. Agave nectar is an ideal unflavored sweetener; however maple syrup and sugar work well also. Salt and pepper do a remarkable job of pointing up flavor.

banana coconut rum
ice cream

1. Cut up **5 very ripe bananas** and put into a food processor. Add ¼ **cup Meyers rum**, ½ **cup sugar**, ½ **teaspoon salt**, ½ **teaspoon fresh ground pepper**, and **1 teaspoon vanilla extract**. Purée.

2. Add **1½ cans (21 oz. total) organic coconut milk** and **1 teaspoon lemon juice**, or to taste. Correct seasoning. Chill and freeze as per ice cream maker's instructions.

---

*See the glossary for more information on coconut milk. Our coconut milk comes in 14 oz. cans.

chocolate ice cream

1. Melt ¾ cup chopped unsweetened good quality chocolate (such as Scharffen Berger or Valhrona) in the contents of **1 can coconut milk** over low heat. When melted, whisk and remove from heat.

2. Combine with **1 more can coconut milk, ¼ cup unsweetened cocoa, 1 tablespoon dried coffee crystals, ¼ teaspoon cinnamon, 1 teaspoon vanilla extract, ½ teaspoon salt, ½ teaspoon fresh grated pepper and ¾ cup light agave nectar.*** Slivered almonds and 2 tablespoons Kahlùa are optional additions. Chill until very cold, and freeze as per ice cream maker's instructions.

---

*Sugar may be substituted for agave: ⅓ to ½ cup sugar for ¼ cup agave, 1 scant cup sugar for ⅔ cup agave, 1 cup sugar for ¾ cup agave. Or you can use maple syrup instead of agave, using the same amount as agave.

coffee almond ice cream

1. Make a coffee concentrate by bringing 1 cup water to a boil. Pass it through a 2¼ oz. package organic coffee (we use Equal Exchange) to yield ¾ cup concentrate.

2. Use toaster oven to bake ¾ cup sliced almonds at 300°F until light tan.

3. Combine contents of 2 cans coconut milk, almonds, coffee concentrate, ½ to ⅔ cup agave nectar, 1 teaspoon vanilla extract, ½ teaspoon salt, ½ teaspoon fresh ground pepper, and 2 tablespoons Kahlua, if desired. Chill until very cold, and freeze as per ice cream maker's instructions.

lemon lotus ice cream

1. Grate the yellow skin of 2 lemons. Squeeze juice to yield ½ cup (4 lemons).

2. Lightly toast ¾ cup whole almonds in a 300°F toaster oven. Cool. Grind finely in a food processor.

3. Combine lemon juice, rind, 2 cans coconut milk, ground almonds, ¾ teaspoon vanilla extract, ½ teaspoon fresh ground pepper, ½ teaspoon almond extract, ½ teaspoon salt, and ½ to ¾ cup agave nectar.
    Chill until very cold.

4. Freeze as per ice cream maker's instructions.

mango ice cream

1. Cut up the flesh of **1 large or 2 small mangoes**. Turn into food processor. Grate rind of **2 to 3 limes** into the processor. Squeeze juice. You will need ½ **cup of lime juice**. Add with the contents of **1 can coconut milk, 1 cup sugar,** ¾ **teaspoon vanilla extract,** ½ **teaspoon salt, 1 tablespoon whole cardamom seed**, freshly ground in a spice mill. You will also need ¼ **cup diced candied ginger** in syrup (available in Asian markets). Purée all together.

2. Combine with the contents of a **second can of coconut milk**. Chill until very cold, and freeze as per ice cream maker's instructions.

strawberry ice cream

1. Clean and trim **2 quarts strawberries**. Turn into food processor. Add **2 tablespoons lemon juice,** ⅔ **cup agave nectar,** ½ **teaspoon salt, 1 teaspoon vanilla extract,** ½ **tablespoon pepper,** and **2 tablespoons Kirschwasser**. Process to yield a coarse mix.

2. Combine strawberry mix with **2 cans coconut milk**. Chill until very cold, and freeze as per ice cream maker's instructions.

peach or nectarine ice cream

1. Peel and remove the seeds of **2½ cups peaches** *or* **nectarines**. Turn into food processor. Add ¼ **cup light agave nectar, 1½ tablespoons lemon juice, ¼ teaspoon almond extract, ½ teaspoon salt,** contents of **1 can coconut milk**, freshly ground **black pepper**, and **1 tablespoon raspberry vinegar**. Add **1 tablespoon Kirschwasser** if you like.

2. Purée fruit and seasonings, chill until very cold, and freeze as per ice cream maker's instructions.

3. A doubled recipe (2 cans of coconut milk, 5 cup peaches, etc.) requires two frozen ice cream bowls.

hot fudge sauce

To use over ice creams or over cake.

1. Weigh **9½ oz. unsweetened chocolate** (we prefer Scharffen Berger) and place in a small pot. Add ⅓ **cup coconut oil.** Cover and turn heat on low. Bring ⅓ **cup water** to a boil. Whisk melted chocolate and add boiling water to it. It will "seize" (coagulate). Turn off heat.

2. Add **1 cup organic sugar,** ¼ **teaspoon salt,** and ½ **cup agave nectar** to pot. Add ¾ **cup coconut milk.** Stir all together and bring to a simmer over low heat while stirring. Dilute as needed with **water.**

3. Serve over **peach** *or* **strawberry ice cream** (see index), or as you like.

3 to 4 cups sauce

blueberry pie

We are fortunate to have our own mesh-enclosed blueberry patch.
It is very time consuming to pick berries, but they are delicious.

1. Choose **coconut oil** *or* **hazelnut pie crust** (see index)
   and prebake completely by first lining crust with foil
   and beans and baking at 350°F until crust seems
   firm and starts to brown. Remove foil and beans and
   complete the baking.

2. Combine in a pot: **1 cup sugar, 3 tablespoons
   cornstarch, ⅛ teaspoon salt, 1 cup water, 1 cup
   blueberries**, the grated **rind** and **juice** of **½ lemon**,
   and a **scant ½ teaspoon cinnamon**. Pick over **3 cups
   blueberries** and set aside.

3. Cook filling, stirring constantly, until mixture comes to
   a boil and begins to thicken. Remove from heat. Add
   reserved blueberries and mix. Let cool a few minutes,
   then turn into baked pie shell.

4. Serve as is, or with **coconut milk whipped cream** *or*
   crème fraîche (see index).

one pie

blueberry tofu mousse

A favorite dessert.

1. In a saucepan combine 1¾ cups of an appropriate fruit juice, 1¾ cups fresh blueberries, and ½ pound tofu. Sprinkle 2½ tablespoons agar-agar (see glossary) over the top and bring to a simmer, then cook 5 to 10 minutes.

2. Meanwhile use a coffee grinder to pulverize ¾ cup nuts (Use walnuts, almonds, filberts [hazelnuts] or a combination. Sometimes we make up part of the measure with coconut flakes. The nuts provide richness and are the base of this dairy free dessert.) Pulverize as finely as possible. Turn into a blender. Add tofu, berries, and juice with ¾ cup grapeseed oil. Turn machine on. Mixture should become thick like mayonnaise. Scrape down. Add ⅓ cup maple syrup, 1 tablespoon lemon juice, 1 teaspoon salt, and 1 teaspoon vanilla extract. The smoothness of this mousse depends on how finely you are able to pulverize the nuts. Taste for lemon juice and for sweetness. Correct seasoning.

3. Oil 8 tea cups or custard molds. Pour mousse into molds. Cool, refrigerate.

4. Use the same pot to simmer ¾ cup blueberries in ⅓ cup juice and 2 tablespoons maple syrup. In a measuring cup stir together ¾ tablespoon potato starch and ¼ cup juice. Add to simmering sauce, stirring until thickened and clear. Thin, if necessary, with more juice. Cool, refrigerate.

5. To serve, run a knife around sides of molds. Turn out onto plates and top with blueberry sauce.

8 servings

lemon lime tofu mousse

1. Grate rind of **1 lemon** and **1 lime**. Turn into a stainless steel pot. Add **½ pound tofu, 1 cup water,** and **⅔ cup maple syrup.** Sprinkle top with **2¼ tablespoons agar-agar flakes.** Cover and slowly bring to a simmer, then simmer 5 minutes.

2. Meanwhile, squeeze lemons and limes and measure juice. You will need ½ cup and will therefore need **2 to 3 more lemons** *or* **limes.** Combine juice with **⅓ cup grapeseed oil** and **⅛ teaspoon salt.** Set aside. Measure **1½ cups soymilk** and set aside.

3. Turn tofu and agar into a food processor or blender. Process. Gradually add juice, oil, and soymilk. When mixture is quite smooth, pour into 7 dessert dishes, or into a fancy glass bowl.

4. Prepare **almond crème** (see index). Toast ⅓ **cup slivered almonds.** Spoon almond crème over the chilled mousse and just before serving, sprinkle with toasted almonds, and, if you like, a few **raspberries** *or* sliced **strawberries**.

7 servings

mango lime pudding

We used to make this dessert using fresh mangoes and a commercial mango drink, no longer available to us. So instead we use a bottled organic clementine juice. Orange juice should work also. The pudding is inspired by one served at Buddha Bodai, a Chinese Buddhist Vegetarian restaurant in Flushing New York. The imaginative chef there is Michael Wong.

1. Measure **2 cups clementine juice** and turn into a pot. Add **2 teaspoons instant agar-agar.*** Bring to a boil, stirring constantly. Once it boils, turn off heat and cool, then refrigerate.

2. Cut sections off of **2 mangoes**. Peel and turn fruit into a processor. Scoring the flesh with a knife and then using a spoon will make this process easier. Add chilled, stiffened juice to processor and turn machine on. Pour **2½ tablespoons grapeseed oil** through the access tube. Also add the **rind** and **juice** of ½ **lime**, ¼ **teaspoon salt** and ⅓ **cup sugar** (*or* **3 tablespoons agave nectar**). Taste for sweet and sour and adjust seasoning accordingly.

3. Remove flesh from **one** more **mango** and cut diced pieces into 8 to 9 small custard cups. Spoon pudding over mango pieces and chill. Serve garnished with a little grated **lime rind** and, if you like, with **gingersnaps** (see index).

4 to 6 servings

---

*Telephone brand, available in Thai markets.

gingered yellow squash cake
with hazelnuts

This is a delicious yellow cake.

1. Bake **1 cup hazelnuts** in a 300°F oven or toaster oven until toasted, 20 to 30 minutes. Set aside. Coarsely grate **yellow summer squash**, using the grater attachment on a food processor, or on a box grater. You will need 3 cups, packed. Also grate **3 tablespoons fresh ginger**. Set both aside.

2. Lightly **oil** three 8″ round cake pans. Dust lightly with flour. Preheat oven to 350°F.

3. Grate hazelnuts coarsely in food processor. Turn out into a bowl.

4. Stir together with a dry whisk: **4 cups all-purpose flour, 1 teaspoon baking soda, 4 teaspoons baking powder, ¾ teaspoon salt**, and **1 cup plus 2 tablespoons organic sugar**. Add nuts and stir again to distribute them.

5. Grate **1 tablespoon lemon rind**. Turn into processor. Add **4 oz. tofu** (this replaces 2 eggs). Add the grated ginger and **1 cup oil**—we use a combination of ⅔ cup coconut oil and ⅓ cup grapeseed oil. Turn machine on. Add **1¼ cups orange juice, 2 teaspoons vanilla**, and the reserved grated squash. Blend briefly. Turn mixture into bowl of dry ingredients and fold all together. Mixture will be rather dry. If necessary, add a tablespoon or two of water. Turn into prepared pans and smooth with a spatula.

6. Bake for 30 to 40 minutes or until edges are browned and pull away from the sides of the pans, and the center is firm when pushed with your finger. Cool on racks for 15 minutes.

7. Turn out cakes. Spread **damson plum** *or* **elderberry jam** between layers and on top of cake.

one 3-layer 8″ cake

LOCAL FEMINIST BOOKSTORE

fresh fruit topping
for sourdough lemon cake

1. Choose a juice appropriate to the fruit you are using. For instance, apple-strawberry juice for strawberries, lingonberry-blueberry for blueberries, papaya nectar for peaches. In a pot place **1½ cups of juice**. Add **2 tablespoons maple syrup** and a **dash salt**. Sprinkle on **2 tablespoons agar-agar**. Do not stir. Cover and bring to a simmer over low heat, then simmer 3 to 4 minutes.

2. Meanwhile, prepare fruit. Measure **2½ cups strawberries, blueberries**, or **peeled**, cut up **peaches**. Set aside.

3. Stir **2 tablespoons kudzu** *or* **1 tablespoon cornstarch** in **3 tablespoons water**. Add to simmering juice and whisk until thickened and clear. Let cool 5 to 10 minutes. Add fruit. Taste and correct seasoning. A sprinkle of **cinnamon** and a few drops of **almond extract** are welcome compliments to peaches.

4. **Sourdough lemon cake** (see index) will rise in the oven and then sink somewhat in the center. Let the cake cool at least 20 minutes before spooning the fruit glaze into the depression. You should have ample glaze to serve over slices of cake as well.

spiced elderberry dessert sauce

1. Strip wild or homegrown **elderberries** from their stems. Measure. Place in a pot with half as much water as berries (e.g. **2 cups berries** to **1 cup water**). Add sticks of **cinnamon** and a few **whole cloves**. Cover and bring to a slow simmer. Cook 10 minutes.

2. Turn out into a cheesecloth-lined colander over a bowl. Twist the cheesecloth closed and press lightly with a potato masher to extract only the juice, not the sticky greenish residue from the elderberry skins.

3. Measure. This recipe uses 3 cups elderberry juice. Return the juice to a pot. Add ¼ **cup lemon juice** and ¼ **cup orange juice**. Sweeten with **1 cup agave nectar** or to your taste. Bring to a boil.

4. Stir **4 tablespoons cornstarch** into ¼ **cup water**. When juice is boiling, add cornstarch mix. Whisk until thickened and clear. Cool and refrigerate. This sauce is delicious over ice cream, cakes, or pancakes.

makes 3 to 4 cups

fresh fruit tart

Very easy, very delicious.

1. Make **coconut oil pie crust** (see index). Preheat oven to 375°F.

2. Stir together **2 to 3 tablespoons sugar, 3 tablespoons cornstarch**, and ½ **teaspoon salt**. If you like, you may add ¼ **teaspoon cinnamon** *or* **cardamom**. Set aside.

3. Prepare **4 cups of mixed fruit**: sliced **peaches, blueberries**, sliced **strawberries**, pitted and halved **cherries**. Any combination will do. Use a slotted spoon to mix fruit with cornstarch and sugar mix. If it tastes too sweet or too bland, add a little lemon juice and rind.

4. Prebake crust, weighted with foil and beans, for 6 to 8 minutes. Remove foil and beans. Add fruit. Continue baking until edges of crust look brown. Remove and cool.

5. If you like, serve with **vegan crème fraîche** *or* **coconut milk whipped cream**. (see index).

one 9″ pie

BREADS & MUFFINS

bread baking

Making your own bread differs from other cooking in that it depends less on accuracy of measured ingredients and time elapsed between steps than it does on learning the "feel" of the dough and sensing how temperature and humidity are affecting it. So bread baking is more subjective and intuitive than calculated. It is very satisfying in that it is hard to produce an inedible loaf. Once you have some practice, there's no reason you can't make excellent bread, and no excuse for over-sweetened and over-yeasted loaves that pass for "good" homemade.

Having a mixer with a dough hook is a necessity for us. Kneading by hand takes time and one is tempted to add more flour than necessary to make the dough stop being sticky sooner than is possible. You can knead by hand if you don't mind the mess and will give the kneading enough time before more flour goes in.

We rise bread twice: once after kneading and once in the pans. We don't make a "sponge" or proof the yeast since both procedures seem a waste of time. The first rising is long, 1½ to 2 hours. This requires a cool place in the kitchen and if that is not possible, then a cool place elsewhere in the house. Rising that is too rapid produces a yeasty-tasting bread with underdeveloped flavor. The second rising should be brief, ½ hour to 45 minutes. The remaining yeast growth takes place in the oven.

Potato cooking water (and mashed potatoes themselves) seems to do something wonderful to bread. Some old-fashioned sourdough starters begin with potatoes, which purportedly attract very particular wild yeasts. We save potato-cooking water in the refrigerator for sourdough pancakes and for bread making.

You will note that except for the whole wheat bread, all others are made with unbleached white flour in combination with whole grains. Producing a well-risen loaf requires high gluten, which the white flour provides. We add gluten flour to the whole wheat to help it up, together with potatoes and a little sourdough starter.

If you have never baked bread before, begin with an easy one like the rye bread. After you have made bread a few times, you can experiment with your own additions. Our recipes here are basic and are restaurant favorites. We always suggest bread for children who are unused to our menu, and they love it.

Bread freezes very well. Place cooled bread in a plastic bag and freeze. To reheat, remove from bag and heat in a 350°F oven for half an hour.

oatmeal sunflower bread

1. Pour **4 cups boiling water** over **3 cups rolled oats** and let cool for ½ hour in a large bowl. Oatmeal must be no more than warm when yeast is added.

2. In a stand mixer or by hand, add **2 tablespoons yeast** to the oatmeal and stir in **2 tablespoons salt**, **¼ cup grapeseed oil**, **½ cup molasses**, and gradually add **5 to 8 cups unbleached white flour**. Knead a good 20 minutes if working by hand and least 10 minutes in a machine. Add enough flour to make dough silky, not tough and dry. When dough seems the right texture, add **½ cup sunflower seeds** and **½ cup sesame seeds**. Mix into bread dough thoroughly and set dough aside to rise for 1½ to 2 hours, covered with a dishtowel. Be sure your kitchen is not too hot. A long slow rising produces best flavor.

3. Use **lecithin oil** (see glossary) to grease 3 small loaf tins (9″ x 5″ x 3″) or 2 larger ones. Punch down bread on a floured board and shape into loaves. Place in pans and let rise ½ hour.

4. Preheat oven to 350°F and bake bread until done, about ¾ hour. Turn out onto racks to cool.

makes 2 to 3 loaves

BREAD

sourdough potato rye bread

You will need to make the rye bread once, then save some of the dough to sour until the next week. Here's how:

1. Wash **4 medium potatoes**. Barely cover with water and cook until tender. Remove and peel. Throw potatoes into a mixer with a dough hook and save potato cooking water.

2. Use the dough hook to mash the potatoes. Add cooking water, **2 tablespoons salt, 2 tablespoons caraway seed**, and **3 cups rye flour**. When mix is cool, add **2 tablespoons dry yeast** and enough **organic high gluten white flour** to form a silky dough. **6 to 7 cups of flour** should make a silky soft dough after about 10 minutes of beating on low speed. Bread dough should clean the sides of the bowl as the dough hook turns.

3. Remove about **1 cup** of the **dough** and put it in a container with ½ **cup water**. Cover and refrigerate to use as the starter for next week's bread.

4. Let the remaining dough rise, preferably in a cool place, for an hour or so.

5. Lightly brush a cookie sheet with **grapeseed oil** and sprinkle heavily with **coarsely ground cornmeal**. Deflate the dough and divide it into 2 to 3 loaves. Shape the dough by tucking in ragged edges and turning round and tucking again. It will feel silky and alive. Place loaves on cookie sheet and let rise again for 20 minutes. Meanwhile boil ½ **cup water** with **1 tablespoon cornstarch**, stirring constantly until thickened. Brush tops of loaves with this mixture for a glaze, and if available, sprinkle with **czerniska seeds**.* Preheat oven to 375°F.

6. Just before baking, make diagonal slashes in the loaves with a sharp knife. Bake until browned. Cool on racks.

7. The following week, combine the refrigerator-stored soured dough with **4 cups rye flour** and water as needed. Stir well. Remove 1 cup of this and refrigerate again. Use the remaining flour and sour mix to make the bread together with the **potatoes**, cooking **water**, **salt**, **caraway** and **white flour**. You can do without the yeast altogether. The bread will then need longer to rise. Or you may add a **scant 1 tablespoon yeast** to help it along. Beat and let it rise as before, and bake the same way after glazing with the cornstarch-water mix. The sour will keep well in the refrigerator, and may be neglected for several weeks without spoiling.

each recipe makes 2 to 3 loaves

BREAD

---

*Indian stores sell this seed as Kolongi. The botanic name is *Nigella sativa*. Those who grow "Love in a mist" will recognize the seeds.

sprouted whole wheat bread

1. Three or four days before making bread, cover **1 cup wheat berries** with water for a few hours, drain and keep in a dark cupboard. Rinse twice a day, draining well each time to produce sprouts by the third or fourth day. Sprouts stop growing quickly when refrigerated. They can be omitted from this bread, but they add protein and texture.

2. Boil **2 cups potatoes**, peeled and cut up, in **water** to cover. Cool to lukewarm. Drain, reserving potato liquid, and mash potatoes. Potatoes add delicious flavor to whole wheat bread. And if you have **sourdough starter*** in your refrigerator, use **1 cup** of it to add additional flavor and leavening.

3. In mixer or bowl, place **3½ cups potato cooking liquid** (tepid) and add **4 tablespoons yeast**. When yeast has dissolved, add **potatoes, ¼ cup oil, 2 tablespoons salt, ½ cup agave nectar, 1 cup gluten flour**** and sourdough starter if available, and begin beating or mixing. Gradually add up to **10 cups whole wheat flour**. Be sure to use hard wheat, not that sold as "pastry flour." The gluten flour will help the bread rise and be light. Now add **2 cups wheat berry sprouts** and **¾ cup sunflower seeds**. When bread is well beaten and silky, turn out to rise for 1½ hours.

*See index for information on sourdough starter.
**Available in health food stores.

4. Preheat oven to 325°F. Use **lecithin oil** (see glossary) to grease 2 to 3 large bread pans. Turn bread out, cut into loaf-sized pieces. Flatten out each one and roll up to make neat loaves. Tuck in ends and place in pans. Let rise 30 minutes more.

5. Bake bread until brown and hollow sounding when you tap on the loaves. Turn out onto racks to cool.

2 to 3 loaves

SELMA

BREAD

quinoa corn bread

Inspired by a trip to Ecuador, where quinoa* originated. Of course corn and potatoes are also "new" world in origin. This makes a bread which is crunchy and moist as well as tasty.

1. Peel and cut into chunks **2 small potatoes**. Put into a pot with **1¼ cups quinoa grain**, rinsed thoroughly first. Cover with **3 cups water** and bring to a boil. Cover pot and simmer until potatoes are quite done and the quinoa is cooked.

2. Turn contents of pot into mixer. Use flat beater, if available, to mash potatoes and to mix with quinoa. Now wait until mixture is cool. Change flat beater to dough hook if you have one. Add **1 cup whole-wheat flour**, ¼ **cup molasses, 1¾ tablespoons salt, ½ cup grapeseed oil, 2 cups cornmeal**, and **1½ cups sourdough starter**** beating on low speed with a dough hook. (Of course, bread may be mixed by hand, in a large bowl, if you like.) Now add up to **4 cups unbleached white flour** and ½ **cup sunflower seeds**, kneading or mixing until batter is smooth and stringy and cleans the sides of the bowl. Taste batter to see if it needs more salt or sweetening.

3. Put bread in a cool room, covered, for 1 to 2 hours to rise.

4. Use **lecithin oil** (see glossary) to grease 4 to 5 bread pans and preheat oven to 375°F.

---

*See the glossary for more information on quinoa.
**See glossary.

5. Turn bread out onto a floured board. Cut and shape into loaves as seems appropriate to the size and shape of your pans. Flatten each loaf slightly and then roll up. Tuck in ends and place in pans. Let rise again for about 30 minutes.

6. Bake bread for about 45 minutes, or until it is well-risen, brown, and hollow sounding when knocked on the crust. Turn out onto racks to cool.

4 to 5 loaves

BREAD

pumpernickel

This bread has a lot of ingredients in it. If unavailable, some may be left out, but each ingredient contributes to its rich, full-bodied flavor.

1. In an oven, toast breadcrumbs until almost burnt. You will need **1 cup crumbs** (**rye** *or* **whole-wheat** are best).

2. Assemble wet ingredients in either a mixing bowl or a mixer with a bread dough hook. Combine: **2 cups brewed decaffeinated coffee** (tepid), **½ cup molasses**, **1 cup potato cooking water** (or plain water), **⅓ cup sourdough starter**, **½ cup barley malt** (available in health food stores), **½ cup grapeseed oil**, and **2 tablespoons tamari**.

3. Add **2 tablespoons dry yeast**. Turn mixer on slow (or stir with a wooden spoon by hand) while adding dry ingredients: Add **1 cup cornmeal, 3 cups whole wheat flour, 1 cup rye flour**, the cooled well-browned crumbs, **⅓ cup carob powder, ¼ cup caraway seed, 1 tablespoon salt, 2 tablespoons cafix, 1 tablespoon fresh ground pepper** and **4 to 6 cups unbleached white flour**. Mix with dough hook or by hand, adding the smaller amount of white flour until dough becomes silky. Add more white flour only if dough is very sticky. Taste for salt and add if necessary.

4. Cover bread with a cloth and let rise in a cool place (not an overly warm kitchen) for two hours, or until doubled in bulk. If it is convenient, bread can be deflated, recovered, and left to rise another 45 minutes. Or it can be shaped. However, best flavor will not develop unless bread rises slowly.

5. Turn dough out onto a floured board and deflate. Divide into 3 parts. Gently shape each into a round, patting in ends, and tucking in sides to get a very round loaf. Lightly oil a baking sheet and sprinkle with cornmeal. Place loaves on sheet. Preheat oven to 400°F.

6. Let bread rise again for no more than 25 minutes. Slash tops of loaves and immediately place in hot oven.

7. If you like, bread may be topped with a glaze: dissolve 1 teaspoon cornstarch in ⅓ cup decaf coffee in a small pot. Bring to a boil, stirring, until thickened. Add ½ teaspoon coarse salt. When bread has baked 20 minutes, brush with the glaze. Bake breads until they sound hollow when tapped, and when the bottoms are browned. Cool on racks.

makes 3 small loaves

BREAD

four grain walnut bread

1. Combine **3 cups oatmeal** and **6 cups water** in a pot. Bring to a boil, remove from heat and let cool.

2. In a mixer or large bowl combine **3 tablespoons salt**, ¾ **cup molasses**, and ¾ **cup coconut oil**. Add oatmeal and mix. When mixture is tepid, add ¼ **cup yeast, 3**¾ **cups water** (potato cooking water, if available), **3 cups rye flour, 3 cups whole wheat flour, 1**½ **cups wheat germ, 1 cup plus 2 tablespoons bran flakes**, and **1**½ **cups cornmeal**. Beat until smooth. Add up to **11 cups unbleached white flour** and beat or knead to make bread silky smooth. Mix in **2**⅔ **cups chopped walnuts**. Turn out into a bowl and let rise 2 hours in a cool place, covered with a dish towel.

3. Preheat oven to 375°F. **Oil** 4 to 5 large loaf pans. Punch down bread and shape into loaves. Pat each piece flat, roll up and tuck in ends. Let rise in pans about 25 minutes.

4. Bake loaves until brown and hollow sounding when rapped. Turn out onto racks to cool.

4 to 5 loaves

flax-oat-raisin bread

We are famous for our oatmeal-sunflower bread, which we sell as small loaves as well as sliced. But this new recipe is even better.

1. Make **flax seed "eggs"** (see glossary). You will need **½ cup**. Set it aside.

2. Warm the contents of **2 (14 oz.) cans coconut milk** and use a can to measure **14 oz. water**. Bring almost to a boil. Pour over **3 cups oat flakes** in a mixer. Add **¾ cup raisins, 2 tablespoons salt, ¼ cup coconut oil** and **scant 1 cup molasses**. Stir all together and let cool until tepid.

3. Add **2 tablespoons dry yeast, ½ cup sunflower seeds**, the flax seed "eggs" and **12 to 14 cups bread flour**. Add flour slowly, beating with a dough hook until the gluten develops long stringy pieces and the dough begins to clean the sides of the mixer. Let rise until doubled.

4. Use **lecithin oil** (see glossary) to grease eight 3½ inch by 6 inch loaf pans (or other pans). Divide dough and shape. Let rise until puffy. Bake in a 350°F preheated oven until well-risen and brown.

makes 8 small loaves

faux croissants

Croissants and puff paste are flaky because the many thin layers of butter interleaved with a flour-based dough create air spaces when baked. The former contain a small amount of yeast; the latter don't. Both are tedious and time-consuming to make. Nevertheless, an ambitious vegan can get a similar, and quite delicious result using these recipes.

1. In a mixer fitted with the flat beater, stir together ⅓ **cup warm water, ⅓ cup all-purpose flour** and **¾ tablespoons dry yeast**. When mix bubbles, add another **½ cup all-purpose flour** and **1½ cups bread flour, 1 tablespoon salt, 2½ tablespoons sugar** and **⅓ cup coconut oil**. Beat well. Dough will be very soft. Dust with **flour**, wrap in plastic wrap or foil and refrigerate until firm—approximately half an hour.

2. Meanwhile, if coconut oil is liquid (in summer), chill it until it is firm. In winter, use as is. Measure ⅔ **cup** of solid **coconut oil** and turn into a food processor. Blend with **½ cup all-purpose flour** until it looks like very soft whipped cream. Scrape sides as needed.

3. Divide chilled dough in half. Roll out on floured board to a ¼ inch to ½ inch thick, shaping dough into a rectangle. Use a spoon to spread the coconut cream over ⅔ of the surface, but not near the edges. Fold in thirds to enclose the fat. Press edges together. Roll into a rectangle again very carefully. The oil-cream should not escape! Again spread the coconut cream over ⅔ of the surface; fold again and pinch edges. Wrap and chill. Repeat with second half of dough, using remaining coconut cream.

4. When dough is firm enough to roll out without the fat breaking through (30 to 45 minutes), but not too stiff to roll out (which could cause breakage), roll out each piece and fold in thirds on a **floured** counter. Repeat step 4 two times again. If you have had to chill dough too long, let it rest at room temperature 10 minutes before rolling out again.

5. Roll out one dough piece to measure 7½ inches by 25 inches. Cut into 5 rectangles (a pizza wheel is effective for this) and divide rectangles into triangles. Roll each triangle to flatten it further. Roll up from the base, stretching widthwise and when nearing the tip, lengthwise. Shape into a crescent and place on an ungreased cookie sheet. Repeat with other half of dough. You should have 20 croissants.

6. Let rise one hour. Preheat oven to 350°F. Bake until well risen and beginning to brown. Brush lightly with **coconut oil**. Continue baking until done. May be frozen and reheated.

makes 20 croissants

BREAD

vegan puff pastry

This recipe is similar to the preceding one in that a flour dough is interleaved with coconut oil. Yeast, however, is omitted.

1. Use a food processor to combine 2½ cups all-purpose flour, 2 tablespoons coconut oil, 1 teaspoon salt, 1 tablespoon sugar, and ⅔ to ¾ cup water. Process until dough is not sticky. Dust lightly with flour, wrap in plastic or foil and refrigerate 30-45 minutes.

2. Use unwashed processor to blend 1 cup coconut oil and 1 cup flour. It should look like very soft whipped cream. If more liquid, chill. Too much chilling will make it unspreadable, but it can be processed again.

3. Divide dough in half. Roll out on a floured board into a ½″ thick rectangle. Spread ⅔ of the dough with approximately 2 tablespoons coconut cream. Fold in thirds to enclose the fat in separate layers. Roll out again careful not to roll over the edges and keep the coconut enclosed. Again spread with coconut cream. Fold and press edges. Repeat with second piece; wrap and chill until firm—approximately half an hour.

4. Roll out again into a rectangle, spread with coconut cream again, and again fold in thirds. Turn, roll out again, spread with cream and fold again. Repeat step 4 two times more, spreading with coconut cream until there is no more of it.

5. Roll out one pastry piece as thinly as possible. Cut into eight 4-inch rounds or cut into 6-inch squares. Wet edges with **water**. Fold up squares to make tarts, or cut lattice strips to edge rounds (fold to make strips turn into a circle). Add topping (see below). Roll out scraps to make lattice strips to top tarts. Repeat with second batch of dough. Bake in a preheated 375°F oven until crisp and lightly brown.

6. Alternatively, roll out each strip into a rectangle 6 inches wide by approximately 22 inches long. Cut 9 crosswise strips from each totaling 18 pieces. Brush the edges of half with water. Fold the others in half and use a knife to slit partway at the fold. Top solid pieces with one topping (below) and top with venetian blind slit pieces. Press edges together. Bake at 375°F until puffed and brown. Sprinkle with **confectioner's sugar**. Cut in half to serve.

7. **Rhubarb topping**: slice **2 cups rhubarb** thinly. Turn into a bowl. Add ⅔ **cup sugar**, ½ **teaspoon ground cardamom** and ½ **teaspoon salt**. Use a spoon to mash slightly. Plan to use this mixture immediately, before it becomes too liquid.

8. Instead of the rhubarb mixture, **strawberry preserves** can be used as a topping.

makes 16 small tarts

spelt croissants

Wheat-free.

1. In a mixer combine the following: **2 pounds spelt flour** (approximately 7 cups), **⅓ cup dry yeast, 2 cups apple juice, 2 very ripe bananas, 1 tablespoon salt, 2 cups cornmeal, ½ cup raisins, ½ cup slivered almonds, ⅓ cup agave nectar,** and **1½ cups dried apples,** cut into dice. You may also add **¾ cup of rye sourdough starter** if available. If not, add **¾ cup rye flour** and **¾ cup water.** Mix with dough hook for 10 minutes. Dough should be very soft. Let rise 1 hour.

2. Preheat oven to 375°F. **Oil** a large cookie sheet. Pat out spelt dough and cut into 10 large rectangles. Divide each diagonally and roll from wide end to the point, to make a croissant shape. Lay the 20 rolls on the baking sheet and let rise 20 minutes more. Bake until puffed and brown.

makes 20 rolls

scones

These are amazingly rich. Adapted from a butter and cream recipe in *Cuisine Magazine* called "Sensational Scones." They are indeed, and ridiculously easy to make.

1. Use a dry whisk to blend 2¾ **cups all-purpose flour,** ⅓ **cup sugar, 2 teaspoons baking powder,** and ½ **teaspoon salt.** Grate 1 **tablespoon orange rind** and set aside, and measure out ¾ **cup dried currants** *or* other dried fruits. Add currants and orange rind to the dry ingredients.

2. Using a 2-cup measure, add **coconut oil** (melted over low heat) to the ⅔ **cup** mark. Now add 1 **cup coconut milk,** making 1⅔ cups liquid total. Use a fork to stir both together. Pour into the dry ingredients and continue using the fork to stir until dough comes together.

3. Preheat oven to 375°F. Turn dough mass onto an unfloured board. Shape into a ¾″ thick round, using your hands. Cut into narrow wedges and place on cookie sheet. If you like, sprinkle tops with **coarse sugar.** Chill in refrigerator 15 minutes. Bake 20 to 25 minutes or until brown.

about 12 large scones

MUFFINS

oatcake scones

1. Over low heat, melt ⅔ cup coconut oil if solid. Combine with 1 cup coconut milk. Add 1 tablespoon lemon juice. Set aside. Preheat oven to 400°F (if you don't have a toaster oven, preheat to 350°F).

2. Toast 1½ cups oat flakes at 350°F in a toaster oven or large oven for 10 minutes. Stir occasionally.

3. In bowl combine 1½ cups flour, ⅓ cup sugar, ½ teaspoon salt and 2 teaspoons baking powder, using dry whisk to stir. Add oat flakes, ⅔ cup currants and the grated rind of ½ orange.

4. Pour coconut oil-milk into dry ingredients and stir all together. Batter will be very wet.

5. Use 2 spoons to drop scones onto ungreased cookie sheet. Bake at 400° 10 to 12 minutes, turning scones once to brown both sides.

makes 30 oat cake scones

best sourdough biscuits

1. Preheat oven to 425°F. In a bowl assemble **3 cups unbleached white flour**, **½ teaspoon salt**, **¾ teaspoon baking soda**, **1 teaspoon baking powder**, and **2½ tablespoons organic sugar.*** Use a dry whisk to briefly mix.

2. Whisk together **1 cup sourdough starter** (see glossary for information on sourdough) and **¾ cup water.** Add **½ cup grapeseed oil** *or* **⅓ cup melted coconut oil.**

3. Stir wet and dry ingredients together. Don't over mix. Batter should be very moist.

4. Turn out onto heavily floured board. Cut into rounds using a glass dipped in flour.

5. Bake. Use spatula to turn once, thereby browning both sides evenly.

makes 1 to 2 dozen biscuits

---

*For dessert biscuits, grated lemon rind and ½ teaspoon ground cardamom may be added.

MUFFINS

orange-cranberry muffins

1. Preheat oven to 400°F. Melt **4 tablespoons coconut oil** (if solid). Set aside to cool. Use a food processor to coarsely chop **¾ cup walnuts**. Turn out and set aside. Now use the processor to coarsely chop **1¼ cups cranberries**. Set aside.

2. Stir together **2½ cups flour**, **⅔ cup sugar**, **1½ teaspoons baking powder**, **½ teaspoon baking soda**, and **½ teaspoon salt**.

3. Grate the rind of **1 orange**. Set aside. Squeeze the juice. You will need **1⅓ cups orange juice**. Combine rind and juice with **½ cup flax seed "eggs"** (see glossary) and cooled melted coconut oil. Use a whisk to blend ingredients. Use **lecithin oil** (see glossary) to grease muffin tins.

4. Combine wet ingredients, dry ingredients, and cranberries and nuts. Spoon into prepared muffin tins. Bake until puffed and brown, about 20 minutes.

one dozen muffins

lemon poppy seed muffins

1. Preheat oven to 400°F. Use **lecithin oil** (see glossary) to lightly grease a 12-compartment muffin tin.

2. Melt ¼ **cup coconut oil** over very low heat. Grate **rind of 2 lemons**. Squeeze ⅔ **cup lemon juice**. Combine rind, juice, and melted oil in a bowl. Add **1 cup coconut milk**, ⅔ **cup agave nectar**, and **1½ teaspoons vanilla extract**. Set aside.

3. In a dry bowl, use a dry whisk to combine **2¾ cups flour**, **1½ teaspoons baking powder**, ½ **teaspoon baking soda**, ¼ **teaspoon salt**, and **3 tablespoons poppy seeds**.

4. Use a spoon to stir wet and dry ingredients together. Don't overmix. Spoon into muffin tin and bake until light brown, about 20 minutes. Cool a few minutes on a rack before turning out.

makes 12 muffins

MUFFINS

banana walnut muffins

1. Melt ½ cup coconut oil (if solid) in a small pot. Combine with ½ cup sourdough starter,* ¼ cup flax seed "eggs"* and ½ teaspoon vanilla extract. Set aside. Heat oven to 375°F. Use lecithin oil* to grease pans for 12 to 15 muffins.

2. Use a fork to mash 3 bananas, leaving them a little lumpy. Set aside.

3. Blend dry ingredients together with a dry whisk: 1½ cups flour, ½ teaspoon salt, ½ teaspoon baking soda and 1½ teaspoons baking powder. Add ¼ cup sugar and chop ¾ cup walnuts and add.

4. Add bananas and wet ingredients to dry ones. Stir to combine. Don't overmix. Spoon batter into greased muffin tins. Bake until light brown.

makes 12 to 15 muffins

*See glossary.

morning glory muffins

From Rachel Portnoy.

1. Preheat oven to 400°F.

2. Combine wet ingredients in a bowl: **1 cup fresh cider,
   ½ cup sourdough** (see glossary), **⅓ cup grapeseed
   oil, ½ cup apples,** peeled, cored, and diced (it's
   preferable to use tart apples such as Macoun or Mutsu),
   ½ cup shredded carrots, ½ cup cranberries,
   coarsely chopped, and **½ cup currants.** Stir well and
   set aside.

3. Combine dry ingredients: **2½ cups unbleached
   white flour, ⅔ cup Sucanat** (*or* **sugar), 1 teaspoon
   baking soda,** sifted, **¼ teaspoon salt, ½ teaspoon
   cinnamon,** and a **grating of nutmeg.** Chop **½ cup
   walnuts** and add.

4. Lightly oil muffin tins using **lecithin oil** (see glossary).

5. Quickly combine wet and dry ingredients, using as
   few strokes as possible to blend. Spoon into muffin
   tins and bake until browned.

makes 1 dozen muffins

sweet potato biscuits

1. Roast **1 to 2 sweet potatoes** for 45 minutes at 400°F, let cool, and peel. You will need **1 cup** roasted sweet potato. Turn into food processor. Add **1½ tablespoons grapeseed oil** and set aside.

2. Blend dry ingredients with a dry whisk: **1⅓ cups flour, ⅔ teaspoon salt, 1 tablespoon sugar, scant tablespoon baking powder.** Heat oven to 425°F.

3. Turn processor on to blend oil and sweet potatoes. Add **3 tablespoons coconut milk.** When mixed, add dry ingredients and mix briefly. Batter should be soft. Dip out 1½″ biscuits onto ungreased baking sheet using 2 spoons. Turn biscuits over after 5 minutes.

makes 2 dozen

BREAKFAST, LUNCH & DRINKS

scrambled tofu

1. Put **1½ pounds tofu** into a pot. Use a fork or potato masher to break up tofu into curds resembling scrambled eggs.

2. In a small bowl, combine **3 tablespoons nutritional yeast, 3 tablespoons white miso**, a **few drops tamari, 3 tablespoons water**, and **¼ teaspoon turmeric**. These ingredients are essential for the good flavor and color of this dish. Mix well with a spoon and fold into tofu. Cover pot and heat gently until tofu is warmed. Stir from time to time. If necessary, a few drops of **water** may be added to prevent burning and to keep tofu creamy.

3. Meanwhile, thinly slice **2 Italian peppers, 6 oyster** *or* **shiitake mushrooms**, and **half 1 small onion**. In a frying pan, fry the vegetables in **2 tablespoons grapeseed oil** over high heat until nicely browned. **Salt** lightly, turn off fire. If you like, deglaze pan with **1 tablespoon tawny port**. Fold cooked vegetables into tofu.

4. Serve with toasted **whole wheat bread** and chopped **straight leaf parsley**.

4 to 5 servings

soysage

A somewhat pungent, Italian-style sausage made from okara (a "waste" by-product of tofu manufacture) instead of pork. If you make your own tofu, you will have okara left over. Otherwise, health food stores that carry fresh tofu in bulk may be able to order some for you. Okara is estimated to be 15 to 20 percent protein. You can store it in a freezer until ready to use. Then be sure to defrost it completely.

1. Prepare 3 to 4 empty tin cans, approximately 3″ diameter by 4½″ high, by removing both ends. Cut 8 squares of aluminum foil to seal top and bottom of each can after filling is added. Set aside.

2. Chop very finely: **1 very large onion** and **¼ cup straight leaf parsley**. Set aside.

3. Combine the following "dry" ingredients in a mixer: **4 cups okara, 1 cup whole wheat flour, ¾ cup bulgar, 1 cup oat flakes, 1 cup nutritional yeast** (available in health food stores), **¼ cup sesame seeds, 2 teaspoons freshly ground pepper, 2¼ teaspoons chili powder, 1 teaspoon red pepper flakes, 1 teaspoon celery seed, 1 tablespoon oregano, 1½ teaspoons salt, 1½ teaspoons whole fennel** (*or* **anise seed**), **¾ teaspoon ground allspice,** and **1 tablespoon dried sage.** Crush **3 cloves garlic** and add, along with chopped vegetables. Mix well.

4. Now add the following "wet" ingredients: **⅓ cup tamari, ⅔ cup grapeseed oil, 1 tablespoon vinegar,** and **1½ tablespoons agave syrup.** Now you can add up to **½ cup water,** but do not make the mixture too moist. You can test by feeling whether you could shape a pattie from the soysage at this point.

5. When soysage is well blended, use a spoon to pack firmly into prepared cans, covering both ends with foil. Use a steamer or a rig a soup kettle with some kind of rack so that soysage can be steamed without standing the cans in water. The rim of a springform pan with a cake rack on top works well if you have the right size pot. Steam soysage 1 hour in the covered pot.

6. Use tongs to remove cans. Cool. Run a knife around sides of each can to turn soysage out. Wrap each cylinder in plastic wrap and store in freezer. To cook for breakfast, defrost overnight in refrigerator.

7. When ready to serve, slice cylinder into 6 to 8 patties. Fry on very hot griddle or in a frying pan, adding just a little **oil**. Brown well on one side and then flip over. Serve with **pancakes** (see index) and **syrup**; topped with **ketchup** or **Spanish sauce** (see following recipe); or accompanied by home fried **potatoes**, as you like.

each cylinder makes 6 to 8 patties

home fried potatoes

Potatoes have to be fresh cooked to make good homefries. Idahos are best. Cook scrubbed **potatoes** in their skins until tender. Peel or not as you like and cut up into small slices. Add chopped **onion** and chopped **green pepper**, **salt** and fresh ground **pepper** and moisten with **grapeseed oil**. Fry potatoes in your largest well-heated cast iron skillet or on a griddle, turning occasionally and sprinkling with **paprika**. When browned and crisp, turn out to serve.

spanish sauce

Chop **1 small onion** fine and sauté in **olive oil** with 2 crushed **cloves garlic, 2 teaspoons oregano, 1 teaspoon basil (dried)**. After a few minutes, add **15 oz.** canned **plain tomato sauce**. Rinse out can with ¼ **cup red wine** and add **1 tablespoon** finely chopped **hot peppers**. Taste for **salt**, and simmer for 10 minutes.

sourdough pancakes

See glossary for information on sourdough starter.

To make pancakes, turn out the **starter** into a bowl the night before and add as much **flour** and **water** as seems necessary to make as much batter as you need. Stir well. Batter will be lumpy. The next morning, return some starter to the refrigerator. The batter should be rather thick. Just before you pour it into the preheated griddle, stir in a splash of **club soda** (*or* **champagne**) to lighten the batter. We use **bananas, strawberries, blueberries, peaches, apples**, and **cranberries** in our pancakes, depending on the time of year. These pancakes will be chewy rather than fluffy, and folks either love them or decide that they aren't done enough for their taste. Be sure to serve them with the best quality **maple syrup**.

uppma

Uppma describes a large group of snack-type cereal dishes popular in India, using various grains. This recipe is made with thin, pounded rice called "poha," obtainable in Indian markets. Uppma makes a gratifying vegan breakfast.

1. Remove stems and seeds from **2 fresh jalapeño** (or other) chilies. Mince. Coarsely chop ⅓ **cup cashews** and ⅓ **cup peanuts.**

2. Heat **3 tablespoons grapeseed oil** and **1 tablespoon dark (toasted) sesame oil** in a frying pan (the combination tastes much like ghee, India's nut-roasted butter). Add ½ **tablespoon black mustard seed** (available in Indian markets), and fry until they begin to pop. Now add the chilies and cook, stirring for a few seconds. Add the chopped nuts, as well as ¼ **cup coconut flakes** (optional), ½ **teaspoon turmeric,** ¾ **teaspoon salt** and **1 tablespoon date sugar** (available in health food stores). Turn off heat.

3. Measure **2 cups thin pounded rice, "poha,"** into a colander. Turn on very hot tap water and rinse the poha. Shake dry and turn poha into the frying pan. Mix all together gently with a slotted spoon. Add ⅔ **cup water,** cover, and simmer 5 minutes.

4. Sprinkle **2 teaspoons lime juice** over the uppma. Serve in a bowl, with chopped **cilantro** on top, and **Apricot Chutney** on the side (see recipe). Uppma may be reheated in a steamer, and will keep in the refrigerator for up to a week.

3 to 4 servings

apricot chutney

1. Cut up ¼ **pound dried apricots.** Cover with **1 cup boiling water** in a bowl, and let soak 1 hour.

2. Place a **1˝ piece** of **fresh ginger** in a food processor with **1 tablespoon vinegar** and process.

3. Turn ginger mix and apricots into a stainless steel pot together with ¼ **cup red wine vinegar, pinch salt, dash cayenne,** and ½ **cup date sugar.** Bring to a boil and simmer over a low flame for half an hour. Add ¼ **cup raisins** and ¼ **cup currants** and cook 20 minutes more. Add **water** as seems necessary. Store in refrigerator.

makes 3 to 4 cups

chinese sticky rice

Adapted from an appetizer recipe from Green Symphony, a
Chinese vegetarian restaurant.

1. Cook **2 cups rice** in **1 cup water** over low heat.

2. Soak **5 black mushrooms** (Chinese dried) in hot
   water. When soft, mince. Save liquid.

3. Use **2 tablespoons grapeseed oil** to sauté
   mushrooms and **2 tablespoons** dry fine-sized
   ground soy protein till very well done (browned).

4. Add mushrooms and liquid to rice. Add **2 tablespoons
   sesame oil** and **1 tablespoon tamari**. Cook together
   till done. Pack into tall narrow ramekins and steam
   all together 10 minutes.

6 breakfast servings

congee
rice porridge

From Buddha Bodai, a Chinese Buddhist vegetarian restaurant in Flushing, New York. We have been told that congee or jook is boat people's food. We find it remarkably comforting to eat for breakfast, or as soup in winter.

1. The best base for congee is a broth made from **soy bean sprouts, carrots,** and **vegetable trimmings** cooked in **water** over low heat for several hours. However, plain water will do.

2. Rinse **2 cups long grain rice** in a strainer. Turn into a pot and add **6 quarts broth** (see above) *or* **water** and **2 tablespoons grapeseed oil.** Let sit without heat several hours.

3. Soak **1½ cups dried shiitakes** in water to cover until soft, about 20 minutes. Slice thinly and add the soaking liquid to the pot. Turn shiitakes and ¼ **cup** very finely slivered peeled **ginger** to pot. Break up approximately **1 cup dried bean curd sticks** (available in Asian markets)—you may need a hammer—and add to pot with a **dash toasted sesame oil, 1 tablespoon soy sauce,** and **2½ tablespoons salt.** Let cook four hours over low heat.

4. Final seasoning: add **1 teaspoon sugar** and **2 teaspoons rice wine.** The consistency should be soupy; add **water** if necessary. Congee may be reheated if necessary. Serve garnished with **toasted peanuts.**

8 to 10 servings

avocado on rye

1. In food processor, pulse ½ **cup semi-soft sun-dried tomatoes**, adding enough **olive oil** to make a thick paste.

2. In a wooden bowl, coarsely chop **1 small avocado** together with ½ **teaspoon balsamic vinegar**. Add **salt** to taste.

3. Toast **2 slices rye bread** and rub lightly with a **clove of garlic**.

4. Spread a thin coat of the sun-dried tomato paste onto the rye toast. Add a little **shredded lettuce**, the avocado, and top with fresh **alfalfa sprouts**. We serve this with **rosemary-olive oil potato chips**.

serves 1 for lunch

chinese steamed buns

from Rachel Portnoy. If you love dumplings, you'll be very pleased with these.

1. **Make filling:** Soak **8 dried shiitake mushrooms** in warm water until softened. Meanwhile shred **1 medium napa cabbage. Grate 2 peeled carrots.** Dice **1 tablespoon fresh ginger.** Peel and slice finely **4 cloves garlic.** Set all vegetables aside. Soak a small **(1 oz.) package cellophane noodles** in water to cover.

2. Squeeze shiitakes and slice thinly. Save juice for other purposes. Sauté mushrooms in **a few tablespoons grapeseed oil** over high heat. Once they begin to brown, add all the vegetables from step 1. Fry until all are well done. Turn into a bowl and let cool. Chop **3 tablespoons cilantro** and add to filling. Drain and coarsely chop cellophane noodles. Add to filling together with **2 tablespoons toasted sesame oil** and **tamari** to taste. A little spicy flavoring, such as **Szechuan hot and spicy sauce,** is welcome. Taste and correct seasoning. Set aside.

3. **Make yeast dough:** In a mixer combine **4½ cups all-purpose flour, 1 tablespoon dry yeast, 1 tablespoon baking powder, ⅓ cup sugar, ⅓ cup grapeseed oil,** and **1⅓ cup water.** Mix with dough hook until dough is silky. Let rest 15 minutes.

4. **Make rolls:** Divide yeast dough into 24 pieces. Roll each out, making a thicker center and thin sides. Roll into rounds. A small Chinese rolling pin works best. Place 4 tablespoon of filling in center, pull up sides, and twist top to make a beggar's sack.

5. Line steamer pans with **lettuce** *or* **cabbage** leaves. Steam buns for 12 minutes. Either serve immediately or cool and freeze. Reheat in steamer on leaf, two per serving for lunch.

6. **Make dipping sauce:** Combine ⅓ **cup rice vinegar, ⅔ cup water, ⅓ cup tamari, 3 to 4 tablespoons sugar, splash toasted sesame oil, 2 scallions,** minced, **and 2 tablespoons cilantro,** chopped fine.

makes 12 lunch servings

broccoli raab calzone

Like other strong-flavored greens (kale, collards, mustard greens), broccoli raab requires a boiling water blanching to minimize bitterness. It is very easy to grow (and tastes best) early in the Spring when the weather is cool. The best greens come from your own garden.

1. Make the dough first. In a mixer combine:
   1 cup water, ¾ cup whole-wheat flour, 2¼ cups unbleached white flour, 1 tablespoon olive oil, 1 tablespoon salt, ½ cup sourdough starter (see glossary), and **2 tablespoons dried yeast**. Use a flat beater or a dough hook to beat this bread dough until it becomes an elastic ball. Let rise in the bowl while you prepare the filling.

2. Thinly slice **4 bunches of broccoli raab** (about **2 quarts**, cut). Turn into a pot of boiling water. After the water returns to a boil, cook about three minutes, then turn into a colander and let drain.

3. Peel and mince **4 cloves garlic**. Cut **16 wrinkled black Italian olives** from their pits and chop coarsely, discarding the pits.

4. Heat **2 tablespoons olive oil** in a large frying pan.
    Add ½ **teaspoon hot pepper flakes** and ¼ **cup
    pignoli nuts.** Sauté a minute or two. Add the garlic
    and the nuts and continue frying over moderate heat
    until the nuts brown just a little and the garlic turns
    golden. Add the drained broccoli raab and turn heat
    to high. Fry until all liquid evaporates and the raab
    begins to brown, stirring when necessary and adding
    olive oil as needed. Finally, turn off heat and season
    with **2 tablespoons balsamic vinegar, 1 teaspoon
    salt,** and **fresh ground pepper.** Let cool 10 minutes.

5. Preheat oven to 450°F. Rub 2 large cookie sheets with
    olive oil and sprinkle generously with **cornmeal.**
    Divide the bread dough into 12 pieces. Use a rolling
    pin and then your hands to stretch each piece into a
    6″ to 7″ diameter circle. Divide the filling and portion
    onto half of each circle. Fold the other half over and
    pinch edges firmly, to make a neat turnover.

6. When all calzones are formed, place on prepared
    cookie sheets and immediately place in the hot oven.
    They should be brown and cooked in less than half
    an hour.

7. Serve calzone with a salad for lunch, or with
    cannelini beans and rice for dinner. They can be
    refrigerated and will reheat in a few minutes in a
    toaster oven.

serves 12

bloodroot burger

A combination of grains, nuts, and a few vegetables make a delicious burger. This recipe makes a lot. We shape the burgers, place each one in plastic wrap, and freeze. Then they are brushed with oil and broiled as needed.

1. In separate pots, cook **1 cup each bulgur, basmati rice,** and well-cleaned **French lentils** until very soft. The lentils take the longest to cook. Toast **1 cup whole almonds** in a 300°F oven until well dried out. When the rice, bulgur, and lentils are done, drain any remaining water off and combine in a large bowl. Turn almonds into a processor to chop finely. Set aside.

2. Dice **1 small onion.** Peel and mince **3 to 4 garlic cloves.** Shred **10 oz. spinach leaves** (or a similar amount of **kale or swiss chard**). Sauté onion, garlic, and greens in **2 tablespoons grapeseed oil** with ½ **teaspoon ground cumin.** When onions turn golden and begin to brown, turn off heat and add to grains. Combine all, including almonds, together with ½ **cup tamari, 2 teaspoons ground black pepper,** and ½ **cup toasted bread crumbs.** Finally, grate **2 small potatoes** (well washed, skins and all) and add to mixture. Mix thoroughly. Potatoes should help burgers stick together better.

3. We weigh approximately 110 grams of mix for each burger. Form into patties. Wrap individually in plastic wrap and freeze.

4. When ready to serve, brush each burger with **grapeseed oil** and broil on both sides. We serve them with toasted **pita bread, salad, raw onions,** and **dill pickles**. Also **catsup** *or* **barbecue sauce** (see index) as you like.

20 burgers

fresh ginger lemonade

This is a delicious cold remedy.

1. You will need **8 oz.** of **fresh baby ginger**. No need to peel it. Cut it up coarsely and place in processor with ¾ **cup organic sugar**. Pulverize.

2. Add **1 cup water** and process thoroughly. Place a strainer in a pot and turn out contents of processor into strainer. Use another **1 cup water** to rinse out processor. Use a spoon to squeeze ginger in strainer. Discard solids.

3. Add **3 more cups water** to pot. Simmer 5 to 10 minutes. This mixture is a concentrate. To serve, measure ¼ cup of it into a glass or cup. Add juice of ¼ **lemon**. Fill with boiling water. Alternatively, fill with ice water and ice cubes for a refreshing summer drink. Store mixture in the refrigerator.

20 servings

iced tea

Bring **1 quart water** to a boil. Add ⅓ **cup loose tea**.
Let steep 4 minutes. Place a strainer over a pitcher
containing **1 quart cold water** and ¼ **cup sugar**
or **2 tablespoons agave syrup**. Pour steeped tea
through strainer. Stir tea mixture well. ½ **orange** and
¼ **lemon** may be squeezed and added to iced tea
pitcher. Let come to room temperature and pour over
ice. Garnish with **fresh mint sprigs**. Refrigerating tea
makes it cloudy.

may wine

1. To make May wine, you will need fresh **sweet
   woodruff**, *asperula odorata*. It is a perennial herb
   easy to grow in semi-shade and in rich humusy soil.
   It is difficult in full sun and in dry or windy places.
   If you find a good spot for it, you will find it a lovely
   ground cover.

2. In May, cut the new growth (including the flowers).
   Open a bottle of **California Rhine wine** and push in
   a handful of woodruff. Close the bottle and leave at
   room temperature overnight. Chill.

3. Strain wine into glasses and add a **strawberry slice** to
   each glass. You can keep May wine in the refrigerator
   for a week or longer. It is thought that woodruff has
   the effect of releasing the alcohol more rapidly into
   the bloodstream, so be careful how much you drink!

sanguinaria*

A non-alcoholic refreshing celebratory drink from Carolanne Curry.

Combine best quality organic juices. You will need
**1 quart organic grape juice, 1 quart organic
cranberry juice** and **1 quart fresh-squeezed
orange juice.** Obviously, a large pitcher is necessary.
Pomegranate juice is now available. **Half a quart**
will make Sanguinaria even better.

15 to 20 servings

mulled wine cider

1. In a large pot combine **4 cups cider, 2 teaspoons
   agave nectar, rind of 1 orange, 3 sticks cinnamon**
   and **5** whole **cloves.** Bring slowly to a boil.

2. Add **2 cups red wine.** Skim out cloves and orange
   rind and ladle into mugs or glasses.

6 to 8 servings

---

*Sanguinaria: a genus with only one known species, *Sanguinaria canadensis*,
the bloodroot; its medicinal rhizome. Sanguine: red, blood. In early
physiology having blood as the dominant humor. Characterized by abundant
and active circulation of blood, as a sanguine temperament; one typically
marked by a ruddy complexion and by cheerful and hopeful spirits. Hence,
warm, ardent; disposed to be hopeful; anticipating the best; confident.

MISCELLANY

almond garlic spread or stuffing for mushrooms

1. Separate cloves of **1 head of garlic** and roast in a toaster oven 10 minutes at 300°F.

2. Grind **2 cups almonds** (skins are okay) in a food processor as fine as possible. Turn off machine. Peel garlic cloves and add to processor. Turn machine on and add: **½ cup extra virgin olive oil**, **½ cup water**, **2 teaspoons salt**, **2 to 3 tablespoons balsamic vinegar**, and **2 to 3 tablespoons tamari**. Taste. This spread should be tart, rich, and salty.

3. Use as is for stuffing, or dilute with up to **½ cup** warm **water** for use as a spread or dip.

4. Pull stems out of **mushroom caps**. Use a fork to fill with garlic almond mixture. Sprinkle with **paprika** and broil until light brown. Mushrooms will not be cooked.

makes about 3 to 4 cups of dip or stuffing

mayonnaise, hollandaise, maltaise and béarnaise sauces

From Mary Prejean. These French sauces are usually made with egg yolks and butter (except for the mayonnaise, made with egg yolk and oil). However, creditable substitutes may be made using almonds.

1. Cover ½ **cup organic almonds** with **water**. Bring to a boil in a small pot. Immediately add cold water to cool the nuts. Slip off the skins and discard.

2. Turn the nuts into a blender or food processor. Squeeze **2 tablespoons lemon juice** and measure ½ **cup water** in one-cup measure and **1 cup grapeseed oil** in another. Turn machine on. Add the water. After 15 seconds, add the lemon juice and then gradually, the oil. The sauce should have a stiff, mayonnaise-like consistency, and may be used as **curried mayonnaise** by adding **1 tablespoon curry powder**, ½ **teaspoon salt, dash Tabasco,** ½ **teaspoon prepared mustard,** and **2 tablespoons catsup.**

3. For **Hollandaise**, add **2 teaspoons Spanish paprika** and ½ **teaspoon turmeric.** Be sure mix is salty and tart, so adjust **lemon juice** and **salt** to taste. Add a little water to give it a softer consistency.

4. For **Maltaise** (great on fresh steamed asparagus), use ½ **cup orange juice** instead of the water and add **1 to 2 teaspoons grated orange rind.** The lemon juice is also necessary. Be sure to season assertively with **salt** and **pepper**, and thin sauce as needed with **orange juice.**

5. **Béarnaise:** Dice **1 to 2 shallots** and simmer in ½ **cup white wine** and ½ **cup white vinegar** with **1 teaspoon dried tarragon** until mix reduces to ½ cup liquid when strained. Add strained mix to blender instead of water and lemon juice. Again, season well with **salt** and **pepper**. Mince **1 tablespoon fresh tarragon leaves** and fold into sauce. Béarnaise is traditionally served over steaks. We use it over our chickpea flour crêpes (see index) that have been filled with wild mushrooms, for a special brunch.

each makes approximately 1½ cups sauce

the three crones

Delicious party food. Coconut oil replaces butter in these filled phyllo appetizers. Fillings may be made in advance and refrigerated for several days.

1. **Spinach:** defrost **1 package frozen spinach** completely in a colander. Squeeze to remove moisture. Dice ½ **large onion** and sauté in a frying pan in a mix of **1 tablespoon olive oil** and **1 tablespoon coconut oil.** Add **3 tablespoons pignoli nuts.** When nuts begin to brown, add the spinach. Cook over moderate heat for a minute or two. Now add **2½ tablespoons flour** and stir for a minute. Add **3 tablespoons coconut milk.** When mixture thickens, add **salt, pepper,** and **tamari** to taste. Set aside.

2. **Mushroom:** soak **4 dried shiitakes** in warm **water** until soft. Chop **2 cups button mushrooms** and **2 cloves garlic.** Squeeze, then slice shiitakes, reserving **liquid.** Sauté over high heat in **1 tablespoon olive oil** and **1 tablespoon coconut oil.** Once shiitakes begin to brown, add the other mushrooms and ½ **cup** chopped **onion** to the pan. When mushrooms begin to brown, add the garlic and cook until softened. Now add **1½ tablespoons flour** and stir well. Add as much shiitake soaking liquid as needed to make a thickened mixture. Add **1 tablespoon tomato paste, salt, pepper,** and **tamari** to taste, and if you like, a splash of **mirin** *or* **white wine.** Set aside.

3. **Sweet potato:** peel **1 large** *or* **2 medium sweet potatoes.** Cut into large chunks. Place on pan. Drizzle with **olive oil** and sprinkle with **2 teaspoons coarse salt** and **1 teaspoon hot pepper flakes.** Bake at

375°F uncovered until potatoes are soft throughout. Let cool a few minutes, then turn potatoes and seasonings into a food processor. Add **1½ tablespoons coconut oil, 2 tablespoons lemon juice** and purée. Now season with **salt, pepper,** and **tamari.** Set aside.

4. **Forming the three crones:** bring **1 pound phyllo pastry** to room temperature. Cut sheets in half lengthwise and then across into quarters. Cover with waxed pepper, a damp paper towel, and then a dry dishcloth. These three layers will help keep the pastry pliable.

5. If **coconut oil** is solid (wintertime), melt ½ **cup** of it over low heat.

6. Lift out 1 sheet of phyllo at a time. Brush lightly with the coconut oil. Place a rounded tablespoon of filling on the bottom middle of the sheet. Fold sides over into thirds, letting the top part flare out somewhat. Brush again with oil, then fold, flag fashion, into a triangle. Place on cookie sheet and repeat. Mushroom and sweet potato fillings form nice triangles. The spinach may be folded so that sides barely reach the center, and then rolled up into a fat cigarette shape. Brush tops lightly with coconut oil and refrigerate until dinnertime. Or, packed carefully in covered containers, the pastries may be frozen.

7. Bake in a preheated oven at 350°F until lightly browned.

45 to 50 pastry appetizers

garlic "butter"

A good dairy-free spread for bread.

1. Pick over ½ **cup red lentils** to remove straw and stones. Cover with **water**, add **3 bay leaves**, and bring to a simmer. Cover and let cook 45 minutes. Remove bay leaves and discard.

2. Separate the cloves of a **whole head** of **garlic**, but do not peel. Lay the cloves in a pan and roast in a 325°F oven (a toaster oven will do) for 30 minutes. Let cool a few minutes, then peel.

3. Steam enough **winter squash** to yield **2 cups** when cooked. Set aside. Sweet potatoes may be substituted.

4. Put the garlic and lentils (drained of excess water) into a food processor. Process. Add the winter squash, ¼ **cup "mellow" white miso**, ¼ **cup olive oil**, approximately **3 tablespoons tofu** and **1 tablespoon horseradish**. Process until very smooth. Grind **black pepper** over the mix generously and mix again.

5. Store in refrigerator.

makes about 2 ½ cups

fried squash flowers

1. Both zucchini and winter **squash** produce two kinds of **flowers**: "female" ones with the fruit (squash) forming behind the blossom, and "male" ones which have no fruit. The latter may be picked and fried.

2. Dilute **sourdough starter** (see glossary) with **beer**. Roll flowers first in the beer-starter mix and then in a 1 to 1 mix of **flour** and **cornmeal** seasoned with **salt** and **pepper**.

3. Sauté flowers immediately in **olive oil**. Sprinkle with **tamari** and **gomahsio** (see glossary) and serve.

MISCELLANY

lynne's sweet and pungent sicilian sauce

Adapted from *The Italian Country Table: Home Cooking from Italy's Farmhouse Kitchens.* ©1999 by Lynne Rossetto Kasper. Published by Scribner, New York, NY. Lynne Rossetto Kasper is the host of *The Splendid Table*® from American Public Media, a favorite radio food program. This delicious sauce defies categorization. It is wonderful (or as Lynne would say, "fabulous!") on bread, crackers, or as a dip.

1. Use a 10" cast iron skillet. Mince ½ **medium onion** and add to heated pan with **1 tablespoon extra virgin olive oil** and ½" **sprig** of **fresh rosemary**. Sauté until onion begins to color over medium heat. Season generously with **salt** and **pepper**. Add **2¼ tablespoons sugar** and stir with a wooden spatula until sugar melts and begins to bubble (taking care not to burn), then finally turns pale amber. Onions should remain light colored.

2. Immediately add ⅛ **teaspoon dried oregano**, ¼ **teaspoon dried basil, 1 large clove garlic**, minced, and the grated **zest of 1 large orange**. Now add ½ **cup red wine vinegar**. Stir and boil down until vinegar is a glaze barely coating the pan. Keep scraping down the pan's sides. Watch for burning.

3. Stir in **1 generous cup** drained **canned whole tomatoes**, crushing them as they go into the pan. Boil and stir, scraping down the sides of the pan until sauce sautés in its own juices. It is done when it becomes a thick jam which mounts on a spoon. Taste for seasoning. A few grinds of **black pepper** will finish the sauce. Cool and refrigerate. Serve cold or at room temperature.

1 to 1½ cups sauce

georgian walnut pâté

From Rachel Portnoy. This recipe makes a lot and is enjoyable even to those who dislike cilantro.

1. Use a heavy French chef's knife to chop **2 bunches cilantro** and **1 bunch basil** *or* a comparable amount of **fresh mint leaves** very fine. Set aside.

2. Chop **2 cups celery**, including leaves and **1 cup onion**. Sauté in **2 tablespoons extra virgin olive oil** until limp, Set aside.

3. In a dry food processor, pulverize **6 cups walnuts** with **4** peeled **cloves garlic**. Add **1½ tablespoons Spanish paprika** and **⅛ teaspoon cayenne**. When mix is well ground, add **1 cup water** and the sautéed onion and celery. Process again until very smooth.

4. Finally add **⅓ cup rice wine vinegar, 1 tablespoon pomegranate molasses** (*or* tamarind concentrate) and **1 tablespoon salt**. Mix to blend. Turn out into a bowl and fold in chopped herbs. Refrigerate. Serve as a spread for bread or crackers, or as a dip with crudités.

makes about 1½ quart

lentil walnut pâté

1. Pick over ½ cup **French lentils** to remove any stones. Cover with **water** and cook over low heat until soft, about 30 minutes. Set aside.

2. Finely chop **1 large onion.** Sauté in ¼ **cup olive oil** with **1 teaspoon dried basil,** crumbled.

3. Turn onions into food processor. Drain lentils and add to processor. Add **1 teaspoon umeboshi** (Japanese salted plum) **paste, 1½ cups walnuts, 1 tablespoon red** or **brown miso, 1 teaspoon salt, 1 tablespoon tamari,** and **1 tablespoon rice wine vinegar.** Process. Correct seasoning. Pâté will be better with more **olive oil,** so drizzle some on top.

about 2 cups pâté

red pepper pâté

From Jim Dunn. Fully ripe red peppers are essential.

1. Broil **6 red peppers.** Turn often, so that they char on all sides. Turn into a paper bag for a few minutes, then pull skins off and discard. Cut into strips. Set aside.

2. Slice **4** peeled **cloves of garlic.** Sauté in ½ **cup olive oil** very gently for five minutes. Remove garlic slices and discard. Pour oil over peppers and refrigerate overnight.

3. The next day, turn peppers into a baking dish. Add ⅓ **cup capers, ½ cup chopped pitted Kalamata olives,** and top with seasoned bread crumbs. Bake at 375°F 20 minutes. Serve warm, as an appetizer, or cool and chill.

makes about 1½ cups pâté

cannelini bean, garlic, and hot pepper pâté

1. Pick over **1 cup cannelini beans** to remove stones. Soak in water overnight or for several hours. Drain soaking water and cover beans with fresh water. Cook until very soft with **1 bay leaf** and **several fresh sage leaves**.

2. Meanwhile, separate **1 whole head of garlic** into cloves, but do not peel. Roast at 300°F on a pan in a toaster oven* together with **1 whole jalapeño chile**. When garlic is quite soft (after about 10 minutes), cool and peel. Drain soft cannelini beans. Turn into processor together with the roasted jalapeño, the garlic, and **3 tablespoons balsamic vinegar**. Purée. Add **¾ cup to 1½ cups extra virgin olive oil**, and **salt** to taste.

about 2 cups pâté

---

*To roast garlic in a regular oven: cut off a thin slice from the top of 1 head of garlic to expose all cloves. Drizzle with olive oil, wrap in foil, and roast at 400°F for 20 minutes, or until soft. Cool. Squeeze garlic flesh from the papery skin.

sourdough spiced deep-fried onion rings

1. Stir together: **1 cup sourdough** (see glossary; if thick, dilute with water), **1½ teaspoons cayenne**, **1½ teaspoons salt**, **½ teaspoon fresh ground black pepper**, **¼ teaspoon dried** crumbled **oregano**, **pinch thyme**, and **⅛ teaspoon ground cumin seed**.

2. Slice and separate into rings **1 large sweet onion**. Turn into the sourdough mix and let soak ½ hour.

3. Remove rings one at a time. Dredge in **flour** *or,* if you like, a **flour and coarse cornmeal mix**. Set rings onto a cookie sheet and refrigerate.

4. Deep fry in **grapeseed oil** at 350°F to 375°F. A large cast iron skillet or a wok works well.

5. If you like, make a **mayonnaise dip**: See recipe for **Curried Mayonnaise** made of almonds (or purchase vegan mayonnaise). Season mayonnaise with **catsup** and **horseradish**.

4 appetizer servings

spiced caramelized almonds

From Rachel Portnoy. Small bags of these make great gifts.

1. Measure **3½ cups unskinned almonds** into a thick-bottomed pot. Add **1⅔ cups sugar, 2 to 3 tablespoons white alcohol** (such as vodka) and **scant ½ cup water.** Also add your choice of a mixture of spices, e.g. **¼ teaspoon each cinnamon, nutmeg, cardamom** and **cayenne, ½ teaspoon each cumin, chili powder** and **5-spice powder.**

2. Turn heat on high and use a wooden spoon to stir occasionally. Once it starts to boil, stir more often. When the syrup gets thick, stir continuously.

3. Eventually the stirring will have encouraged the sugar to crystallize. It will look like sand. Now you must continue stirring constantly so that the sugar will remelt and create enough caramel to coat the nuts. Stirring prevents clumping, but it is tiring! When most of the sandy sugar is restuck onto the nuts, turn the mixture out onto a dry tray to cool. A water soak cleans the pot and spoon.

makes 1½ quart

MISCELLANY

onion chutney

An English tradition to serve with sandwiches. From Rachel Portnoy.

1. Coarsely chop **6 very large onions**. Turn into a soup pot. Add ¼ cup **grapeseed oil, 15 oz. white vinegar, 1 pound brown sugar, 2 tablespoons salt, 1 teaspoon red pepper flakes** and ½ teaspoon **dried ginger**.

2. Turn heat on low and cook 2½ to 3 hours or more, or until mixture is dry and beginning to caramelize. Stir infrequently at the beginning, and more often at the end. Season with **fresh ground black pepper** and refrigerate.

makes 1 quart

ginger jam

Adapted from a Mark Bittman New York Times recipe. This is our favorite accompaniment to Indian curries.

1. Peel and chop finely **1½ cups fresh ginger** (about 1 pound). Coarsely chop **5 cloves garlic** and mince **1** seeded **hot chile pepper**. Turn all into a saucepot. Add **1½ cups water**, ½ **teaspoon salt**, and a generous grind **black pepper**.

2. Bring to a simmer. Add ¾ **cup sugar** and **2** seeded **fresh tomatoes**, coarsely chopped. Stir occasionally, and cook for 30 to 45 minutes, or until quite thick. Cool and refrigerate.

makes about 2 cups

Shopping Trips

Sometimes diners claim they don't know where to find ingredients listed in our recipes. Luckily for us, in Bridgeport we have access to the riches to be found in Latina, Mid-Eastern, Thai, Greek, Italian, Indian and Asian markets. Health food stores are in neighboring communities. Visiting ethnic markets is a great opportunity to experience smells and tastes of diverse cultures.

We try to indicate where to find ingredients as they occur in each recipe. Perhaps however, you will want to plan a shopping trip to a market to stock up on particular ingredients. Following is a very brief guide to what may be purchased in specific markets, listing foods we use at Bloodroot.

Farmers markets will have the best produce, but be sure to ask if it is organic. Community supported agriculture makes a wonderful alliance between the farmer and those who want to eat the best, freshest food.

A good health food store is a must for vegetarians and vegans. There you should be able to find miso, kombu, seitan, tempeh, tofu, tamari or shoyu (quality soy sauce), dried shiitake mushrooms, organically grown grains, beans and lentils, kudzu, agar-agar, quality catsup, organic sugar and Sucanat, quinoa, barley malt, carob, date sugar, nutritional yeast, brown basmati rice, wild rice, pepitas, arame, soy milk, coconut oil and coconut milk.

In Latina groceries you can find fresh jalapeño chiles as well as various dried peppers; ancho, pasilla, mulatto and guajillo, dried corn, fresh cilantro, fresh epazote, calabaza squash, plantains, fresh coconuts, good quality inexpensive long-grain rice (in 10-pound bags), corn tortillas or the masa harina to make them, ready-made corn or wheat tortillas, annatto (achiote), tamarind, jicama, and pigeon peas, as well as excellent mangoes, papayas and watermelons. Not to mention yucca, yautia, batata and many other tropical root vegetables.

A Greek or Middle Eastern market should have bulgar in three sizes and calamata olives; Greek stores will have gigande beans, feta, phyllo pastry leaves, mastica to flavor kouribiedes, green lentils, fides (very fine noodles), and salonika peppers.

Arabic stores have pita bread, Shoosh (pomegranate concentrate), orzo, and meloukhiya.

Italian groceries carry wrinkled olives, large green olives, quality olive oil, good canned tomatoes, quality pasta (look for DeCecco or Rusticella), fresh cavatelli and other pastas, capers, Arborio rice, porcini (dried boletus mushrooms), pignoli nuts, sun-dried tomatoes, arugula and broccoli raab in season, balsamic vinegar, and semolina flour.

Asian markets should have chili-paste-with-garlic in small jars, rice noodles, rice wine vinegar, toasted sesame oil, dried shiitake mushrooms, tree ears (another dried mushroom), fermented black beans, baby eggplants, soy paste (look for Kim Lan brand in Chinese markets), cilantro, mung bean sprouts, rice papers, bean curd skins, mirin (in Japanese stores), Chinese rice wine (in Chinese stores), and in Thai stores: Maesri brand canned Thai red curry paste, lemongrass, Thai basil, green papayas and "Telephone" brand instant agar-agar.

In Indian stores there will be chutneys, dahls (lentils and peas) in variety, kolongi (which are the same as czerniska seed), fresh hot peppers, cilantro, basmati rice, whole mustard seed, poha (pounded rice), fresh ginger, besan (chickpea flour), and cardamom. Quality cumin, coriander, and turmeric can be found in Indian stores, and other spices as well.

Cookbook Shelf

These days there are numerous vegetarian cookbooks available; would that they were more interesting. Mostly they are comparable to a vegetarian meal in a meat-centered restaurant: edible, but scarcely inspirational.

But here are a few which are exceptional: Madhur Jaffrey's *World Vegetarian* is expensive, but a treasure. The fact is that ethnic cooking is the best source for excellent vegetarian food. Jaffrey has collected from many cuisines. *Classic Vegetarian Cooking* from the Middle East and North Africa by Habeeb Salloum is a beautiful array of recipes from that part of the world, and affordable. Another encyclopedic expensive book is *Vegetables from Amaranth to Zucchini* by Elizabeth Schneider. Not vegetarian, it nevertheless lists ways to prepare most any vegetable which crosses your path. The new *Vegetable Love* by Barbara Kafka is similarly encyclopedic and not vegetarian, but has some excellent recipes. Vegans have so few choices in books that they hunger for more options. Of more than casual interest have been *The Candle Café Cookbook* by Joy Pierson and Bart Potenza with Barbara Scott-Goodman, *Rebar Modern Food Cookbook* by Audrey Alsterberg and Wanda Urbanowicz, and *Vegan World Fusion Cuisine* by Mark Reinfeld and Bo Rinaldi.

There are some wonderful books, mostly ethnic or regional cookbooks, that we find useful for vegetarians despite the meat- or fish-laced chapters. The *Breakaway Japanese Kitchen* by Eric Gower is by an American man inspired by Japanese ingredients and techniques. *The Gift of Southern Cooking* by Edna Lewis and Scott Peacock is a book about the traditions of the American South, with beautiful black and white photographs, *Wild Fermentation* by Sandor Katz reads like a novel (at least to a foodie!). We learned how to make delicious sauerkraut and successful Kosher-style dill pickles from him. Since there are so many people in India who are vegetarians, cookbooks written by Indians always have recipes which are appropriate for us. *The Art of Indian Vegetarian Cooking* by Yamuna Devi and *Classic Indian Vegetarian Cooking* by Julie Sahni are most comprehensive. *Savoring the Spice Coast of India* by Maya Kaimal explores foods of the Southern tip of

India; *Dakshin: Vegetarian Cuisine from South India* by Chandra Padmanabhan does also, as does *The New Tastes of India* by Das Sreedbarun.

Of course the best cookbooks from Mexico were written by Diana Kennedy. See *My Mexico* or the *Essential Cuisines of Mexico*. Also, by Zarela Martinez, *The Food and Life of Oaxaca*. None of these is vegetarian, though many recipes are adaptable. However, *The Vegetarian Table: Mexico*, by Victoria Wise is a well done collection of entirely vegetarian dishes. On a trip to Oaxaca, Mexico, the region where corn originated, we had the good fortune to meet Amado Ramirez Leyva. He owns a tortilleria called Itanoni with his wife, where they use ancient corn varieties to make their tortillas. He spoke of the importance of knowing one's identity: what background and what foods your ancestors ate. If you knew about these, you could share. If you don't have an identity, you are merely a consumer. He said that the early development of corn was a task shared by men and women both. He writes:

> Corn in our villages is charged with intimacy, familiarity, air, earth, and water; purified in the fire of the kitchen; it delivers to us its identity, the expression of the mountain, hillside or river valley in which it grew, which comes from its fathers and mothers....aroused by the recent rain, flavors that are gentle, harsh, well defined and enveloping; textures that are elastic and crisp, its youth as tortilla and maturity as tostada; qualities unknown in urban jungles.

> Gastronomy is a marvelous path for us to reencounter this past linked to the matrix of origin, villages and lands; to summon the return of corn means to recognize it and to recognize ourselves in it, to accept ourselves in our genetic, racial, and cultural diversity; to project ourselves with pride in our origin is to show our simple nakedness of flavors, odors and textures that harks back to our origins—the constant synthesis of races.

Our thanks to Pedro Hecht for the translation.

Any and all of the travel cookbooks by Jeffrey Alford and Naomi Duguid are beautiful and useful, though expensive; in particular *Hot Sour Salty Sweet: A Culinary Journey Through Southeast Asia* describes theories of balance useful in cooking Thai and other Asian foods. *Seductions of Rice*, *Home Baking* and *Flatbreads and Flavors* are their other titles.

Finally, we often find inspiration from John Meyer's magazine: *Cuisine at Home*. Since he has respect for ethnic foods, he often features recipes we can use as is or with minor changes. And Lynne Rosetto Kasper's *The Splendid Table*, an American Public Media program, is a must for our listening education. An intelligent and enthusiastic foodie, her programs provide interesting recipes every week, and she is often vegetarian-positive.

glossary

Achiote (annatto)—Rusty red dried seed which colors cooking oil bright yellow-orange. It is necessary for making a "sofrito," seasoning for Puerto Rican and other Latina dishes.

Agar-agar—A thickener also known as kanten. Available in long strips, flakes, or as a powder ("Telephone" brand in Thai markets). It is a seaweed, used as standard growing medium for biological research and for orchid seedlings. The flake or strip form should be softened in cold water without stirring, and then brought slowly to a simmer. The instant powdered form can be boiled with liquid ingredients. Once it dissolves, cool and chill. The texture of agar-agar is somewhat like gelatin (an animal product). Also see **kudzu**.

Agave nectar—A liquid syrup-sweetener which can be used in the same proportion as maple syrup. We prefer it because it has no flavor and is not associated with the genetically modified corn industry as brands such as Karo are. It comes in both light and dark forms.

Avocado Leaves—Will season a black bean purée in an Oaxaca, Mexico manner. Buy dried ones in a Mexican market to be sure to get the right variety of leaves. Rinse and toast in a dry skillet. Sauté with onions and garlic. Purée with beans in a food processor. Add bean cooking water to make a thin purée with wonderful flavor.

Banana leaves—These leaves are available frozen in Latina and Thai markets. They impart a subtle flavor to tamales when used as wrappers, instead of corn husks.

Bragg Liquid Aminos—A non-fermented soy protein used as a flavoring agent. Available in health food stores.

Chickpea flour (besan)—Available in Indian markets and some health food stores. Besan makes pancakes, dumplings, and is an excellent thickener. We use it to make vegan crêpes.

Chilies—Hot peppers come in many forms. Ancho, mulatto, and pasilla are dried. They are sweet and only a little spicy. We like to soak these chilies in hot water after removing the seeds, then we use them and their liquid as gravy bases. Guajillo and ancho chilies make a lovely sauce. Guajillos are Mexican favorites. Poblanos are fresh, undried ancho chilies. They are often stuffed and fried or baked. When we need some heat, we use jalapeños. Hatch chilies are available fresh in the Southwest or canned from New Mexico. They have their own unique flavor. Hungarian paprika, as opposed to Spanish paprika, is essential for Eastern European dishes such as stroganoff.

Chocolate—Chocolate is good for you, argues Rowan Jacobsen in his book *Chocolate Unwrapped* (Invisible Cities Press, 2003). It is the fillers and sugars which are not. Chocolate has very little caffeine in it and is very high in antioxidants, containing twice as much as red wine and seven times as much as green tea. So enjoy it. However, chocolate grown in parts of Africa, especially the Ivory Coast, are products of child slavery and rainforest destruction. Do research where your favorite chocolates come from, and try to buy fair trade and organic certified chocolate if possible. We prefer Scharffen Berger, Valrhona and El Ray.

Coconut milk and coconut oil—See Lagusta's introduction to the vegan volume. We use Thai Kitchen premium organic coconut milk and Omega coconut oil.

Coffee—Use coffee in moderation, and not at all if using homeopathic remedies. Of course the only coffee appropriate is organic and fair trade certified. We use Equal Exchange in our restaurant, and we sell whole beans of Zapatista brand (303-744-7346)—delicious Mexican coffee, putting human values before profit values.

Curry spices—Curry powder is widely available. But try making your own **garam masala** by roasting ⅓ **cup cinnamon, coriander seed**, ¾ **cup cardamom pods**, and ¼ **cup peppercorns** at 200'F 20 minutes. Discard the husks of the cardamom (patience!) and grind all together in a coffee mill. Store in a tightly closed jar. When cooking Indian "style," add **whole cumin seed** to whatever is being sautéed, much **less ground coriander seed**, and **even less ground turmeric** to, say, potatoes and eggplant. This is a delicious and widely adaptable combination.

Czernishka—The seeds of *Nigella sativa* ("love-in-a-mist") used by Poles and Russians to top rye breads, and sometimes in sauerkraut. Mistakenly called black caraway, it belongs to another plant family altogether. It is available in Indian markets as *kolongi*.

Daikon—Very large white radishes used in Japanese cuisine. They are crisp and sweet.

Epazote (*Chenopodium ambrosioides*)—is a weed in our garden. Fresh leaves are a very desirable addition when cooking beans. They impart a clean, pungent flavor. Epazote is usually available in Mexican markets.

Fats and oils—We do not use: corn oil, soy oil, peanut oil, or canola oil. We prefer grapeseed oil for general cooking and frying since it has a high smoke point and delicate flavor. We combine it with quality olive oil for our salad dressing. When sautéing over low heat, we use olive oil in dishes where its flavor will be beneficial. We use toasted sesame oil and pumpkin seed oil for their interesting, intense flavors. We carry organic sweet butter, and often use coconut oil instead of butter for desserts and baked goods.

Flax seed "eggs"—We found this recipe in the *Candle Café Cookbook*: soak ¼ **cup flax seeds** in ¾ **cup hot tap water** in a blender for 15 minutes. Turn machine on and blend until quite thick and most seeds are crushed. It will look like grey caviar. Store these "eggs" covered in the refrigerator. They will keep 2 to 3 weeks. Use a rounded tablespoon to replace 1 egg in cornbreads or cakes.

Gomahsio—Pan-toasted sesame seeds mixed with noniodized salt in a 7:1 ratio, then ground in a spice mill. Sprinkle gomahsio on salads.

gomahsio

1. Rinse **2 cups unhulled sesame seeds** briefly.

2. Pan-roast ¼ **cup sea salt** for a few minutes over low heat. Add drained sesame seeds.

3. Continue pan-roasting, stirring often for 20 minutes or until seeds have absorbed the salt and have dried out.

4. Pulse briefly in a processor, or use as is: Turn into a large open-holed shaker to use on salads.

makes about 2 cups

Jasmine rice blend—Jasmine rice mixed with split baby garbanzo beans and daikon radish seeds. Order from Indian Harvest at 1-800-346-7032.

Jícama (*Pachyrrhizus erosus)*—is a fat root. Peeled and sliced or julienned, it is a crisp, slightly sweet salad addition. Traditionally in Mexico it is sliced, sprinkled with salt, chili powder, and lime juice.

Kudzu—a notorious vine of the South, where it suffocates other vegetation. We use a dried ground Japanese product which thickens much like cornstarch or potato starch. Similarly, it must be softened in cold water. Since when dry it comes in clumps, we estimate amounts. We use it in conjunction with agar-agar to make fruit mousses. It is reputed to have more nutritional value than corn or potato starch.

Lecithin—A natural extract of the fatty part of the soybean. It contains vitamins and minerals and emulsifies fats (keeps them dispersed). This recipe makes an excellent mixture for greasing bread, muffin or cake pans. No flouring is necessary. Use a funnel to pour **1 part lecithin** to **3 parts grapeseed oil**

into a plastic squeeze bottle. Shake well so that oil and lecithin are thoroughly mixed together. Use sparingly—a little goes a long way.

Manioc meal (*Manihot esculenta*)—A grainy flour-like meal made from cassava root. When toasted, it is called *farofa*, and is a staple of Brazilian cuisine. Tapioca is another form of it, and another name for the fresh root is *yucca*. It originated in South America and is used all over the world in its tapioca form.

Masa harina—Dried corn treated with slaked lime. Necessary to make corn tortillas and tamales, as well as for dumplings. Masa dough is sometimes available in Mexican markets. The dry masa harina should be available in the flour section of any supermarket in a Latina community.

Miso—Miso is fermented soy bean paste. We use red or brown misos to flavor gravies as well as to make soup. White (really yellow) miso is delicately sweet, and flavors scrambled tofu. It makes a good soup also.

Mushrooms—There are many wild mushrooms, previously available only to mushrooms hunters that are now under cultivation. Probably our favorite is shiitake (*lentinus edodes*), followed by maitake (hen of the woods, *polyporus frondosus*), chicken of the woods (*polyporus sulfurous*), and oyster (*pleurotus ostreatus*). Portobello and cremini are variations of the button mushroom (*agaricus*) and are less interesting. Dried mushrooms are very valuable for vegetarian cooks. Best are shiitakes and porcini (*ceps* or *boletes*). The latter are very strongly flavored, so use them sparingly.

Organic—We do our best to purchase fruits and vegetables which are organic and locally grown. We think it is critical to use organic lemons and limes. Since we use the zest often from these fruits, we don't want to eat or smell the pesticides used on non-organic citrus. Obviously, lettuce must be organic, and potatoes.

Organic/biodynamic gardening—Attempts to heal land from declines brought about by intensive farming. It also uses natural rhythms such as moon phases to guide planting and harvesting. Biodynamic wines are often exceptional. We particularly like Cooper Mountain Pinot Gris and Pinot Noir (from Beaverton, OR, 503-649-0027).

Pesto—Finely chopped fresh basil, garlic, and olive oil. Traditionally includes nuts such as pignoli or walnuts. Use a food processor to make in the summer and freeze it in ice cube trays, then turn into a plastic bag to store in the freezer. We add the toasted, chopped nuts and sometimes Parmesan at serving time.

Phyllo—Tissue paper-thin pastry sheets originating in Greek and Middle Eastern cuisines. Usually brushed with melted butter, sheets can be brushed with melted coconut oil or grapeseed oil. It must be dealt with quickly or it dries out and becomes too brittle to shape. Keeping it between two sheets of waxed paper and covered with a dampened dishtowel will help retain flexibility.

Pomegranate—An Autumn fruit, the seeds of which are a delicious addition to salads and autumn soups. Pomegranate syrup makes delightful drinks.

Pumpkin seed oil—Dark green pumpkin seed oil is popular in Austrian cuisine. Pumpkin seed oil is high in Omega 3 fatty acids (which are essential for all major bodily functions, and especially useful for optimal brain function and healthy skin), as well as zinc, phosphorus, vitamin A, and calcium. Because it is unrefined, it should not be cooked. It is available in health food stores.

Quinoa—Quinoa (pronounced "keen-wa") is one of the few grains we eat—along with wild rice and a few others—that is native to the Americas. Quinoa cooks very quickly, is high in several nutrients and has a light nutty flavor. It has the highest protein of any grain (16%) and, unlike other grains, is a complete protein. It contains more calcium than milk and is high in lysine, an amino acid that is scarce in the vegetable kingdom. It is also rich in many other vital nutrients, including iron, phosphorus, B-vitamins, and vitamin E. Native to the

Andes, it was once so important to the Incas that they called it their "mother grain." Quinoa is coated with a bitter substance called *saponin*, so it is vital to rinse it well in order to remove any trace of bitterness. With water or stock covering it by 1", quinoa will cook in 15 minutes over low heat.

Seaweeds—Kombu is kelp, necessary as the base of Japanese dipping sauces (dashi). It is also useful in dried bean soups, thickening them slightly. We get ours from Ironbound Island Seaweed (207-963-7016) and add to cannelini bean soup. Wakame also flavors soups, especially hearty winter ones. Nori is used to wrap sushi. And hiziki and arame make interesting salads. The seaweed we use most often is agar-agar. An excellent book (out of print) is *Cooking with Sea Vegetables*, by Sharon Ann Rhoads, Autumn Press.

Seitan—Wheat gluten, available in health food stores. The starch is washed out of wheat so that only the gluten (protein) remains. Stewed in soy sauce with kombu and ginger, it has a texture something like meat, and is therefore useful for vegetarians who sometimes want an approximation of that texture.

Sunchokes or Jerusalem Artichokes (*Helianthus tuberosus*)— A Native American perennial sunflower, less showy than garden varieties. It grows invasively and requires a plot of its own. Dig the tubers after the first frost, wash and refrigerate. Cut in thin slices, they are crisp additions to salads, or they may be roasted for a treat.

Shiso—A Japanese herb which self-sows readily. It is in the mint family. A red form called *perilla* is used as a decorative annual. The green-leafed varieties have superior flavor as an ingredient in tempura, or shredded, as a tofu or soba topping with tamari and shredded baby ginger.

Sourdough—Sourdough starter produces pancakes, biscuits, and breads of wonderful lightness and "clean" flavor. The starter is made up of wild strains of yeast which must be fed fresh water and flour every two to three weeks, so once you have starter, you must use it with some regularity. Always turn it all out, add as much flour and water (potato cooking water, if available) as seems necessary to make a thin batter, and stir well. The batter will be lumpy. Leave overnight. Be sure to remember to return some starter to the refrigerator before adding ingredients such as milk or eggs to the batter. We have had some very close calls. In each instance some of our original starter had been given to a friend who was able to replenish our supply.

You can obtain starter in one of three ways. Getting some from a friend is best, since it will be oldest and therefore will have the best developed flavor. Ours is over 35 years old. Some gourmet or health food stores sell sourdough starter as a dry powder. Or you can try to grow your own: wash, peel, and shred **2 large potatoes**. Add ⅓ **cup sugar** and **flour** and **water** to make a thin mixture. Or, cook the potatoes, mash, and add honey *or* agave syrup, flour and water. Either way, leave this mixture uncovered in a warm place in the kitchen for 5 to 7 days, stirring every day. When it smells fermented and like alcohol, it is ready to use. If it smells rotten, however, discard it and start over. Rye flour will make rye starter.

Once you have the starter, you will note that it has a changeable personality. Weather, humidity, and time of year affect its liveliness. Many times we thought we were preparing a batter which was either too thick or too thin only to have the yeasts grow in the opposite fashion from our expectations. Good luck!

Sweeteners—We have no artificial sweeteners in our restaurant. We use organic sugar, organic honey, and agave nectar. We have stevia packets and use maple syrup, molasses and occasionally barley malt syrup (see the recipe for **pumpernickel bread**) in our baking. Date sugar and Sucanat (both available in health food stores) are delicate sweeteners.

Tamari—We use this traditional wheat-free version of soy sauce to protect any customers who have a severe wheat allergy.

Tamarind—A fruit with pulpy seeds. Used as a souring agent in the way lemon is used. It has its own dark wonderful flavor.

Tea—Our favorite teas are blended by a company called Serendipitea (1-888-832-5433). They are all loose and therefore must be pot brewed. Our favorite herbal teas are made by an Austrian company, Sonnentor (www.sonnentor.com). They sell a number of "moon" teas: rising, full, new, etc. All are organic, delicious blends.

Thickeners—We do love agar-agar and kudzu. However, we also use cornstarch out of habit, and potato starch in Eastern European recipes.

Tomatillos—Originally used by the Aztecs, called *miltomatl*. It is *Physalis ixocarpa*, relatives are Chinese Lanterns, cape gooseberries, and ground cherries. It self-sows readily in our garden, and is available in Mexican markets. Tomatillos sliced thin are tart additions to salads, and grilled, make a fine salsa.

Vinaigrette—The quality of your salad dressing depends on the quality of your oils and vinegar. Note that the oil-vinegar relationship is 4½ to 1.

vinaigrette

Combine in a jar: ⅓ **cup good quality wine vinegar** (you may blend part balsamic vinegar, if you like) *or* ¼ cup fresh-squeezed **lemon juice, ½ teaspoon salt,** and 1½ **cups oil.** We mix **grapeseed oil** with the best **extra virgin olive oil.** Add fresh ground **pepper,** and, if you like, **1 teaspoon prepared mustard.** Shake well.

almost 2 cups

Wasabi—Often thought of as Japanese horseradish, it comes from another plant family altogether. It grows well only at the edges of cold running streams. It is more fragrant and less sharp than Western horseradish. Buy it powdered, mix with a little tepid water and let stand 10 minutes before serving.

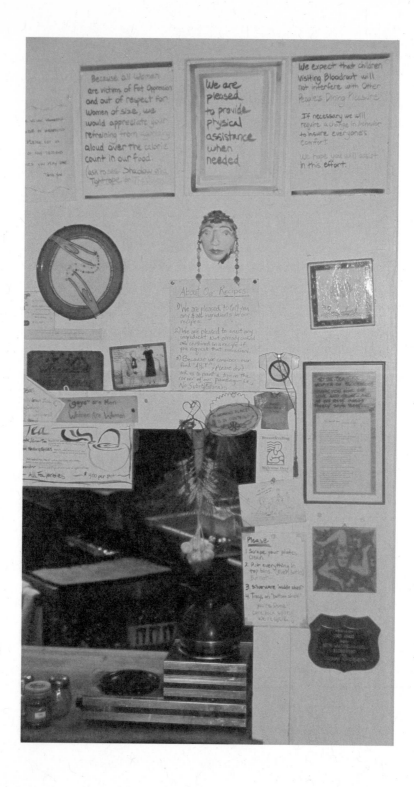

INDEX

Blue color indicates recipe will be found in *The Best of Bloodroot, Volume One, Vegetarian Recipes.*

Blue color indicates recipe will be found in *The Best of Bloodroot, Volume One, Vegetarian Recipes.*

INDEX

Blue color indicates recipe will be found in *The Best of Bloodroot, Volume One, Vegetarian Recipes.*

Blue color indicates recipe will be found in *The Best of Bloodroot, Volume One, Vegetarian Recipes.*

Blue color indicates recipe will be found in *The Best of Bloodroot, Volume One, Vegetarian Recipes.*

INDEX

Blue color indicates recipe will be found in *The Best of Bloodroot, Volume One, Vegetarian Recipes.*

Blue color indicates recipe will be found in *The Best of Bloodroot, Volume One, Vegetarian Recipes.*

Blue color indicates recipe will be found in *The Best of Bloodroot, Volume One, Vegetarian Recipes.*

INDEX

Blue color indicates recipe will be found in *The Best of Bloodroot, Volume One, Vegetarian Recipes.*

Blue color indicates recipe will be found in *The Best of Bloodroot, Volume One, Vegetarian Recipes.*

Index created by Kelly Harran and Carolanne Curry.

Blue color indicates recipe will be found in *The Best of Bloodroot, Volume One, Vegetarian Recipes.*

ABOUT THE TYPE

This book was composed using
ITC Cheltenham, Metro, and Mrs. Eaves.

Typography by Farrington & Favia, Inc.
New York, New York